MODEL LETTERS FOR FAMILY LAWYERS

Third Edition

MODEL LETTERS FOR FAMILY LAWYERS

Third Edition

Mark Harper BA (Hons)

Lisa Fabian Lustigman BA (Hons)

Andrea Woelke BA (Hons)

Family Law

2006

Published by
Jordan Publishing Limited
21 St Thomas Street
Bristol BS1 6JS

British Library Cataloguing-in-Publication Data

A catalogue record for this book is available from the British Library.

ISBN 0 85308 977 9

Typeset by The Partnership Publishing Solutions Limited, Glasgow www.the-pps.co.uk

Printed in Great Britain by Antony Rowe Limited, Chippenham, Wilts

PREFACE

Model Letters for Family Lawyers was first published in 1996. Family law has changed dramatically since then; who would have thought that 10 years later same-sex couples would be able to register their partnership under the Civil Partnership Act 2004?

The aim of my co-authors and myself remains to help busy practitioners avoid having to dictate over and over again standard letters. Where possible the letters aim to comply with the obligations imposed on the few remaining solicitors who valiantly do battle with the Legal Services Commission to try to earn a living and provide a vital service to clients on public funding.

This edition, as before, does not cover adoption or public law children issues. New letters have been introduced to deal with the changes introduced to private law children issues by the Adoption and Children Act 2002.

There is a new letter which deals with rights arising under Civil Partnership. New letters are included to deal with the new costs rules in ancillary relief introduced in 2006.

The book is divided into sections. The sections and the authors responsible for them are as follows:

Section 1: Client Care – *Andrea Woelke*
Section 2: Divorce – *Andrea Woelke*
Section 3: Ancillary Relief – *Mark Harper*
Section 4: Children – *Lisa Fabian Lustigman*
Section 5: Injunctions – *Lisa Fabian Lustigman*
Section 6: Costs – *Andrea Woelke*
Section 7: Cohabitation – *Andrea Woelke*
Section 8: Civil Partnership – *Mark Harper*

Andrea Woelke is enormously grateful for the help he has received in dealing with Sections 1 and 2, in particular on public funding issues, from Andy King of Foster & Partners in Bristol.

At the beginning of each section is a list of the letters in that section. The letters throughout the book are numbered individually. The number is prefaced by an initial, noting the subject matter of it, for example CC1 is the first letter in the book and relates to client care. There are in many cases initials after the number and the following is a key to their meaning:

P   refers to a letter where a solicitor who is a partner in the firm is acting

S   refers to a letter where an assistant solicitor is acting

T   refers to a letter where a trainee solicitor is acting

H   refers to a letter addressed to a husband

W   refers to a letter addressed to a wife

LH   refers to a letter addressed to a Petitioner on Legal Help

A   refers to a letter dealing with adultery

B   refers to a letter dealing with behaviour

D   refers to a letter dealing with two years' separation

E   refers to a letter dealing with five years' separation

C   refers to a letter to a client with children

PC   refers to a letter addressed to a private client

PF   refers to a letter addressed to a publicly funded client

A final caution. As with all precedents, it is essential that they are adapted and tailored to fit the individual's circumstances. If they are not amended appropriately more harm than good may be caused and might lead to a complaint or worse still a negligence action.

Mark Harper
Withers LLP
July 2006

CONTENTS

Section 2 Divorce

Section 3 Ancillary Relief

Section 4 Children

Section 7 Cohabitation

Section 8 Civil Partnership

SECTION 1

CLIENT CARE

Andrea Woelke

Client Care

CC1P Terms of business letter to client on Legal Help for preparation of divorce: partner acting

Dear [client]

I am a partner in this firm and will have overall conduct of your case although I will ask my trainee solicitor [   ] to help on the day-to-day running of your case.

This firm has a Community Legal Service Franchise. This means that this office has been approved by the Legal Services Commission to provide a quality service to you. This firm has also been awarded a contract to provide advice and assistance under the Legal Help scheme.

Since I am advising you under the Legal Help scheme, my firm's costs will be paid for by the Legal Services Commission. The hourly charging rate is fixed by the Government, currently at £[   ].

There are restrictions on the amount of work I can do under the Legal Help scheme.

Initially I can give you three hours of advice under the Legal Help scheme. In circumstances where the criteria laid down by the Legal Services Commission are satisfied and there is a sufficient benefit to you to do so this limit may be extended. I estimate that the overall costs for your divorce will amount to three hours of the hourly rate stated above plus VAT. I will notify you at least every six months of the actual costs incurred in your case. It is difficult to predict how much time I will have to spend on your matter. Much will depend on the other person in your case and their solicitors. Costs will also depend on your input into the matter. I will always try to give you my best estimate of the likely costs of your matter, but the estimates are not fixed.

Wherever possible, please try to write a short letter to me to answer any questions I have raised rather than telephone me.

Although under the Legal Help scheme I can advise and assist you in the divorce to prepare the necessary papers, I am not permitted to represent you in court, since technically you are representing yourself. It is, however, rare for someone to have to go to any court hearings about the divorce itself.

If it becomes necessary to represent you in court proceedings dealing with children or finances, I will have to apply for Legal Representation for you.

If in subsequent financial proceedings you recover or preserve any money or property, my firm's costs including all costs incurred under the Legal Help Scheme will be paid for out of that, but not out of maintenance. This is known as the Legal Services Commission's contractual charge. If you start court proceedings under the Legal Representation Scheme, I will explain more about the contractual charge to you.

I will keep you regularly informed of progress in your case and explain any delay and the reason for it. I will explain the effect of any important and relevant papers. Also, if a different person takes over your case, I will tell you the name of that person and the reason for the change.

Proceeds of Crime Act

Under the Proceeds of Crime Act we have to take full proof of ID from you. We usually do this at the first meeting. However, if we have not yet done so for whatever reason, we will ask you to make an appointment for this as soon as possible.

Ending instructing me

You may terminate your instructions to me in writing at any time, but I will be entitled to keep all your papers and documents while there is money owing to the firm for our charges and expenses. I may decide to stop acting for you only with good reason, for example:

1. if you do not give me clear or proper instructions;
2. if I cannot continue to act without being in breach of rules of professional conduct; or
3. if there has been an irretrievable breakdown in trust and confidence.

At the end of your case

My firm will keep your file of papers (except for any papers that you ask to be returned to you) for at least six years from the date of the last bill. My firm will keep the file on the understanding that we have the authority to destroy it after this period. My firm will not destroy documents that you ask us to deposit in safe custody.

If you require the file during the period while it is in storage, we can provide this to you on payment of our reasonable fees for delivery, locating any specific documents and making any copies for you. As you will appreciate, we hold a number of files in storage and it may take some time to retrieve your particular papers.

Procedure for resolving problems

If a problem arises at any time, please contact me so that we can talk about your concerns. If that does not provide the solution, please contact my client care partner, [   ], who can supply you with this firm's written complaints procedure if you require this.

All solicitors must attempt to resolve problems that may arise with their services. It is therefore important that you immediately raise with me any concerns you may have. I would be disappointed if you thought that you had reason to be unhappy with the service that I am providing.

In the unlikely event that a mistake is made by my firm, we have professional indemnity insurance in the sum of £[   ] per claim. We do require that you limit any claim you may have in respect of professional negligence against this firm to the amount of that sum.

If you continue to instruct me, this will mean that you accept the terms of business set out in this letter.

Yours sincerely

CC1S Terms of business letter to client on Legal Help for preparation of divorce: solicitor or trainee acting

Dear [*client*]

I am a [*trainee*] solicitor in this firm and will have overall conduct of your case subject to the supervision of my supervising partner [   ].

This firm has a Community Legal Service Franchise. This means that this office has been approved by the Legal Services Commission to provide a quality service to you. This firm has also been awarded a contract to provide advice and assistance under the Legal Help scheme.

Since I am advising you under the Legal Help scheme, my firm's costs will be paid for by the Legal Services Commission. The hourly charging rate is fixed by the Government, currently at £[   ].

There are restrictions on the amount of work I can do under the Legal Help scheme.

Initially I can give you three hours of advice under the Legal Help scheme. In circumstances where the criteria laid down by the Legal Services Commission are satisfied and there is a sufficient benefit to you to do so this limit may be extended. I estimate that the overall costs for your divorce will amount to three hours of the hourly rate stated above plus VAT. I will notify you at least every six months of the actual costs incurred in your case. It is difficult to predict how much time I will have to spend on your matter. Much will depend on the other person in your case and their solicitors. Costs will also depend on your input into the matter. I will always try to give you my best estimate of the likely costs of your matter, but the estimates are not fixed.

Wherever possible, please try to write a short letter to me to answer any questions I have raised rather than telephone me.

Although under the Legal Help scheme I can advise and assist you in the divorce to prepare the necessary papers, I am not permitted to represent you in court, since technically you are representing yourself. It is, however, rare for someone to have to go to any court hearings about the divorce itself.

If it becomes necessary to represent you in court proceedings dealing with children or finances, I will have to apply for Legal Representation for you.

If in subsequent financial proceedings you recover or preserve any money or property, my firm's costs including all costs incurred under the Legal Help Scheme will be paid for out of that, but not out of maintenance. This is known as the Legal Services Commission's contractual charge. If you start court proceedings under the Legal Representation Scheme, I will explain more about the contractual charge to you.

I will keep you regularly informed of progress in your case and explain any delay and the reason for it. I will explain the effect of any important and relevant papers. Also, if a different person takes over your case, I will tell you the name of that person and the reason for the change.

Proceeds of Crime Act

Under the Proceeds of Crime Act we have to take full proof of ID from you. We usually do this at the first meeting. However, if we have not yet done so for whatever reason, we will ask you to make an appointment for this as soon as possible.

Ending instructing me

You may terminate your instructions to me in writing at any time, but I will be entitled to keep all your papers and documents while there is money owing to the firm for our charges and expenses. I may decide to stop acting for you only with good reason, for example:

1. if you do not give me clear or proper instructions;
2. if I cannot continue to act without being in breach of rules of professional conduct; or
3. if there has been an irretrievable breakdown in trust and confidence.

At the end of your case

My firm will keep your file of papers (except for any papers that you ask to be returned to you) for at least six years from the date of the last bill. My firm will keep the file on the understanding that we have the authority to destroy it after this period. My firm will not destroy documents that you ask us to deposit in safe custody.

If you require the file during the period while it is in storage, we can provide this to you on payment of our reasonable fees for delivery, locating any specific documents and making any copies for you. As you will appreciate, we hold a number of files in storage and it may take some time to retrieve your particular papers.

Procedure for resolving problems

If a problem arises at any time, please contact me or my supervising partner so that we can talk about your concerns. If that does not provide the solution, please contact the client care partner, [   ], who can supply you with this firm's written complaints procedure if you require this.

All solicitors must attempt to resolve problems that may arise with their services. It is therefore important that you immediately raise with me any concerns you may have. I would be disappointed if you thought that you had reason to be unhappy with the service that I am providing.

section **7** CLIENT CARE

In the unlikely event that a mistake is made by my firm, we have professional indemnity insurance in the sum of £[   ] per claim. We do require that you limit any claim you may have in respect of professional negligence against this firm to the amount of that sum.

If you continue to instruct me, this will mean that you accept the terms of business set out in this letter.

Yours sincerely

CC2P Terms of business letter to client on Legal Help other than divorce: partner acting

Dear [*client*]

I am a partner in this firm and will have overall conduct of your case although I will ask my trainee solicitor [   ] to help on the day-to-day running of your case.

This firm has a Community Legal Service Franchise. This means that this office has been approved by the Legal Services Commission to provide a quality service to you. This firm has also been awarded a contract to provide advice and assistance under the Legal Help scheme.

Since I am advising you under the Legal Help scheme, my firm's costs will be paid for by the Legal Services Commission. The hourly charging rate is fixed by the Government, currently at £[   ].

There are restrictions on the amount of work I can do under the Legal Help scheme.

Initially I can give you two hours of advice under the Legal Help scheme. I estimate that I will carry out at least two hours' worth of work at the rate stated above (plus VAT) until the matter can be settled or you have justification to apply for General Family Help or Legal Representation. I will notify you at least every six months of the actual costs incurred in your case. It is difficult to predict how much time I will have to spend on your matter. Much will depend on the other person in your case and their solicitors. Costs will also depend on your input into the matter. I will always try to give you my best estimate of the likely costs of your matter, but the estimates are not fixed.

Wherever possible, please try to write a short letter to me to answer any questions I have raised rather than telephone me.

If in subsequent financial proceedings you recover or preserve any money or property, my firm's costs including all costs incurred under the Legal Help Scheme will be paid for out of that, but not out of maintenance. This is known as the Legal Services Commission's contractual charge. If you start court proceedings under the Legal Representation Scheme, I will explain more about the contractual charge to you.

I will keep you regularly informed of progress in your case and explain any delay and the reason for it. I will explain the effect of any important and relevant papers. Also, if a different person takes over your case, I will tell you the name of that person and the reason for the change.

Proceeds of Crime Act

Under the Proceeds of Crime Act we have to take full proof of ID from you. We usually do this at the first meeting. However, if we have not yet done so for whatever reason, we will ask you to make an appointment for this as soon as possible.

Ending instructing me

You may terminate your instructions to me in writing at any time, but I will be entitled to keep all your papers and documents while there is money owing to the firm for our charges and expenses. I may decide to stop acting for you only with good reason, for example:

1.   if you do not give me clear or proper instructions;
2.   if I cannot continue to act without being in breach of rules of professional conduct; or
3.   if there has been an irretrievable breakdown in trust and confidence.

At the end of your case

My firm will keep your file of papers (except for any papers that you ask to be returned to you) for at least six years from the date of the last bill. My firm will keep the file on the understanding that we have the authority to destroy it after this period. My firm will not destroy documents that you ask us to deposit in safe custody.

If you require the file during the period while it is in storage, we can provide this to you on payment of our reasonable fees for delivery, locating any specific documents and making any copies for you. As you will appreciate, we hold a number of files in storage and it may take some time to retrieve your particular papers.

Procedure for resolving problems

If a problem arises at any time, please contact me so that we can talk about your concerns. If that does not provide the solution, please contact my client care partner, [   ], who can supply you with this firm's written complaints procedure if you require this.

All solicitors must attempt to resolve problems that may arise with their services. It is therefore important that you immediately raise with me any concerns you may have. I would be disappointed if you thought that you had reason to be unhappy with the service that I am providing.

In the unlikely event that a mistake is made by my firm, we have professional indemnity insurance in the sum of £[   ] per claim. We do require that you limit any claim you may have in respect of professional negligence against this firm to the amount of that sum.

If you continue to instruct me, this will mean that you accept the terms of business set out in this letter.

Yours sincerely

CC2S Terms of business letter to client on Legal Help other than divorce: solicitor or trainee acting

Dear [*client*]

I am a [*trainee*] solicitor in this firm and will have overall conduct of your case subject to the supervision of my supervising partner [   ].

This firm has a Community Legal Service Franchise. This means that this office has been approved by the Legal Services Commission to provide a quality service to you. This firm has also been awarded a contract to provide advice and assistance under the Legal Help scheme.

Since I am advising you under the Legal Help scheme, my firm's costs will be paid for by the Legal Services Commission. The hourly charging rate is fixed by the Government, currently at £[   ].

There are restrictions on the amount of work I can do under the Legal Help scheme.

Initially I can give you two hours of advice under the Legal Help scheme. I estimate that I will carry out at least two hours' worth of work at the rate stated above (plus VAT) until the matter can be settled or you have justification to apply for General Family Help or Legal Representation. I will notify you at least every six months of the actual costs incurred in your case. It is difficult to predict how much time I will have to spend on your matter. Much will depend on the other person in your case and their solicitors. Costs will also depend on your input into the matter. I will always try to give you my best estimate of the likely costs of your matter, but the estimates are not fixed.

Wherever possible, please try to write a short letter to me to answer any questions I have raised rather than telephone me.

If in subsequent financial proceedings you recover or preserve any money or property, my firm's costs including all costs incurred under the Legal Help Scheme will be paid for out of that, but not out of maintenance. This is known as the Legal Services Commission's contractual charge. If you start court proceedings under the Legal Representation Scheme, I will explain more about the contractual charge to you.

I will keep you regularly informed of progress in your case and explain any delay and the reason for it. I will explain the effect of any important and relevant papers. Also, if a different person takes over your case, I will tell you the name of that person and the reason for the change.

Proceeds of Crime Act

Under the Proceeds of Crime Act we have to take full proof of ID from you. We usually do this at the first meeting. However, if we have not yet done so for whatever reason, we will ask you to make an appointment for this as soon as possible.

Ending instructing me

You may terminate your instructions to me in writing at any time, but I will be entitled to keep all your papers and documents while there is money owing to the firm for our charges and expenses. I may decide to stop acting for you only with good reason, for example:

1. if you do not give me clear or proper instructions;
2. if I cannot continue to act without being in breach of rules of professional conduct; or
3. if there has been an irretrievable breakdown in trust and confidence.

At the end of your case

My firm will keep your file of papers (except for any papers that you ask to be returned to you) for at least six years from the date of the last bill. My firm will keep the file on the understanding that we have the authority to destroy it after this period. My firm will not destroy documents that you ask us to deposit in safe custody.

If you require the file during the period while it is in storage, we can provide this to you on payment of our reasonable fees for delivery, locating any specific documents and making any copies for you. As you will appreciate, we hold a number of files in storage and it may take some time to retrieve your particular papers.

Procedure for resolving problems

If a problem arises at any time, please contact me or my supervising partner so that we can talk about your concerns. If that does not provide the solution, please contact my client care partner, [   ], who can supply you with this firm's written complaints procedure if you require this.

All solicitors must attempt to resolve problems that may arise with their services. It is therefore important that you immediately raise with me any concerns you may have. I would be disappointed if you thought that you had reason to be unhappy with the service that I am providing.

In the unlikely event that a mistake is made by my firm, we have professional indemnity insurance in the sum of £[   ] per claim. We do require that you limit any claim you may have in respect of professional negligence against this firm to the amount of that sum.

If you continue to instruct me, this will mean that you accept the terms of business set out in this letter.

Yours sincerely

CC3P Terms of business for Help with Mediation: partner acting

Dear [*client*]

I am a partner in this firm and will have overall conduct of your case although I will ask my trainee solicitor [   ] to help on the day-to-day running of your case.

I have now received confirmation from your mediator that you are receiving publicly funded mediation.

[*I have submitted your application to the Legal Services Commission for a Help with Mediation Certificate.*

Once the Legal Services Commission has dealt with your application you will receive the confirmation of their decision and the certificate at the same time that it is sent to my firm. However, there are often considerable delays in processing applications and it may be several weeks before you receive these documents.

or

I have used the devolved powers awarded to my firm by the Legal Services Commission to issue a Help with Mediation Certificate for you immediately. The certificate covers [   ] and has a financial limit of £[   ].]

The Certificate enables me to give you legal advice while you are involved in the mediation process and to help you with the work required to conclude and implement any arrangements made at mediation.

My firm will be paid by the Legal Services Commission for any work that I carry out on your behalf under this certificate at the rate of £[   ] per hour plus VAT. The certificate is limited to dealing with issues involving [your children/finances/the family law aspects of the issues between you including financial and children matters]. There is an initial costs limit on the work that I can carry out for you under the terms of this certificate although the Legal Services Commission can extend the limit if they decide it is appropriate to do so.

To get the most benefit out of it, I suggest that you contact me by letter and keep me up to date with the mediation process and let me have any questions you have. I can then advise you in the most efficient way.

In most cases if money or property is recovered or preserved while your case is funded by the Legal Services Commission, you will have to repay the legal costs that have been incurred on your behalf. However, this does not apply to the costs incurred under a Help with Mediation Certificate. You will still have to repay the costs incurred under the Legal Help Scheme or a General Family Help or Legal Representation Certificate.

Proceeds of Crime Act

Under the Proceeds of Crime Act we have to take full proof of ID from you. We usually do this at the first meeting. However, if we have not yet done so for whatever reason, we will ask you to make an appointment for this as soon as possible.

As part of mediation you will be giving full and frank disclosure of your financial and personal circumstances. The Proceeds of Crime Act 2002 in certain circumstances makes it a criminal offence for you to enter into a financial settlement with your [spouse/civil partner] if you know that any income or capital of whatever nature which you or your [spouse/civil partner] uses or retains represents the proceeds of crime. The proceeds of crime are any money which has arisen as a result of any crime and include, for example, money saved as a result of tax evasion or undeclared cash taken out of a business. If you are aware of such money in your family's circumstances, you should tell me about it as soon as possible. We can then discuss what steps need to be taken.

Ending instructing me

You may terminate your instructions to me in writing at any time, but I will be entitled to keep all your papers and documents while there is money owing to the firm for our charges and expenses. I may decide to stop acting for you only with good reason, for example:

1.　if you do not give me clear or proper instructions;
2.　if I cannot continue to act without being in breach of rules of professional conduct; or
3.　if there has been an irretrievable breakdown in trust and confidence.

At the end of your case

My firm will keep your file of papers (except for any papers that you ask to be returned to you) for at least six years from the date of the last bill. My firm will keep the file on the understanding that we have the authority to destroy it after this period. My firm will not destroy documents that you ask us to deposit in safe custody.

If you require the file during the period while it is in storage, we can provide this to you on payment of our reasonable fees for delivery, locating any specific documents and making any copies for you. As you will appreciate, we hold a number of files in storage and it may take some time to retrieve your particular papers.

Procedure for resolving problems

If a problem arises at any time, please contact me so that we can talk about your concerns. If that does not provide the solution, please contact my client care partner, [   ], who can supply you with this firm's written complaints procedure if you require this.

All solicitors must attempt to resolve problems that may arise with their services. It is therefore important that you immediately raise with me any concerns you may have. I would be disappointed if you thought that you had reason to be unhappy with the service that I am providing.

In the unlikely event that a mistake is made by my firm, we have professional indemnity insurance in the sum of £[   ] per claim. We do require that you limit any claim you may have in respect of professional negligence against this firm to the amount of that sum.

If you continue to instruct me, this will mean that you accept the terms of business set out in this letter.

Yours sincerely

CC3S Terms of business for Help with Mediation: solicitor or trainee acting

Dear [*client*]

I am a [*trainee*] solicitor in this firm and will have overall conduct of your case subject to the supervision of my supervising partner [   ].

I have now received confirmation from your mediator that you are receiving publicly funded mediation.

[I have submitted your application to the Legal Services Commission for a Help with Mediation Certificate.

Once the Legal Services Commission has dealt with your application you will receive the confirmation of their decision and the certificate at the same time that it is sent to my firm. However, there are often considerable delays in processing applications and it may be several weeks before you receive these documents.

or

I have made the application for a Help with Mediation Certificate to the partner with devolved powers awarded to this firm by the Legal Services Commission, who has issued a Help with Mediation Certificate for you immediately. The certificate covers [   ] and has a financial limit of £[   ].]

The Certificate enables me to give you legal advice while you are involved in the mediation process and to help you with the work required to conclude and implement any arrangements made at mediation.

My firm will be paid by the Legal Services Commission for any work that I carry out on your behalf under this certificate at the rate of £[   ] per hour plus VAT. The certificate is limited to dealing with issues involving [your children/finances/the family law aspects of the issues between you including financial and children matters]. There is an initial costs limit on the work that I can carry out for you under the terms of this certificate although the Legal Services Commission can extend the limit if they decide it is appropriate to do so.

To get the most benefit out of it, I suggest that you contact me by letter and keep me up to date with the mediation process and let me have any questions you have. I can then advise you in the most efficient way.

In most cases if money or property is recovered or preserved while your case is funded by the Legal Services Commission, you will have to repay the legal costs that have been incurred on your behalf. However, this does not apply to the costs incurred under a Help with Mediation Certificate. You will still have to repay the costs incurred under the Legal Help Scheme or a General Family Help or Legal Representation Certificate.

Proceeds of Crime Act

Under the Proceeds of Crime Act we have to take full proof of ID from you. We usually do this at the first meeting. However, if we have not yet done so for whatever reason, we will ask you to make an appointment for this as soon as possible.

As part of mediation you will be giving full and frank disclosure of your financial and personal circumstances. The Proceeds of Crime Act 2002 in certain circumstances makes it a criminal offence for you to enter into a financial settlement with your [spouse/civil partner] if you know that any income or capital of whatever nature which you or your [spouse/civil partner] uses or retains represents the proceeds of crime. The proceeds of crime are any money which has arisen as a result of any crime and include, for example, money saved as a result of tax evasion or undeclared cash taken out of a business. If you are aware of such money in your family's circumstances, you should tell me about it as soon as possible. We can then discuss what steps need to be taken.

Ending instructing me

You may terminate your instructions to me in writing at any time, but I will be entitled to keep all your papers and documents while there is money owing to the firm for our charges and expenses. I may decide to stop acting for you only with good reason, for example:

1. if you do not give me clear or proper instructions;
2. if I cannot continue to act without being in breach of rules of professional conduct; or
3. if there has been an irretrievable breakdown in trust and confidence.

At the end of your case

My firm will keep your file of papers (except for any papers that you ask to be returned to you) for at least six years from the date of the last bill. My firm will keep the file on the understanding that we have the authority to destroy it after this period. My firm will not destroy documents that you ask us to deposit in safe custody.

If you require the file during the period while it is in storage, we can provide this to you on payment of our reasonable fees for delivery, locating any specific documents and making any copies for you. As you will appreciate, we hold a number of files in storage and it may take some time to retrieve your particular papers.

Procedure for resolving problems

If a problem arises at any time, please contact me or my supervising partner so that we can talk about your concerns. If that does not provide the solution, please contact my client care partner, [   ], who can supply you with this firm's written complaints procedure if you require this.

All solicitors must attempt to resolve problems that may arise with their services. It is therefore important that you immediately raise with me any concerns you may have. I would be disappointed if you thought that you had reason to be unhappy with the service that I am providing.

In the unlikely event that a mistake is made by my firm, we have professional indemnity insurance in the sum of £[   ] per claim. We do require that you limit any claim you may have in respect of professional negligence against this firm to the amount of that sum.

If you continue to instruct me, this will mean that you accept the terms of business set out in this letter.

Yours sincerely

CC4P Terms of business for clients on General Family Help or Legal Representation: partner acting

Dear [*client*]

I am a solicitor and a partner in the firm. I will have the overall management and responsibility for your case and other solicitors or trainee solicitors may help me under my supervision.

1. Introduction

This firm has a Community Legal Service Franchise and a contract with the Legal Services Commission to provide General Family Help and Legal Representation. This means that this office has been specially approved by the Legal Services Commission to provide a quality service to you.

You are making an application for General Family Help or Legal Representation to assist you in funding your case. You will recall that I explained to you a number of points about General Family Help and Legal Representation when you completed the application forms. I am writing to confirm these and other important points.

Initially you will probably be granted General Family Help only. This will allow me to state your case, give financial disclosure to the other person in your case (if your case concerns finances), and to negotiate a settlement. It will also cover the initial stages of court proceedings. However if matters cannot be resolved and it is necessary to proceed towards a final hearing you will need to upgrade to a Legal Representation Certificate. At that stage the Legal Services Commission will look at the merits and your financial position again. It may then decide that you can use any savings or other assets that you have to finance the final hearing or that you should apply for a bank loan to cover the costs of the final hearing rather than to continue to receive public funding. I will explain the procedure and requirements to you if it appears that this is likely to apply in your case. In most other aspects the conditions that apply under a General Family Help Certificate and Legal Representation Certificate are very similar and I will explain them together and point out any differences if appropriate.

2. Criteria for General Family Help and Legal Representation

The Legal Services Commission will not only assess your financial eligibility but also your prospects of success and make a cost-benefit analysis of your case.

Generally, you will not be granted General Family Help or Legal Representation if you have not attempted to reach a settlement or if your prospects of success are poor. If your case concerns something other than domestic violence or children, for example finances, your application will also be refused if your prospects of success are borderline or uncertain, unless the case has overwhelming importance to you or a significant wider public interest.

Your application will also be refused unless the likely benefits to be gained from the proceedings for you justify the likely costs, are such that a reasonable private paying client would be prepared to take or defend the proceedings in all the circumstances.

3.   Mediation

In most family cases you are required to discuss with a mediator the way in which mediation may be able to assist you in resolving the dispute. If you agree to mediation, the mediator will ask the other person to attend mediation with you to explore the prospects of a settlement. In some types of family cases or depending on individual circumstances this may not be required. In your case you have now satisfied the requirements imposed by the Legal Services Commission concerning mediation and you can therefore proceed with your application for a General Family Help or Legal Representation Certificate. If it appears likely that mediation would be beneficial to you at a later stage in the case then I will consider the options with you again at that time.

4.   Delays

Unfortunately, there tend to be considerable delays at the Legal Services Commission due to, amongst other things, pressure of work. It may take about four to six weeks for the average General Family Help or Legal Representation application to be determined and a Funding Certificate to be issued. Similar delays occur at all stages whenever we have to deal with the Legal Services Commission.

Delays may also be caused at court or for other reasons. However, we will try and do all we can to minimise delays and will always keep you informed.

5.   Scope

Until you accept an offer of General Family Help or Legal Representation and the Funding Certificate is in our possession, I am unable to carry out any work under the General Family Help or Legal Representation schemes. I know that this is frustrating but this is outside my control. If there is an emergency, it may be appropriate for you to receive Emergency Representation. I will explain this in section 6 below. A Funding Certificate is not retrospective so it does not cover work done before the date of the Funding Certificate.

Similarly, a Funding Certificate will have a costs limitation attached to it. This means that I will only be allowed to carry out work up to that limitation, including incidental expenses. Once the limitation is reached, I will have to apply for an extension and I will not be able to do any further work for you until the extension is granted. At that stage the Legal Services Commission will also look at whether it is still reasonable for you to receive Legal Representation and you will have to convince them that it is.

The work that the firm can do under a Funding Certificate is strictly limited by the wording of that Certificate. Occasionally it may be necessary to obtain an amendment to the Certificate from the Legal Services Commission to carry out work which is outside the scope of the original description. Frequently, there are delays at the Legal Services Commission in granting amendments to Certificates.

6. Emergency representation

If your case is very urgent, it may be appropriate to make an application for Emergency Representation. This is only appropriate in extremely urgent cases requiring immediate court action and will not be appropriate in the vast majority of cases. I can make an application for Emergency Representation only if this is justifiable in the particular circumstances of your case.

If you obtain an Emergency Certificate you are under an obligation to accept a full Funding Certificate on such terms as to contributions as the Legal Services Commission imposes (see section 7 below). An Emergency Representation Certificate may be revoked or discharged if:

1. you do not provide information or documents when requested; or
2. you do not attend the Legal Services Commission for an interview (if this is required) to assess your means; or
3. you are not financially eligible; or
4. you do not accept an offer of a full Funding Certificate to replace the Emergency Representation Certificate.

It can be revoked or discharged for these reasons even if the case comes to an end before your application for Public Funding has been fully dealt with by the Legal Services Commission. You will have to pay all the legal costs that the Legal Services Commission has paid to this firm and any expenses (for example barrister's fees) yourself if your Emergency Representation Certificate is revoked or discharged or if you do not get a full Funding Certificate to replace the Emergency Certificate.

7. Your duties to the Legal Services Commission

You are under a duty to the Legal Services Commission:

1. to complete and return as soon as possible any forms received from the Legal Services Commission and, in particular, any forms about assessment of your income and assets;
2. to notify the Legal Services Commission of any increase in your income or capital;
3. to notify the Legal Services Commission of any change in your address;

4.   to notify the Legal Services Commission if you start to live with or stop living with a partner, whether of the same sex or the opposite sex.

8.   Our duties to the Legal Services Commission

You are my client and I will of course act in your best interests. However, as you are in receipt of General Family Help or Legal Representation I also have duties to the Legal Services Commission.

If you ask me to act in a way which could cause unreasonable expense to the Community Legal Service fund, I am under a duty to notify the Legal Services Commission which could result in your Funding Certificate being discharged.

I am also under a duty to inform the Legal Services Commission of any material changes in your prospects of success.

If you do not accept a reasonable offer to settle the case, I must tell the Legal Services Commission and they will probably stop your public funding by discharging the Funding Certificate. An offer is reasonable if a privately paying client in your position would accept it.

If any information comes to my knowledge about your financial eligibility to General Family Help or Legal Representation, I am under a duty to notify the Legal Services Commission.

9.   Contributions

The Legal Services Commission will assess whether or not you are liable to pay a contribution towards the cost of the case. You do not pay any money to this firm, but if contributions are assessed you will have to pay the monthly instalments to the Legal Services Commission. If your income or capital changes, the contribution may increase or decrease.

You have to pay your contributions for the duration of your case, until your Funding Certificate is discharged; this normally happens after the end of your case.

If at the end of the case your total contributions are more than what the Legal Services Commission has paid out, you will get a refund.

10.   Charges

The court or the Legal Services Commission assesses whether our charges are reasonable. In most family cases, the hourly rate which we can charge is fixed by the Government.

[Because I am an accredited specialist the hourly rate that the Legal Services Commission pays this firm for my time is 15% higher than those for other lawyers. This also applies to my colleagues who are accredited specialists and may work on your case from time to time.]

Our charges, like those of all solicitors, are based on a number of different factors.

Factors which will be taken into account are:

1. the time spent;
2. the skills, specialised knowledge and responsibility required of the members of the firm handling the matter;
3. the complexities and difficulty or novelty of the questions involved;
4. the circumstances in which the business involved is transacted (for instance if, due to the urgency, evening or weekend work is required);
5. the number and importance of any documents prepared or considered;
6. the amount or value of any money or property involved;
7. the importance of the matter to you.

The most important of these factors is the amount of time spent by members of the firm in dealing with your case. We have a computer-based time recording system which records the time spent by each member of the firm on your case.

Time is recorded for all work done on your case including time spent on the telephone, reading incoming post or emails, writing or dictating outgoing letters or emails, preparing file notes of meetings, considering and drafting documents, reviewing your file, considering your case, preparing instructions and briefs to barristers, researching law where necessary, attending conferences with barristers, attending court, meetings with you, meetings with the lawyers acting for the other person in your case or other people connected with the case, taking statements from witnesses and so on.

This firm's charges are exclusive of VAT at the current rate which will be added to the bill.

In cases involving court proceedings it is always difficult to forecast the amount of time that will be spent since much will depend on the attitude of the other person in your case and their solicitors, the volume and complexity of the documents disclosed and the time required for preparation and in court.

In general, costs are likely to be as follows.

- In domestic violence injunctions, when two court hearings are required, depending on whether it is easy to serve the other person with the court documents, it is unlikely to cost less than £[3,000].

- If there is a dispute about where children are to live and/or how often one parent is to see the children, and the case proceeds to a final hearing without an agreement being reached, the total costs are unlikely to be less than £[10,000]. A complex case may cost even more. If the case settles at an early stage, the total costs are much less.

- If there is a dispute about financial matters, and the case proceeds to a final hearing without an agreement being reached, the total costs are unlikely to be less than £[15,000]. A complex case may cost even more. If the case settles at an early stage, the total costs are much less.

If you require a forecast for your own case at any time, please ask and I will do my best to give one. It is unlikely that I will be able to make a firmer prediction until I can assess the issues in detail and until I know the position of the other person in your case.

I will always try to give you my best estimate of the likely costs of your case, but the estimates are not fixed. Sometimes I may only be able to give you my best estimate of the costs of the next stage of your case. I will notify you at least every six months of the actual costs incurred in your case and give you an estimate of the total costs.

As well as the charges made by this firm, incidental expenses such as the fees of barristers and experts (if instructed) and court fees will be added to the bill.

I will tell you about any changes in the likely cost of your case.

At the end of the case I will have a detailed bill prepared for assessment by the court or the Commission and if:

- you have paid contributions; or
- you have preserved or recovered money or property and the statutory charge applies,

I will send a copy to you. You then have the right to request a detailed assessment and you will have the right to be heard or to write to the court with your views.

11. Recovering costs incurred from the other person in your case

The general rule in family cases is that each party pays their own lawyer's costs. By contrast to other court cases, in family cases courts do not automatically order the 'loser' to pay the 'winner's' costs. This is because it is not often apparent that there is a 'winner' or a 'loser'. In cases involving children or finances, the court will only order one party to pay the other's costs in exceptional circumstances, for example if one party has conducted the court case in a way that has wasted considerable resources or if a party has tried to mislead the court. If necessary, please ask me as to whether an order for costs is likely to be made in your case.

Even in the rare cases where another person has to pay your costs it is unlikely that they will have to pay all of your costs and you will still have to pay any shortfall.

There can be additional problems with orders for costs for example:

- The person who has been ordered to pay the costs may not do so. If they do not pay, you will have to try to enforce the costs order (for example by sending in the bailiffs or obtaining a charge over property owned by them) and this itself costs more money and takes time.

- The other person in your case may have very little or no money and the court may not order them to pay your costs for this reason.

- The person who has been ordered to pay the costs may then turn out to have no money or they may disappear.

In any event, no matter how successful you are at the final hearing of your case and no matter that the other person is good for all the money which they are ordered to pay, they will only have to pay those costs which the court assesses as reasonable and proportionate. This will vary from case to case, but may only amount to as little as 60% of your costs or less. The rest will still be paid from any contributions you have paid or via the statutory charge.

Generally speaking, whilst you receive General Family Help or Legal Representation, the other person in your case will not have to pay for the time spent dealing with the Legal Services Commission and related work. The shortfall will also be paid from any contributions you have paid or via the statutory charge.

12. Statutory charge

At the end of the case the Legal Services Commission will pay all your legal costs including my firm's charges (under the Legal Help scheme, Funding Certificate and under the Help with Mediation scheme). The statutory charge will apply to all of these costs except for costs spent on mediation or Help with Mediation.

If the other person in your case has been ordered to pay all or some of your costs, the Legal Services Commission will seek to recover those costs from the other person. As I explained, there is likely to be a shortfall between the costs that the other person has to pay and your overall costs.

You will still have to pay your costs out of any money or property you recover or preserve in a financial case

- if, as is usual in family cases, no order for costs has been made and therefore you have to pay your own costs,
- if the person who has been ordered to pay your costs does not pay, or
- if there is a shortfall.

If there are court proceedings relating to children and domestic violence and later there are proceedings relating to finances under the same Funding Certificate, the whole costs will be liable to the statutory charge. Maintenance is exempt from the provisions of the statutory charge. This means that your costs will be deducted from any money recovered before you receive it. If property or money is preserved or recovered, the Legal Services Commission has a discretion, in certain circumstances, to postpone the operation of the Statutory Charge until the property is sold, providing you agree to pay interest on your costs and you live in the property. Where the operation of the Statutory Charge is postponed, interest is charged on your costs at the rate of [8%] per year.

There are other special rules which mean that:

- you can use money you get in a financial case to buy a home for yourself;
- you can use a property which you get in a financial case as your home; or
- you can move from one such home to a new home

and the statutory charge is put as a mortgage on that home. When it considers whether to postpone the operation of the statutory charge in such a case the Legal Services Commission may require you to prove that you cannot raise a bank loan that would enable you to repay the statutory charge immediately and may require you to continue with monthly payments you made as a contribution to your public funding so that the statutory charge can be repaid more quickly.

Please contact me if you would like me to explain any aspects of the statutory charge to you again.

I have to pay any money I recover for you to the Legal Services Commission. The Legal Services Commission will deduct any money they have paid and not yet got back in another way from the money before it sends the balance of the money to you.

If in a case about finances you do not preserve or recover money or property, you will not be refunded any contributions you pay to the Legal Services Commission (unless your overall costs are less than your contributions). The rest of my firm's costs will be paid out of the Community Legal Service fund.

13. Costs against you

The court has power to make an order that you pay some or all of the other person's costs, although this is quite unusual in family cases. If the court makes an order for costs, it may order that there will be a further hearing when the court will assess whether and, if so, how much you are able to afford to pay.

There is, however, still a risk that you have to pay some or all of the costs of the other person in your case. It is therefore important that you consider carefully any proposals and that you make reasonable proposals yourself to settle the matter. In addition, if you do not accept reasonable proposals made by the other person in your case, your Certificate may be stopped. If you then continue with your case, either by acting in person or by paying for legal representation yourself, the statutory charge will still apply and you may be ordered to pay the other person's costs too.

14. During your case

I will keep you informed regularly of progress in your case, especially if I decide I need to do something which I have not yet discussed with you. I will explain the effect of any important or relevant papers in your case. I may need to instruct a barrister to advise about your case and to represent you in court. I will explain this to you if this happens and, where appropriate, discuss the choice with you. Your file may be seen by staff from the Legal Services Commission as part of their assessment of the quality of this firm's work. The staff at the Legal Services Commission are bound by law to keep information confidential.

15. Proceeds of Crime Act

Under the Proceeds of Crime Act we have to take full proof of ID from you. We usually do this at the first meeting. However, if we have not yet done so for whatever reason, we will ask you to make an appointment for this as soon as possible.

In financial family proceedings you are obliged to give full and frank disclosure of your financial and personal circumstances. The Proceeds of Crime Act 2002 in certain circumstances makes it a criminal offence for you to enter into a financial settlement with your [spouse/civil partner] if you know that any income or capital of whatever nature which you or your [spouse/civil partner] uses or retains represents the proceeds of crime. The proceeds of crime are any money which has arisen as a result of any crime and include, for example, money saved as a result of tax evasion or undeclared cash taken out of a business. If you are aware of such money in your family's circumstances, you should tell me about it as soon as possible. We can then discuss what steps need to be taken.

16. Ending instructing me

You may terminate your instructions to me in writing at any time. I may decide to stop acting for you only with good reason, for example:

1. if you do not give me clear or proper instructions;
2. if I cannot continue to act without being in breach of rules of professional conduct;
3. if there has been an irretrievable breakdown in trust and confidence; or
4. if your funding is withdrawn.

If this happens and court proceedings are ongoing, this firm will have to come off the court record. [*To avoid having to attend court for this reason, we require all clients to sign a 'Notice of Acting in Person' which we can then send to the court and all other parties. We will let you know in advance if we ever have to make use of this.*]

17. At the end of your case

My firm will keep your file of papers (except for any papers that you ask to be returned to you) for at least six years from the date of the last bill. My firm will keep the file on the understanding that we have the authority to destroy it after this period. My firm will not destroy documents that you ask us to deposit in safe custody.

If you require the file during the period while it is in storage, we can provide this to you on payment of our reasonable fees for delivery, locating any specific documents and making any copies for you. As you will appreciate, we hold a number of files in storage and it may take some time to retrieve your particular papers.

18. Procedure for resolving problems

If a problem arises at any time, please contact me so that we can talk about your concerns. If that does not provide the solution, please contact my client care partner, [   ], who can supply you with this firm's written complaints procedure if you require this.

All solicitors must attempt to resolve problems that may arise with their services. It is therefore important that you immediately raise with me any concerns you may have. I would be disappointed if you thought that you had reason to be unhappy with the service that I am providing.

In the unlikely event that a mistake is made by my firm, we have professional indemnity insurance in the sum of £[   ] per claim. We do require that you limit any claim you may have in respect of professional negligence against this firm to the amount of that sum.

If you continue to instruct me, this will mean that you accept the terms of business set out in this letter.

Yours sincerely

CC4S   Terms of business for clients on General Family Help or Legal Representation: solicitor or trainee acting

Dear [*client*]

I am a [*trainee*] solicitor employed in the firm. The partner in the firm responsible for supervising my management of your case is [   ].

1.   Introduction

This firm has a Community Legal Service Franchise and a contract with the Legal Services Commission to provide General Family Help and Legal Representation. This means that this office has been specially approved by the Legal Services Commission to provide a quality service to you.

You are making an application for General Family Help or Legal Representation to assist you in funding your case. You will recall that I explained to you a number of points about General Family Help and Legal Representation when you completed the application forms. I am writing to confirm these and other important points.

Initially you will probably be granted General Family Help only. This will allow me to state your case, give financial disclosure to the other person in your case (if your case concerns finances), and to negotiate a settlement. It will also cover the initial stages of court proceedings. However if matters cannot be resolved and it is necessary to proceed towards a final hearing you will need to upgrade to a Legal Representation Certificate. At that stage the Legal Services Commission will look at the merits and your financial position again. It may then decide that you can use any savings or other assets that you have to finance the final hearing or that you should apply for a bank loan to cover the costs of the final hearing rather than to continue to receive public funding. I will explain the procedure and requirements to you if it appears that this is likely to apply in your case. In most other aspects the conditions that apply under a General Family Help Certificate and Legal Representation Certificate are very similar and I will explain them together and point out any differences if appropriate.

2.   Criteria for General Family Help and Legal Representation

The Legal Services Commission will not only assess your financial eligibility but also your prospects of success and make a cost-benefit analysis of your case.

Generally, you will not be granted General Family Help or Legal Representation if you have not attempted to reach a settlement or if your prospects of success are poor. If your case concerns something other than domestic violence or children, for example finances, your application will also be refused if your prospects of success are borderline or uncertain, unless the case has overwhelming importance to you or a significant wider public interest.

Your application will also be refused unless the likely benefits to be gained from the proceedings for you justify the likely costs, are such that a reasonable private paying client would be prepared to take or defend the proceedings in all the circumstances.

3. Mediation

In most family cases you are required to discuss with a mediator the way in which mediation may be able to assist you in resolving the dispute. If you agree to mediation, the mediator will ask the other person to attend mediation with you to explore the prospects of a settlement. In some types of family cases or depending on individual circumstances this may not be required. In your case you have now satisfied the requirements imposed by the Legal Services Commission concerning mediation and you can therefore proceed with your application for a General Family Help or Legal Representation Certificate. If it appears likely that mediation would be beneficial to you at a later stage in the case then I will consider the options with you again at that time.

4. Delays

Unfortunately, there tend to be considerable delays at the Legal Services Commission due to, amongst other things, pressure of work. It may take about four to six weeks for the average General Family Help or Legal Representation application to be determined and a Funding Certificate to be issued. Similar delays occur at all stages whenever we have to deal with the Legal Services Commission.

Delays may also be caused at court or for other reasons. However, we will try and do all we can to minimise delays and will always keep you informed.

5. Scope

Until you accept an offer of General Family Help or Legal Representation and the Funding Certificate is in our possession, I am unable to carry out any work under the General Family Help or Legal Representation schemes. I know that this is frustrating but this is outside my control. If there is an emergency, it may be appropriate for you to receive Emergency Representation. I will explain this in section 6 below. A Funding Certificate is not retrospective so it does not cover work done before the date of the Funding Certificate.

Similarly, a Funding Certificate will have a costs limitation attached to it. This means that I will only be allowed to carry out work up to that limitation, including incidental expenses. Once the limitation is reached, I will have to apply for an extension and I will not be able to do any further work for you until the extension is granted. At that stage the Legal Services Commission will also look at whether it is still reasonable for you to receive Legal Representation and you will have to convince them that it is.

The work that the firm can do under a Funding Certificate is strictly limited by the wording of that Certificate. Occasionally it may be necessary to obtain an amendment to the Certificate from the Legal Services Commission to carry out work which is outside the scope of the original description. Frequently, there are delays at the Legal Services Commission in granting amendments to Certificates.

6. Emergency representation

If your case is very urgent, it may be appropriate to make an application for Emergency Representation. This is only appropriate in extremely urgent cases requiring immediate court action and will not be appropriate in the vast majority of cases. I can make an application for Emergency Representation only if this is justifiable in the particular circumstances of your case.

If you obtain an Emergency Certificate you are under an obligation to accept a full Funding Certificate on such terms as to contributions as the Legal Services Commission imposes (see section 7 below). An Emergency Representation Certificate may be revoked or discharged if:

1. you do not provide information or documents when requested; or
2. you do not attend the Legal Services Commission for an interview (if this is required) to assess your means; or
3. you are not financially eligible; or
4. you do not accept an offer of a full Funding Certificate to replace the Emergency Representation Certificate.

It can be revoked or discharged for these reasons even if the case comes to an end before your application for Public Funding has been fully dealt with by the Legal Services Commission. You will have to pay all the legal costs that the Legal Services Commission has paid to this firm and any expenses (for example barrister's fees) yourself if your Emergency Representation Certificate is revoked or discharged or if you do not get a full Funding Certificate to replace the Emergency Certificate.

7. Your duties to the Legal Services Commission

You are under a duty to the Legal Services Commission:

1. to complete and return as soon as possible any forms received from the Legal Services Commission and, in particular, any forms about assessment of your income and assets;
2. to notify the Legal Services Commission of any increase in your income or capital;
3. to notify the Legal Services Commission of any change in your address;
4. to notify the Legal Services Commission if you start to live with or stop

living with a partner, whether of the same sex or the opposite sex.

8.   Our duties to the Legal Services Commission

You are my client and I will of course act in your best interests. However, as you are in receipt of General Family Help or Legal Representation I also have duties to the Legal Services Commission.

If you ask me to act in a way which could cause unreasonable expense to the Community Legal Service fund, I am under a duty to notify the Legal Services Commission which could result in your Funding Certificate being discharged.

I am also under a duty to inform the Legal Services Commission of any material changes in your prospects of success.

If you do not accept a reasonable offer to settle the case, I must tell the Legal Services Commission and they will probably stop your public funding by discharging the Funding Certificate. An offer is reasonable if a privately paying client in your position would accept it.

If any information comes to my knowledge about your financial eligibility to General Family Help or Legal Representation, I am under a duty to notify the Legal Services Commission.

9.   Contributions

The Legal Services Commission will assess whether or not you are liable to pay a contribution towards the cost of the case. You do not pay any money to this firm, but if contributions are assessed you will have to pay the monthly instalments to the Legal Services Commission. If your income or capital changes, the contribution may increase or decrease.

You have to pay your contributions for the duration of your case, until your Funding Certificate is discharged; this normally happens after the end of your case.

If at the end of the case your total contributions are more than what the Legal Services Commission has paid out, you will get a refund.

10. Charges

The court or the Legal Services Commission assesses whether our charges are reasonable. In most family cases, the hourly rate which we can charge is fixed by the Government.

[*Because I am an accredited specialist the hourly rate that the Legal Services Commission pays this firm for my time is 15% higher than those for other lawyers. This also applies to my colleagues who are accredited specialists and may work on your case from time to time.*]

Our charges, like those of all solicitors, are based on a number of different factors.

Factors which will be taken into account are:

1.   the time spent;
2.   the skills, specialised knowledge and responsibility required of the members of the firm handling the matter;
3.   the complexities and difficulty or novelty of the questions involved;
4.   the circumstances in which the business involved is transacted (for instance if, due to the urgency, evening or weekend work is required);
5.   the number and importance of any documents prepared or considered;
6.   the amount or value of any money or property involved;
7.   the importance of the matter to you.

The most important of these factors is the amount of time spent by members of the firm in dealing with your case. We have a computer-based time recording system which records the time spent by each member of the firm on your case.

Time is recorded for all work done on your case including time spent on the telephone, reading incoming post or emails, writing or dictating outgoing letters or emails, preparing file notes of meetings, considering and drafting documents, reviewing your file, considering your case, preparing instructions and briefs to barristers, researching law where necessary, attending conferences with barristers, attending court, meetings with you, meetings with the lawyers acting for the other person in your case or other people connected with the case, taking statements from witnesses and so on.

This firm's charges are exclusive of VAT at the current rate which will be added to the bill.

In cases involving court proceedings it is always difficult to forecast the amount of time that will be spent since much will depend on the attitude of the other person in your case and their solicitors, the volume and complexity of the documents disclosed and the time required for preparation and in court.

In general, costs are likely to be as follows.

●   In domestic violence injunctions, when two court hearings are required, depending on whether it is easy to serve the other person with the court documents, it is unlikely to cost less than £[3,000].

●   If there is a dispute about where children are to live and/or how often one parent is to see the children, and the case proceeds to a final hearing without an agreement being reached, the total costs are unlikely to be less than £[10,000]. A complex case may cost even more. If the case settles at an early stage, the total costs are much less.

●   If there is a dispute about financial matters, and the case proceeds to a final hearing without an agreement being reached, the total costs are unlikely to be less than £[15,000]. A complex case may cost even more. If the case settles at an early stage, the total costs are much less.

If you require a forecast for your own case at any time, please ask and I will do my best to give one. It is unlikely that I will be able to make a firmer prediction until I can assess the issues in detail and until I know the position of the other person in your case.

I will always try to give you my best estimate of the likely costs of your case, but the estimates are not fixed. Sometimes I may only be able to give you my best estimate of the costs of the next stage of your case. I will notify you at least every six months of the actual costs incurred in your case and give you an estimate of the total costs.

As well as the charges made by this firm, incidental expenses such as the fees of barristers and experts (if instructed) and court fees will be added to the bill.

I will tell you about any changes in the likely cost of your case.

At the end of the case I will have a detailed bill prepared for assessment by the court or the Commission and if:

- you have paid contributions; or
- you have preserved or recovered money or property and the statutory charge applies,

I will send a copy to you. You then have the right to request a detailed assessment and you will have the right to be heard or to write to the court with your views.

11. Recovering costs incurred from the other person in your case

The general rule in family cases is that each party pays their own lawyer's costs. By contrast to other court cases, in family cases courts do not automatically order the 'loser' to pay the 'winner's' costs. This is because it is not often apparent that there is a 'winner' or a 'loser'. In cases involving children or finances, the court will only order one party to pay the other's costs in exceptional circumstances, for example if one party has conducted the court case in a way that has wasted considerable resources or if a party has tried to mislead the court. If necessary, please ask me as to whether an order for costs is likely to be made in your case.

Even in the rare cases where another person has to pay your costs it is unlikely that they will have to pay all of your costs and you will still have to pay any shortfall.

There can be additional problems with orders for costs for example:

- The person who has been ordered to pay the costs may not do so. If they do not pay, you will have to try to enforce the costs order (for example by sending in the bailiffs or obtaining a charge over property owned by them) and this itself costs more money and takes time.

- The other person in your case may have very little or no money and the court may not order them to pay your costs for this reason.

- The person who has been ordered to pay the costs may then turn out to have no money or they may disappear.

In any event, no matter how successful you are at the final hearing of your case and no matter that the other person is good for all the money which they are ordered to pay, they will only have to pay those costs which the court assesses as reasonable and proportionate. This will vary from case to case, but may only amount to as little as 60% of your costs or less. The rest will still be paid from any contributions you have paid or via the statutory charge.

Generally speaking, whilst you receive General Family Help or Legal Representation, the other person in your case will not have to pay for the time spent dealing with the Legal Services Commission and related work. The shortfall will also be paid from any contributions you have paid or via the statutory charge.

12. Statutory charge

At the end of the case the Legal Services Commission will pay all your legal costs including my firm's charges (under the Legal Help scheme, Funding Certificate and under the Help with Mediation scheme). The statutory charge will apply to all of these costs except for costs spent on mediation or Help with Mediation.

If the other person in your case has been ordered to pay all or some of your costs, the Legal Services Commission will seek to recover those costs from the other person. As I explained, there is likely to be a shortfall between the costs that the other person has to pay and your overall costs.

You will still have to pay your costs out of any money or property you recover or preserve in a financial case

- if, as is usual in family cases, no order for costs has been made and therefore you have to pay your own costs,
- if the person who has been ordered to pay your costs does not pay, or
- if there is a shortfall.

If there are court proceedings relating to children and domestic violence and later there are proceedings relating to finances under the same Funding Certificate, the whole costs will be liable to the statutory charge. Maintenance is exempt from the provisions of the statutory charge. This means that your costs will be deducted from any money recovered before you receive it. If property or money is preserved or recovered, the Legal Services Commission has a discretion, in certain circumstances, to postpone the operation of the Statutory Charge until the property is sold, providing you agree to pay interest on your costs and you live in the property. Where the operation of the Statutory Charge is postponed, interest is charged on your costs at the rate of [8%] per year.

There are other special rules which mean that:

- you can use money you get in a financial case to buy a home for yourself;
- you can use a property which you get in a financial case as your home; or
- you can move from one such home to a new home

and the statutory charge is put as a mortgage on that home. When it considers whether to postpone the operation of the statutory charge in such a case the Legal Services Commission may require you to prove that you cannot raise a bank loan that would enable you to repay the statutory charge immediately and may require you to continue with monthly payments you made as a contribution to your public funding so that the statutory charge can be repaid more quickly.

Please contact me if you would like me to explain any aspects of the statutory charge to you again.

I have to pay any money I recover for you to the Legal Services Commission. The Legal Services Commission will deduct any money they have paid and not yet got back in another way from the money before it sends the balance of the money to you.

If in a case about finances you do not preserve or recover money or property, you will not be refunded any contributions you pay to the Legal Services Commission (unless your overall costs are less than your contributions). The rest of my firm's costs will be paid out of the Community Legal Service fund.

13. Costs against you

The court has power to make an order that you pay some or all of the other person's costs, although this is quite unusual in family cases. If the court makes an order for costs, it may order that there will be a further hearing when the court will assess whether and, if so, how much you are able to afford to pay.

There is, however, still a risk that you have to pay some or all of the costs of the other person in your case. It is therefore important that you consider carefully any proposals and that you make reasonable proposals yourself to settle the matter. In addition, if you do not accept reasonable proposals made by the other person in your case, your Certificate may be stopped. If you then continue with your case, either by acting in person or by paying for legal representation yourself, the statutory charge will still apply and you may be ordered to pay the other person's costs too.

14. During your case

I will keep you informed regularly of progress in your case, especially if I decide I need to do something which I have not yet discussed with you. I will explain the effect of any important or relevant papers in your case. I may need to instruct a barrister to advise about your case and to represent you in court. I will explain this to you if this happens and, where appropriate, discuss the choice with you. Your file may be seen by staff from the Legal Services Commission as part of their assessment of the quality of this firm's work. The staff at the Legal Services Commission are bound by law to keep information confidential.

15. Proceeds of Crime Act

Under the Proceeds of Crime Act we have to take full proof of ID from you. We usually do this at the first meeting. However, if we have not yet done so for whatever reason, we will ask you to make an appointment for this as soon as possible.

In financial family proceedings you are obliged to give full and frank disclosure of your financial and personal circumstances. The Proceeds of Crime Act 2002 in certain circumstances makes it a criminal offence for you to enter into a financial settlement with your [spouse/civil partner] if you know that any income or capital of whatever nature which you or your [spouse/civil partner] uses or retains represents the proceeds of crime. The proceeds of crime are any money which has arisen as a result of any crime and include, for example, money saved as a result of tax evasion or undeclared cash taken out of a business. If you are aware of such money in your family's circumstances, you should tell me about it as soon as possible. We can then discuss what steps need to be taken.

16. Ending instructing me

You may terminate your instructions to me in writing at any time. I may decide to stop acting for you only with good reason, for example:

1. if you do not give me clear or proper instructions;
2. if I cannot continue to act without being in breach of rules of professional conduct;
3. if there has been an irretrievable breakdown in trust and confidence; or
4. if your funding is withdrawn.

If this happens and court proceedings are ongoing, this firm will have to come off the court record. [*To avoid having to attend court for this reason, we require all clients to sign a 'Notice of Acting in Person' which we can then send to the court and all other parties. We will let you know in advance if we ever have to make use of this.*]

17. At the end of your case

My firm will keep your file of papers (except for any papers that you ask to be returned to you) for at least six years from the date of the last bill. My firm will keep the file on the understanding that we have the authority to destroy it after this period. My firm will not destroy documents that you ask us to deposit in safe custody.

If you require the file during the period while it is in storage, we can provide this to you on payment of our reasonable fees for delivery, locating any specific documents and making any copies for you. As you will appreciate, we hold a number of files in storage and it may take some time to retrieve your particular papers.

18. Procedure for resolving problems

If a problem arises at any time, please contact me or my supervising partner so that we can talk about your concerns. If that does not provide the solution, please contact my client care partner, [   ], who can supply you with this firm's written complaints procedure if you require this.

All solicitors must attempt to resolve problems that may arise with their services. It is therefore important that you immediately raise with me any concerns you may have. I would be disappointed if you thought that you had reason to be unhappy with the service that I am providing.

In the unlikely event that a mistake is made by my firm, we have professional indemnity insurance in the sum of £[   ] per claim. We do require that you limit any claim you may have in respect of professional negligence against this firm to the amount of that sum.

If you continue to instruct me, this will mean that you accept the terms of business set out in this letter.

Yours sincerely

CC5P Terms of business for clients on Public Funding for a Trust of Land Act or Inheritance Act claim: partner acting

Dear [*client*]

I am a solicitor and a partner in the firm. I will have the overall management and responsibility for your case and other solicitors or trainee solicitors may help me under my supervision.

1. Introduction

This firm has a Community Legal Service Franchise and a contract with the Legal Services Commission to provide General Family Help and Legal Representation. This means that this office has been specially approved by the Legal Services Commission to provide a quality service to you.

You are making an application for General Family Help or Legal Representation to assist you in funding your case. You will recall that I explained to you a number of points about General Family Help and Legal Representation when you completed the application forms. I am writing to confirm these and other important points.

Initially you will probably be granted General Family Help only. This will allow me to state your case, give disclosure of relevant documents and to negotiate a settlement. It will also cover the initial stages of court proceedings. However if matters cannot be resolved and it is necessary to proceed towards a final hearing you will need to upgrade to a Legal Representation Certificate. At that stage the Legal Services Commission will look at the merits and your financial position again. It may then decide that you can use any savings or other assets that you have to finance the final hearing or that you should apply for a bank loan to cover the costs of the final hearing rather than to continue to receive public funding. I will explain the procedure and requirements to you if it appears that this is likely to apply in your case. In most other aspects the conditions that apply under a General Family Help Certificate and Legal Representation Certificate are very similar and I will explain them together and point out any differences if appropriate.

2. Criteria for General Family Help and Legal Representation

The Legal Services Commission will not only assess your financial eligibility but also your prospects of success and make a cost-benefit analysis of your case.

Generally you will not be granted General Family Help or Legal Representation if you have not attempted to reach a settlement or if your prospects of success are poor, borderline or uncertain, unless the case has overwhelming importance to you or a significant wider public interest.

Your application will also be refused unless the likely benefits to be gained from the proceedings for you justify the likely costs, such that a reasonable privately-paying client would be prepared to take or defend the proceedings in all the circumstances.

3.   Mediation

In most family cases you are required to discuss with a mediator the way in which mediation may be able to assist you in resolving the dispute. If you agree to mediation, the mediator will ask the other person to attend mediation with you to explore the prospects of a settlement. In some types of family cases or depending on individual circumstances this may not be required. In your case you have now satisfied the requirements imposed by the Legal Services Commission concerning mediation and you can therefore proceed with your application for a General Family Help or Legal Representation Certificate. If it appears likely that mediation would be beneficial to you at a later stage in the case then I will consider the options with you again at that time.

4.   Delays

Unfortunately, there tend to be considerable delays at the Legal Services Commission due to, amongst other things, pressure of work. It may take about four to six weeks for the average General Family Help or Legal Representation application to be determined and a Funding Certificate to be issued. Similar delays occur at all stages whenever we have to deal with the Legal Services Commission.

Delays may also be caused at court or for other reasons. However, we will try and do all we can to minimise delays and will always keep you informed.

5.   Scope

Until you accept an offer of General Family Help or Legal Representation and the Funding Certificate is in our possession, I am unable to carry out any work under the General Family Help or Legal Representation schemes. I know that this is frustrating but this is outside my control. If there is an emergency, it may be appropriate for you to receive Emergency Representation. I will explain this in section 6 below. A Funding Certificate is not retrospective so it does not cover work done before the date of the Funding Certificate.

Similarly, a Funding Certificate will have a costs limitation attached to it. This means that I will only be allowed to carry out work up to that limitation, including incidental expenses. Once the limitation is reached, I will have to apply for an extension and I will not be able to do any further work for you until the extension is granted. At that stage the Legal Services Commission will also look at whether it is still reasonable for you to receive Legal Representation and you will have to convince them that it is.

The work that the firm can do under a Funding Certificate is strictly limited by the wording of that Certificate. Occasionally it may be necessary to obtain an amendment to the Certificate from the Legal Services Commission to carry out work which is outside the scope of the original description. Frequently, there are delays at the Legal Services Commission in granting amendments to Certificates.

6. Emergency representation

If your case is very urgent, it may be appropriate to make an application for Emergency Representation. This is only appropriate in extremely urgent cases requiring immediate court action and will not be appropriate in the vast majority of cases. I can make an application for Emergency Representation only if this is justifiable in the particular circumstances of your case.

If you obtain an Emergency Certificate you are under an obligation to accept a full Funding Certificate on such terms as to contributions as the Legal Services Commission imposes (see section 7 below). An Emergency Representation Certificate may be revoked or discharged if:

1. you do not provide information or documents when requested; or
2. you do not attend the Legal Services Commission for an interview (if this is required) to assess your means; or
3. you are not financially eligible; or
4. you do not accept an offer of a full Funding Certificate to replace the Emergency Representation Certificate.

It can be revoked or discharged for these reasons even if the case comes to an end before your application for Public Funding has been fully dealt with by the Legal Services Commission. You will have to pay all the legal costs that the Legal Services Commission has paid to this firm and any expenses (for example barrister's fees) yourself if your Emergency Representation Certificate is revoked or discharged or if you do not get a full Funding Certificate to replace the Emergency Certificate.

7. Your duties to the Legal Services Commission

You are under a duty to the Legal Services Commission:

1. to complete and return as soon as possible any forms received from the Legal Services Commission and, in particular, any forms about assessment of your income and assets;
2. to notify the Legal Services Commission of any increase in your income or capital;
3. to notify the Legal Services Commission of any change in your address;
4. to notify the Legal Services Commission if you start to live with or stop living with a partner, whether of the same sex or the opposite sex.

8. Our duties to the Legal Services Commission

You are my client and I will of course act in your best interests. However, as you are in receipt of General Family Help or Legal Representation I also have duties to the Legal Services Commission.

If you ask me to act in a way which could cause unreasonable expense to the Community Legal Service fund, I am under a duty to notify the Legal Services Commission which could result in your Funding Certificate being discharged.

I am also under a duty to inform the Legal Services Commission of any material changes in your prospects of success.

If you do not accept a reasonable offer to settle the case, I must tell the Legal Services Commission and they will probably stop your public funding by discharging the Funding Certificate. An offer is reasonable if a privately paying client in your position would accept it.

If any information comes to my knowledge about your financial eligibility to General Family Help or Legal Representation, I am under a duty to notify the Legal Services Commission.

9. Contributions

The Legal Services Commission will assess whether or not you are liable to pay a contribution towards the cost of the case. You do not pay any money to this firm, but if contributions are assessed you will have to pay the monthly instalments to the Legal Services Commission. If your income or capital changes, the contribution may increase or decrease.

You have to pay your contributions for the duration of your case, until your Funding Certificate is discharged; this normally happens after the end of your case.

If at the end of the case your total contributions are more than what the Legal Services Commission has paid out, you will get a refund.

10. Charges

The court or the Legal Services Commission assess whether our charges are reasonable. In most family cases, the hourly rate which we can charge is fixed by the Government.

[*Because I am an accredited specialist the hourly rate that the Legal Services Commission pays this firm for my time is 15% higher than those for other lawyers. This also applies to my colleagues who are accredited specialists and may work on your case from time to time.*]

Our charges, like those of all solicitors, are based on a number of different factors.

Factors which will be taken into account are:

1. the time spent;
2. the skills, specialised knowledge and responsibility required of the members of the firm handling the matter;
3. the complexities and difficulty or novelty of the questions involved;
4. the circumstances in which the business involved is transacted (for instance if, due to the urgency, evening or weekend work is required);
5. the number and importance of any documents prepared or considered;
6. the amount or value of any money or property involved;
7. the importance of the matter to you.

The most important of these factors is the amount of time spent by members of the firm in dealing with your case. We have a computer-based time recording system which records the time spent by each member of the firm on your case.

Time is recorded for all work done on your case including time spent on the telephone, reading incoming post or emails, writing or dictating outgoing letters or emails, preparing file notes of meetings, considering and drafting documents, reviewing your file, considering your case, preparing instructions and briefs to barristers, researching law where necessary, attending conferences with barristers, attending court, meetings with you, meetings with the lawyers acting for the other person in your case or other people connected with the case, taking statements from witnesses and so on.

This firm's charges are exclusive of VAT at the current rate which will be added to the bill.

In court cases it is always difficult to forecast the amount of time that will be spent since much will depend on the attitude of the other person in your case and their solicitors, the volume and complexity of the documents disclosed and the time required for preparation and in court.

In general, costs are likely to be as follows.

*   If a case is resolved by agreement, it could cost as little as £[1,000], but sometimes it will be necessary to consider a great volume of documents such as solicitors' files and correspondence before it is possible to provide you with the advice that is necessary for you to be able to make an informed decision about proposals for settlement. Therefore, even if the matter is resolved by agreement, the costs can be higher and could be £[5,000] or more.

*   If the case is not resolved by agreement and the case proceeds to a final hearing, the costs could be up to £[10,000] or more. A complex case may cost £[15,000–20,000] or even more.

I enclose a costs schedule forecasting the costs up to a stage where it will be possible for me to advise you where your case may be going. I should be able to give you a forecast for the costs after that stage then. Please note that the schedule is not a quote, but simply my best guess of what your costs are likely to be. Your costs may be higher or lower and will depend on the factors set out above. If you require a forecast for your own case at any time, please ask and I will do my best to give one. It is unlikely that I will be able to make a firmer prediction until I can assess the issues in detail and until I know the position of the other person in your case.

I will always try to give you my best estimate of the likely costs of your case, but the estimates are not fixed. Sometimes I may only be able to give you my best estimate of the costs of the next stage of your case. I will notify you at least every six months of the actual costs incurred in your case and give you an estimate of the total costs.

As well as the charges made by this firm, incidental expenses such as the fees of barristers and experts (if instructed) and court fees will be added to the bill.

I will tell you about any changes in the likely cost of your case.

At the end of the case I will have a detailed bill prepared for assessment by the court or the Commission and if:

- you have paid contributions; or
- you have preserved or recovered money or property and the statutory charge applies,

I will send a copy to you. You then have the right to request a detailed assessment and you will have the right to be heard or to write to the court with your views.

11. Recovering costs incurred from the other person in your case

If you decide not to proceed with your case before court proceedings are commenced, or if the case is settled before then, there is no rule of law requiring the other person in your case to make any payment towards your legal costs, and you are unlikely to recover them.

In all court cases the court has a discretion to decide who should pay the costs and it can apportion and decide who should pay for a particular part of the case.

In general the 'loser' will be ordered to pay the 'winner's' costs and in Inheritance Act cases the estate would normally be ordered to pay the costs if the claimant is awarded something out of the estate. However, the costs rules are designed to encourage parties to settle their disputes as early as possible. Therefore, it is necessary to consider at an appropriate stage whether to make or to accept proposals for settlement. The court will consider such proposals and the conduct of the parties in general when making a decision on costs. So, for example, the court may order the 'loser' to pay the 'winner's' costs up to the point at which the 'winner' rejected some reasonable proposals for settlement that the 'loser' made. The 'winner' may in such a situation very well be ordered to pay the 'loser's' costs after that date.

You will have to bear this in mind throughout the case in order to minimise your risk of being ordered to pay any costs.

If the other person in your case is ordered to pay your costs, unfortunately, this will not be all the costs that would have been incurred under the Funding Certificate. There can be additional problems with orders for costs for example:

- The person who has been ordered to pay the costs may not do so. If they do not pay, you will have to try to enforce the costs order (for example by sending in the bailiffs or obtaining a charge over property owned by them) and this itself costs more money and takes time.

- The other person in your case may have very little or no money and the court may not order them to pay your costs for this reason.

- The person who has been ordered to pay the costs may then turn out to have no money or they may disappear.

In any event, no matter how successful you are at the final hearing of your case and no matter that the other person is good for all the money which they are ordered to pay, they will only have to pay those costs which the court assesses as reasonable and proportionate. This will vary from case to case, but may only amount to as little as 60% of your costs or less. The rest will still be paid from any contributions you have paid or via the statutory charge.

Generally speaking, whilst you receive General Family Help or Legal Representation, the other person in your case will not have to pay for the time spent dealing with the Legal Services Commission and related work. The shortfall will also be paid from any contributions you have paid or via the statutory charge.

12. Statutory charge

At the end of the case the Legal Services Commission will pay all your legal costs including my firm's charges (under the Legal Help scheme, Funding Certificate and under the Help with Mediation scheme). The statutory charge will apply to all of these costs except for costs spent on mediation or Help with Mediation.

If the other person in your case has been ordered to pay all or some of your costs, the Legal Services Commission will seek to recover those costs from the other person. As I explained, there is likely to be a shortfall between the costs that the other person has to pay and your overall costs.

You will still have to pay your costs out of any money or property you recover or preserve in a financial case

- if no order for costs has been made and therefore you have to pay your own costs,

- if the person who has been ordered to pay your costs does not pay, or
- if there is a shortfall.

If there are court proceedings relating to children and domestic violence and later there are proceedings relating to finances under the same Funding Certificate, the whole costs will be liable to the statutory charge. Maintenance is exempt from the provisions of the statutory charge. This means that your costs will be deducted from any money recovered before you receive it. If property or money is preserved or recovered, the Legal Services Commission has a discretion, in certain circumstances, to postpone the operation of the Statutory Charge until the property is sold, providing you agree to pay interest on your costs and you live in the property. Where the operation of the Statutory Charge is postponed, interest is charged on your costs at the rate of [8%] per year.

There are other special rules which mean that:

- you can use money you get in a financial case to buy a home for yourself;
- you can use a property which you get in a financial case as your home; or
- you can move from one such home to a new home

and the statutory charge is put as a mortgage on that home. When it considers whether to postpone the operation of the statutory charge in such a case the Legal Services Commission may require you to prove that you cannot raise a bank loan that would enable you to repay the statutory charge immediately and may require you to continue with monthly payments you made as a contribution to your public funding so that the statutory charge can be repaid more quickly.

Please contact me if you would like me to explain any aspects of the statutory charge to you again.

I have to pay any money I recover for you to the Legal Services Commission. The Legal Services Commission will deduct any money they have paid and not yet got back in another way from the money before it sends the balance of the money to you.

If you do not preserve or recover money or property, you will not be refunded any contributions you pay to the Legal Services Commission (unless your overall costs are less than your contributions). The rest of my firm's costs will be paid out of the Community Legal Service fund.

13. Costs against you

The court has power to make an order that you pay some or all of the other person's costs. The main principle in property or inheritance disputes is that the successful party gets their costs paid by the unsuccessful party. When the court makes an order for costs, it may order that there will be a further hearing when the court will assess whether and, if so, how much you are able to afford to pay.

Even if you receive public funding now because you do not have the money to pay your legal fees, you may be ordered to pay another person's costs if you have not accepted reasonable proposals for settlement or in other circumstances. You may then have received property or money in the case and be ordered to pay the costs order from those assets. It is therefore important that you consider carefully any proposals and that you make reasonable proposals yourself to settle the matter. In addition, if you do not accept reasonable proposals made by the other person in your case, your Certificate may be stopped. If you then continue with your case, either by acting in person or by paying for legal representation yourself, the statutory charge will still apply and you may be ordered to pay the other person's costs too.

14. During your case

I will keep you informed regularly of progress in your case, especially if I decide I need to do something which I have not yet discussed with you. I will explain the effect of any important or relevant papers in your case. I may need to instruct a barrister to advise about your case and to represent you in court. I will explain this to you if this happens and, where appropriate, discuss the choice with you. Your file may be seen by staff from the Legal Services Commission as part of their assessment of the quality of this firm's work. The staff at the Legal Services Commission are bound by law to keep information confidential.

15. Proceeds of Crime Act

Under the Proceeds of Crime Act we have to take full proof of ID from you. We usually do this at the first meeting. However, if we have not yet done so for whatever reason, we will ask you to make an appointment for this as soon as possible.

In financial family proceedings you are obliged to give full and frank disclosure of your financial and personal circumstances. The Proceeds of Crime Act 2002 in certain circumstances makes it a criminal offence for you to enter into a financial settlement with someone if you know that any income or capital of whatever nature which you or the other person uses or retains represents the proceeds of crime. The proceeds of crime are any money which has arisen as a result of any crime and include, for example, money saved as a result of tax evasion or undeclared cash taken out of a business. If you are aware of such money in your circumstances, you should tell me about it as soon as possible. We can then discuss what steps need to be taken.

16. Ending instructing me

You may terminate your instructions to me in writing at any time. I may decide to stop acting for you only with good reason, for example:

1.   if you do not give me clear or proper instructions;

2.   if I cannot continue to act without being in breach of rules of professional conduct;
3.   if there has been an irretrievable breakdown in trust and confidence; or
4.   if your funding is withdrawn.

If this happens and court proceedings are ongoing, this firm will have to come off the court record. [*To avoid having to attend court for this reason, we require all clients to sign a 'Notice of Acting in Person' which we can then send to the court and all other parties. We will let you know in advance if we ever have to make use of this.*]

17.   At the end of your case

My firm will keep your file of papers (except for any papers that you ask to be returned to you) for at least six years from the date of the last bill. My firm will keep the file on the understanding that we have the authority to destroy it after this period. My firm will not destroy documents that you ask us to deposit in safe custody.

If you require the file during the period while it is in storage, we can provide this to you on payment of our reasonable fees for delivery, locating any specific documents and making any copies for you. As you will appreciate, we hold a number of files in storage and it may take some time to retrieve your particular papers.

18.   Procedure for resolving problems

If a problem arises at any time, please contact me so that we can talk about your concerns. If that does not provide the solution, please contact my client care partner, [   ], who can supply you with this firm's written complaints procedure if you require this.

All solicitors must attempt to resolve problems that may arise with their services. It is therefore important that you immediately raise with me any concerns you may have. I would be disappointed if you thought that you had reason to be unhappy with the service that I am providing.

In the unlikely event that a mistake is made by my firm, we have professional indemnity insurance in the sum of £[   ] per claim. We do require that you limit any claim you may have in respect of professional negligence against this firm to the amount of that sum.

If you continue to instruct me, this will mean that you accept the terms of business set out in this letter.

Yours sincerely

Enc. costs schedule

CC5S Terms of business for clients on Public Funding for a Trust of Land Act or Inheritance Act claim: solicitor or trainee acting

Dear [*client*]

I am a [*trainee*] solicitor employed in the firm. The partner in the firm responsible for supervising my management of your case is [   ].

1. Introduction

This firm has a Community Legal Service Franchise and a contract with the Legal Services Commission to provide General Family Help and Legal Representation. This means that this office has been specially approved by the Legal Services Commission to provide a quality service to you.

You are making an application for General Family Help or Legal Representation to assist you in funding your case. You will recall that I explained to you a number of points about General Family Help and Legal Representation when you completed the application forms. I am writing to confirm these and other important points.

Initially you will probably be granted General Family Help only. This will allow me to state your case, give disclosure of relevant documents and to negotiate a settlement. It will also cover the initial stages of court proceedings. However if matters cannot be resolved and it is necessary to proceed towards a final hearing you will need to upgrade to a Legal Representation Certificate. At that stage the Legal Services Commission will look at the merits and your financial position again. It may then decide that you can use any savings or other assets that you have to finance the final hearing or that you should apply for a bank loan to cover the costs of the final hearing rather than to continue to receive public funding. I will explain the procedure and requirements to you if it appears that this is likely to apply in your case. In most other aspects the conditions that apply under a General Family Help Certificate and Legal Representation Certificate are very similar and I will explain them together and point out any differences if appropriate.

2. Criteria for General Family Help and Legal Representation

The Legal Services Commission will not only assess your financial eligibility but also your prospects of success and make a cost-benefit analysis of your case.

Generally you will not be granted General Family Help or Legal Representation if you have not attempted to reach a settlement or if your prospects of success are poor, borderline or uncertain, unless the case has overwhelming importance to you or a significant wider public interest.

Your application will also be refused unless the likely benefits to be gained from the proceedings for you justify the likely costs, such that a reasonable privately-paying client would be prepared to take or defend the proceedings in all the circumstances.

3.   Mediation

In most family cases you are required to discuss with a mediator the way in which mediation may be able to assist you in resolving the dispute. If you agree to mediation, the mediator will ask the other person to attend mediation with you to explore the prospects of a settlement. In some types of family cases or depending on individual circumstances this may not be required. In your case you have now satisfied the requirements imposed by the Legal Services Commission concerning mediation and you can therefore proceed with your application for a General Family Help or Legal Representation Certificate. If it appears likely that mediation would be beneficial to you at a later stage in the case then I will consider the options with you again at that time.

4.   Delays

Unfortunately, there tend to be considerable delays at the Legal Services Commission due to, amongst other things, pressure of work. It may take about four to six weeks for the average General Family Help or Legal Representation application to be determined and a Funding Certificate to be issued. Similar delays occur at all stages whenever we have to deal with the Legal Services Commission.

Delays may also be caused at court or for other reasons. However, we will try and do all we can to minimise delays and will always keep you informed.

5.   Scope

Until you accept an offer of General Family Help or Legal Representation and the Funding Certificate is in our possession, I am unable to carry out any work under the General Family Help or Legal Representation schemes. I know that this is frustrating but this is outside my control. If there is an emergency, it may be appropriate for you to receive Emergency Representation. I will explain this in section 6 below. A Funding Certificate is not retrospective so it does not cover work done before the date of the Funding Certificate.

Similarly, a Funding Certificate will have a costs limitation attached to it. This means that I will only be allowed to carry out work up to that limitation, including incidental expenses. Once the limitation is reached, I will have to apply for an extension and I will not be able to do any further work for you until the extension is granted. At that stage the Legal Services Commission will also look at whether it is still reasonable for you to receive Legal Representation and you will have to convince them that it is.

The work that the firm can do under a Funding Certificate is strictly limited by the wording of that Certificate. Occasionally it may be necessary to obtain an amendment to the Certificate from the Legal Services Commission to carry out work which is outside the scope of the original description. Frequently, there are delays at the Legal Services Commission in granting amendments to Certificates.

6. Emergency representation

If your case is very urgent, it may be appropriate to make an application for Emergency Representation. This is only appropriate in extremely urgent cases requiring immediate court action and will not be appropriate in the vast majority of cases. I can make an application for Emergency Representation only if this is justifiable in the particular circumstances of your case.

If you obtain an Emergency Certificate you are under an obligation to accept a full Funding Certificate on such terms as to contributions as the Legal Services Commission imposes (see section 7 below). An Emergency Representation Certificate may be revoked or discharged if:

1. you do not provide information or documents when requested; or
2. you do not attend the Legal Services Commission for an interview (if this is required) to assess your means; or
3. you are not financially eligible; or
4. you do not accept an offer of a full Funding Certificate to replace the Emergency Representation Certificate.

It can be revoked or discharged for these reasons even if the case comes to an end before your application for Public Funding has been fully dealt with by the Legal Services Commission. You will have to pay all the legal costs that the Legal Services Commission has paid to this firm and any expenses (for example barrister's fees) yourself if your Emergency Representation Certificate is revoked or discharged or if you do not get a full Funding Certificate to replace the Emergency Certificate.

7. Your duties to the Legal Services Commission

You are under a duty to the Legal Services Commission:

1. to complete and return as soon as possible any forms received from the Legal Services Commission and, in particular, any forms about assessment of your income and assets;
2. to notify the Legal Services Commission of any increase in your income or capital;
3. to notify the Legal Services Commission of any change in your address;
4. to notify the Legal Services Commission if you start to live with or stop living with a partner, whether of the same sex or the opposite sex.

8.   Our duties to the Legal Services Commission

You are my client and I will of course act in your best interests. However, as you are in receipt of General Family Help or Legal Representation I also have duties to the Legal Services Commission.

If you ask me to act in a way which could cause unreasonable expense to the Community Legal Service fund, I am under a duty to notify the Legal Services Commission which could result in your Funding Certificate being discharged.

I am also under a duty to inform the Legal Services Commission of any material changes in your prospects of success.

If you do not accept a reasonable offer to settle the case, I must tell the Legal Services Commission and they will probably stop your public funding by discharging the Funding Certificate. An offer is reasonable if a privately paying client in your position would accept it.

If any information comes to my knowledge about your financial eligibility to General Family Help or Legal Representation, I am under a duty to notify the Legal Services Commission.

9.   Contributions

The Legal Services Commission will assess whether or not you are liable to pay a contribution towards the cost of the case. You do not pay any money to this firm, but if contributions are assessed you will have to pay the monthly instalments to the Legal Services Commission. If your income or capital changes, the contribution may increase or decrease.

You have to pay your contributions for the duration of your case, until your Funding Certificate is discharged; this normally happens after the end of your case.

If at the end of the case your total contributions are more than what the Legal Services Commission has paid out, you will get a refund.

10.   Charges

The court or the Legal Services Commission assesses whether our charges are reasonable. In most family cases, the hourly rate which we can charge is fixed by the Government.

[*Because I am an accredited specialist the hourly rate that the Legal Services Commission pays this firm for my time is 15% higher than those for other lawyers. This also applies to my colleagues who are accredited specialists and may work on your case from time to time.*]

Our charges, like those of all solicitors, are based on a number of different factors.

Factors which will be taken into account are:

1. the time spent;
2. the skills, specialised knowledge and responsibility required of the members of the firm handling the matter;
3. the complexities and difficulty or novelty of the questions involved;
4. the circumstances in which the business involved is transacted (for instance if, due to the urgency, evening or weekend work is required);
5. the number and importance of any documents prepared or considered;
6. the amount or value of any money or property involved;
7. the importance of the matter to you.

The most important of these factors is the amount of time spent by members of the firm in dealing with your case. We have a computer-based time recording system which records the time spent by each member of the firm on your case.

Time is recorded for all work done on your case including time spent on the telephone, reading incoming post or emails, writing or dictating outgoing letters or emails, preparing file notes of meetings, considering and drafting documents, reviewing your file, considering your case, preparing instructions and briefs to barristers, researching law where necessary, attending conferences with barristers, attending court, meetings with you, meetings with the lawyers acting for the other person in your case or other people connected with the case, taking statements from witnesses and so on.

This firm's charges are exclusive of VAT at the current rate which will be added to the bill.

In court cases it is always difficult to forecast the amount of time that will be spent since much will depend on the attitude of the other person in your case and their solicitors, the volume and complexity of the documents disclosed and the time required for preparation and in court.

In general, costs are likely to be as follows.

- If a case is resolved by agreement, it could cost as little as £[1,000], but sometimes it will be necessary to consider a great volume of documents such as solicitors' files and correspondence before it is possible to provide you with the advice that is necessary for you to be able to make an informed decision about proposals for settlement. Therefore, even if the matter is resolved by agreement, the costs can be higher and could be £[5,000] or more.

- If the case is not resolved by agreement and the case proceeds to a final hearing, the costs could be up to £[10,000] or more. A complex case may cost £[15,000–20,000] or even more.

I enclose a costs schedule forecasting the costs up to a stage where it will be possible for me to advise you where your case may be going. I should be able to give you a forecast for the costs after that stage then. Please note that the schedule is not a quote, but simply my best guess of what your costs are likely to be. Your costs may be higher or lower and will depend on the factors set out above. If you require a forecast for your own case at any time, please ask and I will do my best to give one. It is unlikely that I will be able to make a firmer prediction until I can assess the issues in detail and until I know the position of the other person in your case.

I will always try to give you my best estimate of the likely costs of your case, but the estimates are not fixed. Sometimes I may only be able to give you my best estimate of the costs of the next stage of your case. I will notify you at least every six months of the actual costs incurred in your case and give you an estimate of the total costs.

As well as the charges made by this firm, incidental expenses such as the fees of barristers and experts (if instructed) and court fees will be added to the bill.

I will tell you about any changes in the likely cost of your case.

At the end of the case I will have a detailed bill prepared for assessment by the court or the Commission and if:

- you have paid contributions; or
- you have preserved or recovered money or property and the statutory charge applies,

I will send a copy to you. You then have the right to request a detailed assessment and you will have the right to be heard or to write to the court with your views.

11.   Recovering costs incurred from the other person in your case

If you decide not to proceed with your case before court proceedings are commenced, or if the case is settled before then, there is no rule of law requiring the other person in your case to make any payment towards your legal costs, and you are unlikely to recover them.

In all court cases the court has a discretion to decide who should pay the costs and it can apportion and decide who should pay for a particular part of the case.

In general the 'loser' will be ordered to pay the 'winner's' costs and in Inheritance Act cases the estate would normally be ordered to pay the costs if the claimant is awarded something out of the estate. However, the costs rules are designed to encourage parties to settle their disputes as early as possible. Therefore, it is necessary to consider at an appropriate stage whether to make or to accept proposals for settlement. The court will consider such proposals and the conduct of the parties in general when making a decision on costs. So, for example, the court may order the 'loser' to pay the 'winner's' costs up to the point at which the 'winner' rejected some reasonable proposals for settlement that the 'loser' made. The 'winner' may in such a situation very well be ordered to pay the 'loser's' costs after that date.

You will have to bear this in mind throughout the case in order to minimise your risk of being ordered to pay any costs.

If the other person in your case is ordered to pay your costs, unfortunately, this will not be all the costs that would have been incurred under the Funding Certificate. There can be additional problems with orders for costs for example:

- The person who has been ordered to pay the costs may not do so. If they do not pay, you will have to try to enforce the costs order (for example by sending in the bailiffs or obtaining a charge over property owned by them) and this itself costs more money and takes time.

- The other person in your case may have very little or no money and the court may not order them to pay your costs for this reason.

- The person who has been ordered to pay the costs may then turn out to have no money or they may disappear.

In any event, no matter how successful you are at the final hearing of your case and no matter that the other person is good for all the money which they are ordered to pay, they will only have to pay those costs which the court assesses as reasonable and proportionate. This will vary from case to case, but may only amount to as little as 60% of your costs or less. The rest will still be paid from any contributions you have paid or via the statutory charge.

Generally speaking, whilst you receive General Family Help or Legal Representation, the other person in your case will not have to pay for the time spent dealing with the Legal Services Commission and related work. The shortfall will also be paid from any contributions you have paid or via the statutory charge.

12. Statutory charge

At the end of the case the Legal Services Commission will pay all your legal costs including my firm's charges (under the Legal Help scheme, Funding Certificate and under the Help with Mediation scheme). The statutory charge will apply to all of these costs except for costs spent on mediation or Help with Mediation.

If the other person in your case has been ordered to pay all or some of your costs, the Legal Services Commission will seek to recover those costs from the other person. As I explained, there is likely to be a shortfall between the costs that the other person has to pay and your overall costs.

You will still have to pay your costs out of any money or property you recover or preserve in a financial case

- if no order for costs has been made and therefore you have to pay your own costs,

- if the person who has been ordered to pay your costs does not pay, or
- if there is a shortfall.

If there are court proceedings relating to children and domestic violence and later there are proceedings relating to finances under the same Funding Certificate, the whole costs will be liable to the statutory charge. Maintenance is exempt from the provisions of the statutory charge. This means that your costs will be deducted from any money recovered before you receive it. If property or money is preserved or recovered, the Legal Services Commission has a discretion, in certain circumstances, to postpone the operation of the Statutory Charge until the property is sold, providing you agree to pay interest on your costs and you live in the property. Where the operation of the Statutory Charge is postponed, interest is charged on your costs at the rate of [8%] per year.

There are other special rules which mean that:

- you can use money you get in a financial case to buy a home for yourself;
- you can use a property which you get in a financial case as your home; or
- you can move from one such home to a new home

and the statutory charge is put as a mortgage on that home. When it considers whether to postpone the operation of the statutory charge in such a case the Legal Services Commission may require you to prove that you cannot raise a bank loan that would enable you to repay the statutory charge immediately and may require you to continue with monthly payments you made as a contribution to your public funding so that the statutory charge can be repaid more quickly.

Please contact me if you would like me to explain any aspects of the statutory charge to you again.

I have to pay any money I recover for you to the Legal Services Commission. The Legal Services Commission will deduct any money they have paid and not yet got back in another way from the money before it sends the balance of the money to you.

If in case about finances you do not preserve or recover money or property, you will not be refunded any contributions you pay to the Legal Services Commission (unless your overall costs are less than your contributions). The rest of my firm's costs will be paid out of the Community Legal Service fund.

13. Costs against you

The court has power to make an order that you pay some or all of the other person's costs. The main principle in property or inheritance disputes is that the successful party gets their costs paid by the unsuccessful party. When the court makes an order for costs, it may order that there will be a further hearing when the court will assess whether and, if so, how much you are able to afford to pay.

Even if you receive public funding now because you do not have the money to pay your legal fees, you may be ordered to pay another person's costs if you have not accepted reasonable proposals for settlement or in other circumstances. You may then have received property or money in the case and be ordered to pay the costs order from those assets. It is therefore important that you consider carefully any proposals and that you make reasonable proposals yourself to settle the matter. In addition, if you do not accept reasonable proposals made by the other person in your case, your Certificate may be stopped. If you then continue with your case, either by acting in person or by paying for legal representation yourself, the statutory charge will still apply and you may be ordered to pay the other person's costs too.

14. During your case

I will keep you informed regularly of progress in your case, especially if I decide I need to do something which I have not yet discussed with you. I will explain the effect of any important or relevant papers in your case. I may need to instruct a barrister to advise about your case and to represent you in court. I will explain this to you if this happens and, where appropriate, discuss the choice with you. Your file may be seen by staff from the Legal Services Commission as part of their assessment of the quality of this firm's work. The staff at the Legal Services Commission are bound by law to keep information confidential.

15. Proceeds of Crime Act

Under the Proceeds of Crime Act we have to take full proof of ID from you. We usually do this at the first meeting. However, if we have not yet done so for whatever reason, we will ask you to make an appointment for this as soon as possible.

In financial family proceedings you are obliged to give full and frank disclosure of your financial and personal circumstances. The Proceeds of Crime Act 2002 in certain circumstances makes it a criminal offence for you to enter into a financial settlement with someone if you know that any income or capital of whatever nature which you or the other person uses or retains represents the proceeds of crime. The proceeds of crime are any money which has arisen as a result of any crime and include, for example, money saved as a result of tax evasion or undeclared cash taken out of a business. If you are aware of such money in your circumstances, you should tell me about it as soon as possible. We can then discuss what steps need to be taken.

16. Ending instructing me

You may terminate your instructions to me in writing at any time. I may decide to stop acting for you only with good reason, for example:

1.   if you do not give me clear or proper instructions;

2.   if I cannot continue to act without being in breach of rules of professional conduct;
3.   if there has been an irretrievable breakdown in trust and confidence; or
4.   if your funding is withdrawn.

If this happens and court proceedings are ongoing, this firm will have to come off the court record. [*To avoid having to attend court for this reason, we require all clients to sign a "Notice of Acting in Person" which we can then send to the court and all other parties. We will let you know in advance if we ever have to make use of this.*]

17.   At the end of your case

My firm will keep your file of papers (except for any papers that you ask to be returned to you) for at least six years from the date of the last bill. My firm will keep the file on the understanding that we have the authority to destroy it after this period. My firm will not destroy documents that you ask us to deposit in safe custody.

If you require the file during the period while it is in storage, we can provide this to you on payment of our reasonable fees for delivery, locating any specific documents and making any copies for you. As you will appreciate, we hold a number of files in storage and it may take some time to retrieve your particular papers.

18.   Procedure for resolving problems

If a problem arises at any time, please contact me or my supervising partner so that we can talk about your concerns. If that does not provide the solution, please contact my client care partner, [   ], who can supply you with this firm's written complaints procedure if you require this.

All solicitors must attempt to resolve problems that may arise with their services. It is therefore important that you immediately raise with me any concerns you may have. I would be disappointed if you thought that you had reason to be unhappy with the service that I am providing.

In the unlikely event that a mistake is made by my firm, we have professional indemnity insurance in the sum of £[   ] per claim. We do require that you limit any claim you may have in respect of professional negligence against this firm to the amount of that sum.

If you continue to instruct me, this will mean that you accept the terms of business set out in this letter.

Yours sincerely

Enc. costs schedule

CC6P Terms of business for private client: general family: partner acting

Dear [*client*]

1. Introduction

I am a solicitor and a partner in the firm and I will have the overall management and responsibility for your case. Other solicitors or trainee solicitors may help me under my supervision and deal with some of the day-to-day work. I set out in this letter the terms of business for clients of this firm as they apply to you.

2. Standards

Every solicitor in our offices endeavours to maintain certain minimum standards of case management. If you find that the standards set out below are not maintained, please speak to me.

I will try to return your telephone calls as soon as possible. I have a personal voicemail facility, so if for any reason I am not at my desk, please leave a message on my voicemail.

3. Charges

Our charges, like those of all solicitors, are based on a number of different factors.

Factors which will be taken into account are:

1. the time spent;
2. the skills, specialised knowledge and responsibility required of the members of the firm handling the matter;
3. the complexities and difficulty or novelty of the questions involved;
4. the circumstances in which the business involved is transacted (for instance if, due to the urgency, evening or weekend work is required or if an unusually large amount of documentation needs to be considered).

The most important of these factors is the amount of time spent by members of the firm in dealing with your case. We have a computer-based time recording system on which each member of the firm records the time spent on your case. Each individual has an hourly charge-out rate based on an hour of their time.

My own current charge-out rate is £[   ] per hour. The current charge-out rate for my assistant solicitors is £[   ] and the rate for my trainee solicitor is £[   ] per hour. I will let you know the charge-out rates of any other individual members of the firm dealing with your case whenever you request. The charge-out rates are exclusive of VAT.

Figures given to you for charge-out rates of any individuals in the firm are of

course subject to periodic review (for example to take into account inflation or any increase in the level of qualification or responsibility of any member of the firm dealing with the case).

Charge-out rates may also be increased if any of the factors mentioned at the beginning of this section apply.

Charge-out rates will apply to all the work done on your case including time spent on the telephone, reading incoming post or emails, writing or dictating outgoing letters or emails, preparing file notes of meetings, considering and drafting documents, reviewing your file, considering your case, preparing instructions and briefs to barristers, researching law where necessary, attending conferences with barristers, attending court, meetings with you, meetings with the lawyers acting for the other person in your case or other people connected with the case, taking statements from witnesses and so on.

As well as the charges made by this firm, incidental expenses such as the fees of any barristers or experts and court fees will be added to the bill.

Our charges are not contingent upon the result of your case. They are payable 'win or lose'. You are primarily liable for the charges. Even if the court orders someone else to pay your costs, you will have to pay in the first instance and may then be reimbursed when funds clear from the person ordered to pay your costs.

In cases involving court proceedings it is always difficult to forecast the amount of time that will be spent since much will depend on the attitude of the other person in your case and their solicitors, the volume and complexity of the documents disclosed and the time required for preparation and in court.

In general, costs are likely to be as follows.

- For a straightforward divorce, it is unlikely that the total costs will be less than £[600] plus VAT and the costs will be more if there are problems with the other person co-operating or if the divorce is contested. The court fees are currently £[340].

- In domestic violence injunctions, when two court hearings are required, depending on whether it is easy to serve the other person with the court documents, it is unlikely to cost less than £[5,000].

- If there is a dispute about where children are to live and/or how often one parent is to see the children, and the case proceeds to a final hearing without an agreement being reached, the total costs are unlikely to be less than £[15,000]. A complex case may cost even more. If the case settles at an early stage, the total costs are much less.

- If there is a dispute about financial matters, and the case proceeds to a final hearing without an agreement being reached, the total costs are unlikely to be less than £[25,000]. A complex case may cost even more. If the case settles at an early stage, the total costs are much less.

If you require a forecast for your own case at any time, please ask and I will do my best to give one. It is unlikely that I will be able to make a firmer prediction until I can assess the issues in detail and until I know the position of the other person in your case.

I will always try to give you my best estimate of the likely costs of your case, but the estimates are not fixed. Sometimes I may only be able to give you my best estimate of the costs of the next stage of your case. I will give you an estimate at least every six months.

Unfortunately, because of delays in the court system, court proceedings can often take a long time to conclude. If we did not require payment until the end of a case, our staff and overhead costs involved in financing your case would become prohibitive. It is for this reason that it is our standard practice both to require money on account and to deliver regular interim bills on account where appropriate. Because of the nature of family work, however, it is likely that at certain times during the case we will give you (without any further notification) varying amounts of credit which reflects on-going work which has not yet been billed.

[The interim bills on account are based on an estimate of the costs incurred to the date of that bill. These will be a guide to the total cost to that date, although they may require some adjustment at the end of a case.

or

All interim bills are based on the time spent and recorded over a period, and are final for the period stated on the bill. This may include incidental expenses not yet paid, but will not always include all incidental expenses for that period (for example if we have not yet received a bill from someone). We will send you a breakdown of the time spent with the bill.]

You must pay all bills within 14 days. Unless the work on your file is complete, you will also have to pay (or replenish) money we hold on account for you. Sometimes we will need to ask you for more money on account, for example if there is a court hearing coming up. For any bills that are not paid within 1 month from the date of the bill you will have to pay interest at the rate of 8% per year on the outstanding sum.

You have a right to ask for your overall costs to be limited to a maximum. Since it is difficult to predict the work involved in family cases, I do not recommend you to do so. It could mean that I would have to stop acting for you half way through the case.

The final total costs will depend on all the circumstances, in particular the total amount of time involved on the matter, which cannot be foreseen with any certainty, although I will keep you informed as to the costs incurred as the case progresses.

You may be ordered to pay the costs of someone else. In such a case, you must provide this firm with funds within seven days.

4.   Recovering costs from the other person in your case

The general rule in family cases is that each party pays their own lawyer's costs. By contrast to other court cases, in family cases courts do not automatically order the 'loser' to pay the 'winner's' costs. This is because it is not often apparent that there is a 'winner' or a 'loser'. In cases involving children or finances, the court will only order one party to pay the other's costs in exceptional circumstances, for example if one party has conducted the court case in a way that has wasted considerable resources or if a party has tried to mislead the court. If necessary, please ask me as to whether an order for costs is likely to be made in your case.

If there is no order for costs, each person will pay their own costs. You may have been paying costs as the case goes on, in which case you will not have any money returned to you unless there is surplus money on account.

The court may order you to pay some or all of the costs of another person in your case either as a fixed sum or to be assessed by the court. If you are ordered to pay costs to another person in court proceedings at any stage in your case you must do so within 14 days from the order. I will not pay other people's costs on your behalf.

You are primarily liable for the fees charged by this firm and any incidental expenses, no matter what the result and even if someone else is ordered to pay your costs in court proceedings.

Even in the rare cases where another person has to pay your costs it is unlikely that they will have to pay all of your costs and you will still have to pay any shortfall.

There can be additional problems with orders for costs for example:

- The person who has been ordered to pay the costs may not do so. If they do not pay, you will have to try to enforce the costs order (for example by sending in the bailiffs or obtaining a charge over property owned by them) and this itself costs more money and takes time.

- The other person in your case may have very little or no money and the court may not order them to pay your costs for this reason.

- The person who has been ordered to pay the costs may then turn out to have no money or they may disappear.

In any event, no matter how successful you are at the final hearing of your case and no matter that the other person is good for all the money which they are ordered to pay, they will only have to pay those costs which the court assesses as reasonable and proportionate. This will vary from case to case, but may only amount to as little as 60% of your costs or less. You will still remain liable to pay the remainder of the costs and incidental expenses.

5. Proceeds of Crime Act

Under the Proceeds of Crime Act we have to take full proof of ID from you. We usually do this at the first meeting. However, if we have not yet done so for whatever reason, we will ask you to make an appointment for this as soon as possible.

In financial family proceedings you are obliged to give full and frank disclosure of your financial and personal circumstances. The Proceeds of Crime Act 2002 in certain circumstances makes it a criminal offence for you to enter into a financial settlement with your [spouse/civil partner] if you know that any income or capital of whatever nature which you or your [spouse/civil partner] uses or retains represents the proceeds of crime. The proceeds of crime are any money which has arisen as a result of any crime and include, for example, money saved as a result of tax evasion or undeclared cash taken out of a business. If you are aware of such money in your family's circumstances, you should tell me about it as soon as possible. We can then discuss what steps need to be taken.

6. Ending instructing me

You may terminate your instructions to me in writing at any time, but I will be entitled to keep all your papers and documents while there is money owing to the firm for our charges and expenses. I may decide to stop acting for you only with good reason, for example:

1. if you do not pay a bill;
2. if you fail to comply with a request for payment of money on account;
3. if you do not give me clear or proper instructions;
4. if I cannot continue to act without being in breach of rules of professional conduct; or
5. if there has been an irretrievable breakdown in trust and confidence.

If this happens and court proceedings are ongoing, this firm will have to come off the court record. [*To avoid having to attend court for this reason, we require all clients to sign a 'Notice of Acting in Person' which we can then send to the court and all other parties. We will let you know in advance if we ever have to make use of this.*]

7. At the end of your case

My firm will keep your file of papers (except for any papers that you ask to be returned to you) for at least six years from the date of the last bill. My firm will keep the file on the understanding that we have the authority to destroy it after this period. My firm will not destroy documents that you ask us to deposit in safe custody.

If you require the file during the period while it is in storage, we can provide this to you on payment of our reasonable fees for delivery, locating any specific documents and making any copies for you. As you will appreciate, we hold a number of files in storage and it may take some time to retrieve your particular papers.

8.   Procedure for resolving problems

If a problem arises at any time, please contact me so that we can talk about your concerns. If that does not provide the solution, please contact my client care partner, [   ], who can supply you with this firm's written complaints procedure if you require this.

All solicitors must attempt to resolve problems that may arise with their services. It is therefore important that you immediately raise with me any concerns you may have. I would be disappointed if you thought that you had reason to be unhappy with the service that I am providing.

In the unlikely event that a mistake is made by my firm, we have professional indemnity insurance in the sum of £[   ] per claim. We do require that you limit any claim you may have in respect of professional negligence against this firm to the amount of that sum.

If you continue to instruct me, this will mean that you accept the terms of business set out in this letter.

Yours sincerely

CC6S Terms of business for private client: general family: solicitor acting

Dear [*client*]

1. Introduction

I am a solicitor and I will have the overall management and responsibility for your case. A trainee solicitor under my supervision may help me and deal with some of the day-to-day work. The partner with overall responsibility for your case is [   ]. I set out in this letter the terms of business for clients of this firm as they apply to you.

2. Standards

Every solicitor in our offices endeavours to maintain certain minimum standards of case management. If you find that the standards set out below are not maintained, please speak to me.

I will try to return your telephone calls as soon as possible. I have a personal voicemail facility, so if for any reason I am not at my desk, please leave a message on my voicemail.

3. Charges

Our charges, like those of all solicitors, are based on a number of different factors.

Factors which will be taken into account are:

1. the time spent;
2. the skills, specialised knowledge and responsibility required of the members of the firm handling the matter;
3. the complexities and difficulty or novelty of the questions involved;
4. the circumstances in which the business involved is transacted (for instance if, due to the urgency, evening or weekend work is required or if an unusually large amount of documentation needs to be considered).

The most important of these factors is the amount of time spent by members of the firm in dealing with your case. We have a computer-based time recording system on which each member of the firm records the time spent on your case. Each individual has an hourly charge-out rate based on an hour of their time.

My own current charge-out rate is £[   ] per hour. The current charge-out rate for my trainee solicitor is £[   ] per hour and the rate for the partner responsible for your case is £[   ] per hour. I will let you know the charge-out rates of any other individual members of the firm dealing with your case whenever you request. The charge-out rates are exclusive of VAT.

Figures given to you for charge-out rates of any individuals in the firm are of

course subject to periodic review (for example to take into account inflation or any increase in the level of qualification or responsibility of any member of the firm dealing with the case).

Charge-out rates may also be increased if any of the factors mentioned at the beginning of this section apply.

Charge-out rates will apply to all the work done on your case including time spent on the telephone, reading incoming post or emails, writing or dictating outgoing letters or emails, preparing file notes of meetings, considering and drafting documents, reviewing your file, considering your case, preparing instructions and briefs to barristers, researching law where necessary, attending conferences with barristers, attending court, meetings with you, meetings with the lawyers acting for the other person in your case or other people connected with the case, taking statements from witnesses and so on.

As well as the charges made by this firm, incidental expenses such as the fees of any barristers or experts and court fees will be added to the bill.

Our charges are not contingent upon the result of your case. They are payable 'win or lose'. You are primarily liable for the charges. Even if the court orders someone else to pay your costs, you will have to pay in the first instance and may then be reimbursed when funds clear from the person ordered to pay your costs.

In cases involving court proceedings it is always difficult to forecast the amount of time that will be spent since much will depend on the attitude of the other person in your case and their solicitors, the volume and complexity of the documents disclosed and the time required for preparation and in court.

In general, costs are likely to be as follows.

- For a straightforward divorce, it is unlikely that the total costs will be less than £[600] plus VAT and the costs will be more if there are problems with the other person co-operating or if the divorce is contested. The court fees are currently £[340].

- In domestic violence injunctions, when two court hearings are required, depending on whether it is easy to serve the other person with the court documents, it is unlikely to cost less than £[5,000].

- If there is a dispute about where children are to live and/or how often one parent is to see the children, and the case proceeds to a final hearing without an agreement being reached, the total costs are unlikely to be less than £[15,000]. A complex case may cost even more. If the case settles at an early stage, the total costs are much less.

- If there is a dispute about financial matters, and the case proceeds to a final hearing without an agreement being reached, the total costs are unlikely to be less than £[25,000]. A complex case may cost even more. If the case settles at an early stage, the total costs are much less.

If you require a forecast for your own case at any time, please ask and I will do my best to give one. It is unlikely that I will be able to make a firmer prediction until I can assess the issues in detail and until I know the position of the other person in your case.

I will always try to give you my best estimate of the likely costs of your case, but the estimates are not fixed. Sometimes I may only be able to give you my best estimate of the costs of the next stage of your case. I will give you an estimate at least every six months.

Unfortunately, because of delays in the court system, court proceedings can often take a long time to conclude. If we did not require payment until the end of a case, our staff and overhead costs involved in financing your case would become prohibitive. It is for this reason that it is our standard practice both to require money on account and to deliver regular interim bills on account where appropriate. Because of the nature of family work, however, it is likely that at certain times during the case we will give you (without any further notification) varying amounts of credit which reflects on-going work which has not yet been billed.

[The interim bills on account are based on an estimate of the costs incurred to the date of that bill. These will be a guide to the total cost to that date, although they may require some adjustment at the end of a case.

or

All interim bills are based on the time spent and recorded over a period, and are final for the period stated on the bill. This may include incidental expenses not yet paid, but will not always include all incidental expenses for that period (for example if we have not yet received a bill from someone). We will send you a breakdown of the time spent with the bill.]

You must pay all bills within 14 days. Unless the work on your file is complete, you will also have to pay (or replenish) money we hold on account for you. Sometimes we will need to ask you for more money on account, for example if there is a court hearing coming up. For any bills that are not paid within 1 month from the date of the bill you will have to pay interest at the rate of 8% per year on the outstanding sum.

You have a right to ask for your overall costs to be limited to a maximum. Since it is difficult to predict the work involved in family cases, I do not recommend you to do so. It could mean that I would have to stop acting for you half way through the case.

The final total costs will depend on all the circumstances, in particular the total amount of time involved on the matter, which cannot be foreseen with any certainty, although I will keep you informed as to the costs incurred as the case progresses.

You may be ordered to pay the costs of someone else. In such a case, you must provide this firm with funds within seven days.

4. Recovering costs from the other person in your case

The general rule in family cases is that each party pays their own lawyer's costs. By contrast to other court cases, in family cases courts do not automatically order the 'loser' to pay the 'winner's' costs. This is because it is not often apparent that there is a 'winner' or a 'loser'. In cases involving children or finances, the court will only order one party to pay the other's costs in exceptional circumstances, for example if one party has conducted the court case in a way that has wasted considerable resources or if a party has tried to mislead the court. If necessary, please ask me as to whether an order for costs is likely to be made in your case.

If there is no order for costs, each person will pay their own costs. You may have been paying costs as the case goes on, in which case you will not have any money returned to you unless there is surplus money on account.

The court may order you to pay some or all of the costs of another person in your case either as a fixed sum or to be assessed by the court. If you are ordered to pay costs to another person in court proceedings at any stage in your case you must do so within 14 days from the order. I will not pay other people's costs on your behalf.

You are primarily liable for the fees charged by this firm and any incidental expenses, no matter what the result and even if someone else is ordered to pay your costs in court proceedings.

Even in the rare cases where another person has to pay your costs it is unlikely that they will have to pay all of your costs and you will still have to pay any shortfall.

There can be additional problems with orders for costs for example:

- The person who has been ordered to pay the costs may not do so. If they do not pay, you will have to try to enforce the costs order (for example by sending in the bailiffs or obtaining a charge over property owned by them) and this itself costs more money and takes time.

- The other person in your case may have very little or no money and the court may not order them to pay your costs for this reason.

- The person who has been ordered to pay the costs may then turn out to have no money or they may disappear.

In any event, no matter how successful you are at the final hearing of your case and no matter that the other person is good for all the money which they are ordered to pay, they will only have to pay those costs which the court assesses as reasonable and proportionate. This will vary from case to case, but may only amount to as little as 60% of your costs or less. You will still remain liable to pay the remainder of the costs and incidental expenses.

5. Proceeds of Crime Act

Under the Proceeds of Crime Act we have to take full proof of ID from you. We usually do this at the first meeting. However, if we have not yet done so for whatever reason, we will ask you to make an appointment for this as soon as possible.

In financial family proceedings you are obliged to give full and frank disclosure of your financial and personal circumstances. The Proceeds of Crime Act 2002 in certain circumstances makes it a criminal offence for you to enter into a financial settlement with your [spouse/civil partner] if you know that any income or capital of whatever nature which you or your [spouse/civil partner] uses or retains represents the proceeds of crime. The proceeds of crime are any money which has arisen as a result of any crime and include, for example, money saved as a result of tax evasion or undeclared cash taken out of a business. If you are aware of such money in your family's circumstances, you should tell me about it as soon as possible. We can then discuss what steps need to be taken.

6. Ending instructing me

You may terminate your instructions to me in writing at any time, but I will be entitled to keep all your papers and documents while there is money owing to the firm for our charges and expenses. I may decide to stop acting for you only with good reason, for example:

1. if you do not pay a bill;
2. if you fail to comply with a request for payment of money on account;
3. if you do not give me clear or proper instructions;
4. if I cannot continue to act without being in breach of rules of professional conduct; or
5. if there has been an irretrievable breakdown in trust and confidence.

If this happens and court proceedings are ongoing, this firm will have to come off the court record. [*To avoid having to attend court for this reason, we require all clients to sign a 'Notice of Acting in Person' which we can then send to the court and all other parties. We will let you know in advance if we ever have to make use of this.*]

7. At the end of your case

My firm will keep your file of papers (except for any papers that you ask to be returned to you) for at least six years from the date of the last bill. My firm will keep the file on the understanding that we have the authority to destroy it after this period. My firm will not destroy documents that you ask us to deposit in safe custody.

If you require the file during the period while it is in storage, we can provide this to you on payment of our reasonable fees for delivery, locating any specific documents and making any copies for you. As you will appreciate, we hold a number of files in storage and it may take some time to retrieve your particular papers.

8. Procedure for resolving problems

If a problem arises at any time, please contact me or my supervising partner so that we can talk about your concerns. If that does not provide the solution, please contact my client care partner, [   ], who can supply you with this firm's written complaints procedure if you require this.

All solicitors must attempt to resolve problems that may arise with their services. It is therefore important that you immediately raise with me any concerns you may have. I would be disappointed if you thought that you had reason to be unhappy with the service that I am providing.

In the unlikely event that a mistake is made by my firm, we have professional indemnity insurance in the sum of £[   ] per claim. We do require that you limit any claim you may have in respect of professional negligence against this firm to the amount of that sum.

If you continue to instruct me, this will mean that you accept the terms of business set out in this letter.

Yours sincerely

CC6T Terms of business for private client: general family: trainee solicitor acting

Dear [*client*]

1. Introduction

I refer to your recent meeting with my trainee solicitor [   ] who took your instructions. I am writing to you to confirm your instructions as the [partner/solicitor] responsible for supervising the conduct of your case. [*The partner with overall responsibility for your case is [   ].*]

I set out in this letter the terms of business for clients of this firm as they apply to you.

2. Standards

Every solicitor in our offices endeavours to maintain certain minimum standards of case management. If you find that the standards set out below are not maintained, please speak to me.

I will try to return your telephone calls as soon as possible. I have a personal voicemail facility, so if for any reason I am not at my desk, please leave a message on my voicemail.

3. Charges

Our charges, like those of all solicitors, are based on a number of different factors.

Factors which will be taken into account are:

1. the time spent;
2. the skills, specialised knowledge and responsibility required of the members of the firm handling the matter;
3. the complexities and difficulty or novelty of the questions involved;
4. the circumstances in which the business involved is transacted (for instance if, due to the urgency, evening or weekend work is required or if an unusually large amount of documentation needs to be considered).

The most important of these factors is the amount of time spent by members of the firm in dealing with your case. We have a computer-based time recording system on which each member of the firm records the time spent on your case. Each individual has an hourly charge-out rate based on an hour of their time.

[   ]'s current charge-out rate is £[   ] per hour. My own current charge-out rate is £[ ] per hour [*and the rate for the partner supervising your case is £[ ] per hour*]. I will let you know the charge-out rates of any other individual members of the firm dealing with your case whenever you request. The charge-out rates are exclusive of VAT.

Figures given to you for charge-out rates of any individuals in the firm are of course subject to periodic review (for example to take into account inflation or any increase in the level of qualification or responsibility of any member of the firm dealing with the case).

Charge-out rates may also be increased if any of the factors mentioned at the beginning of this section apply.

Charge-out rates will apply to all the work done on your case including time spent on the telephone, reading incoming post or emails, writing or dictating outgoing letters or emails, preparing file notes of meetings, considering and drafting documents, reviewing your file, considering your case, preparing instructions and briefs to barristers, researching law where necessary, attending conferences with barristers, attending court, meetings with you, meetings with the lawyers acting for the other person in your case or other people connected with the case, taking statements from witnesses and so on.

As well as the charges made by this firm, incidental expenses such as the fees of any barristers or experts and court fees will be added to the bill.

Our charges are not contingent upon the result of your case. They are payable 'win or lose'. You are primarily liable for the charges. Even if the court orders someone else to pay your costs, you will have to pay in the first instance and may then be reimbursed when funds clear from the person ordered to pay your costs.

In cases involving court proceedings it is always difficult to forecast the amount of time that will be spent since much will depend on the attitude of the other person in your case and their solicitors, the volume and complexity of the documents disclosed and the time required for preparation and in court.

In general, costs are likely to be as follows.

- For a straightforward divorce, it is unlikely that the total costs will be less than £[600] plus VAT and the costs will be more if there are problems with the other person co-operating or if the divorce is contested. The court fees are currently £[340].

- In domestic violence injunctions, when two court hearings are required, depending on whether it is easy to serve the other person with the court documents, it is unlikely to cost less than £[5,000].

- If there is a dispute about where children are to live and/or how often one parent is to see the children, and the case proceeds to a final hearing without an agreement being reached, the total costs are unlikely to be less than £[15,000]. A complex case may cost even more. If the case settles at an early stage, the total costs are much less.

- If there is a dispute about financial matters, and the case proceeds to a final hearing without an agreement being reached, the total costs are unlikely to be less than £[25,000]. A complex case may cost even more. If the case settles at an early stage, the total costs are much less.

If you require a forecast for your own case at any time, please ask and I will do my best to give one. It is unlikely that I will be able to make a firmer prediction until I can assess the issues in detail and until I know the position of the other person in your case.

I will always try to give you my best estimate of the likely costs of your case, but the estimates are not fixed. Sometimes I may only be able to give you my best estimate of the costs of the next stage of your case. I will give you an estimate at least every six months.

Unfortunately, because of delays in the court system, court proceedings can often take a long time to conclude. If we did not require payment until the end of a case, our staff and overhead costs involved in financing your case would become prohibitive. It is for this reason that it is our standard practice both to require money on account and to deliver regular interim bills on account where appropriate. Because of the nature of family work, however, it is likely that at certain times during the case we will give you (without any further notification) varying amounts of credit which reflects on-going work which has not yet been billed.

[The interim bills on account are based on an estimate of the costs incurred to the date of that bill. These will be a guide to the total cost to that date, although they may require some adjustment at the end of a case.

or

All interim bills are based on the time spent and recorded over a period, and are final for the period stated on the bill. This may include incidental expenses not yet paid, but will not always include all incidental expenses for that period (for example if we have not yet received a bill from someone). We will send you a breakdown of the time spent with the bill.]

You must pay all bills within 14 days. Unless the work on your file is complete, you will also have to pay (or replenish) money we hold on account for you. Sometimes we will need to ask you for more money on account, for example if there is a court hearing coming up. For any bills that are not paid within 1 month from the date of the bill you will have to pay interest at the rate of 8% per year on the outstanding sum.

You have a right to ask for your overall costs to be limited to a maximum. Since it is difficult to predict the work involved in family cases, I do not recommend you to do so. It could mean that I would have to stop acting for you half way through the case.

The final total costs will depend on all the circumstances, in particular the total amount of time involved on the matter, which cannot be foreseen with any certainty, although I will keep you informed as to the costs incurred as the case progresses.

You may be ordered to pay the costs of someone else. In such a case, you must provide this firm with funds within seven days.

4. Recovering costs from the other person in your case

The general rule in family cases is that each party pays their own lawyer's costs. By contrast to other court cases, in family cases courts do not automatically order the 'loser' to pay the 'winner's' costs. This is because it is not often apparent that there is a 'winner' or a 'loser'. In cases involving children or finances, the court will only order one party to pay the other's costs in exceptional circumstances, for example if one party has conducted the court case in a way that has wasted considerable resources or if a party has tried to mislead the court. If necessary, please ask me as to whether an order for costs is likely to be made in your case.

If there is no order for costs, each person will pay their own costs. You may have been paying costs as the case goes on, in which case you will not have any money returned to you unless there is surplus money on account.

The court may order you to pay some or all of the costs of another person in your case either as a fixed sum or to be assessed by the court. If you are ordered to pay costs to another person in court proceedings at any stage in your case you must do so within 14 days from the order. I will not pay other people's costs on your behalf.

You are primarily liable for the fees charged by this firm and any incidental expenses, no matter what the result and even if someone else is ordered to pay your costs in court proceedings.

Even in the rare cases where another person has to pay your costs it is unlikely that they will have to pay all of your costs and you will still have to pay any shortfall.

There can be additional problems with orders for costs for example:

- The person who has been ordered to pay the costs may not do so. If they do not pay, you will have to try to enforce the costs order (for example by sending in the bailiffs or obtaining a charge over property owned by them) and this itself costs more money and takes time.

- The other person in your case may have very little or no money and the court may not order them to pay your costs for this reason.

- The person who has been ordered to pay the costs may then turn out to have no money or they may disappear.

In any event, no matter how successful you are at the final hearing of your case and no matter that the other person is good for all the money which they are ordered to pay, they will only have to pay those costs which the court assesses as reasonable and proportionate. This will vary from case to case, but may only amount to as little as 60% of your costs or less. You will still remain liable to pay the remainder of the costs and incidental expenses.

5. Proceeds of Crime Act

Under the Proceeds of Crime Act we have to take full proof of ID from you. We usually do this at the first meeting. However, if we have not yet done so for whatever reason, we will ask you to make an appointment for this as soon as possible.

In financial family proceedings you are obliged to give full and frank disclosure of your financial and personal circumstances. The Proceeds of Crime Act 2002 in certain circumstances makes it a criminal offence for you to enter into a financial settlement with your [spouse/civil partner] if you know that any income or capital of whatever nature which you or your [spouse/civil partner] uses or retains represents the proceeds of crime. The proceeds of crime are any money which has arisen as a result of any crime and include, for example, money saved as a result of tax evasion or undeclared cash taken out of a business. If you are aware of such money in your family's circumstances, you should tell me about it as soon as possible. We can then discuss what steps need to be taken.

6. Ending instructing me

You may terminate your instructions to me in writing at any time, but I will be entitled to keep all your papers and documents while there is money owing to the firm for our charges and expenses. I may decide to stop acting for you only with good reason, for example:

1. if you do not pay a bill;
2. if you fail to comply with a request for payment of money on account;
3. if you do not give me clear or proper instructions;
4. if I cannot continue to act without being in breach of rules of professional conduct; or
5. if there has been an irretrievable breakdown in trust and confidence.

If this happens and court proceedings are ongoing, this firm will have to come off the court record. [*To avoid having to attend court for this reason, we require all clients to sign a "Notice of Acting in Person" which we can then send to the court and all other parties. We will let you know in advance if we ever have to make use of this.*]

7. At the end of your case

My firm will keep your file of papers (except for any papers that you ask to be returned to you) for at least six years from the date of the last bill. My firm will keep the file on the understanding that we have the authority to destroy it after this period. My firm will not destroy documents that you ask us to deposit in safe custody.

If you require the file during the period while it is in storage, we can provide this to you on payment of our reasonable fees for delivery, locating any specific documents and making any copies for you. As you will appreciate, we hold a number of files in storage and it may take some time to retrieve your particular papers.

8. Procedure for resolving problems

If a problem arises at any time, please contact me so that we can talk about your concerns. If that does not provide the solution, please contact my client care partner, [   ], who can supply you with this firm's written complaints procedure if you require this.

All solicitors must attempt to resolve problems that may arise with their services. It is therefore important that you immediately raise with me any concerns you may have. I would be disappointed if you thought that you had reason to be unhappy with the service that we are providing.

In the unlikely event that a mistake is made by my firm, we have professional indemnity insurance in the sum of £[   ] per claim. We do require that you limit any claim you may have in respect of professional negligence against this firm to the amount of that sum.

If you continue to instruct me, this will mean that you accept the terms of business set out in this letter.

Yours sincerely

CC7P Terms of business for private client envisaging Trust of Land Act or Inheritance Act claim: partner acting

Dear [*client*]

1.   Introduction

I am a solicitor and a partner in the firm and I will have the overall management and responsibility for your case. Other solicitors or trainee solicitors may help me under my supervision and deal with some of the day-to-day work. I set out in this letter the terms of business for clients of this firm as they apply to you.

2.   Standards

Every solicitor in our offices endeavours to maintain certain minimum standards of case management. If you find that the standards set out below are not maintained, please speak to me.

I will try to return your telephone calls as soon as possible. I have a personal voicemail facility, so if for any reason I am not at my desk, please leave a message on my voicemail.

3.   Charges

Our charges, like those of all solicitors, are based on a number of different factors.

Factors which will be taken into account are:

1.   the time spent;
2.   the skills, specialised knowledge and responsibility required of the members of the firm handling the matter;
3.   the complexities and difficulty or novelty of the questions involved;
4.   the circumstances in which the business involved is transacted (for instance if, due to the urgency, evening or weekend work is required or if an unusually large amount of documentation needs to be considered).

The most important of these factors is the amount of time spent by members of the firm in dealing with your case. We have a computer-based time recording system on which each member of the firm records the time spent on your case. Each individual has an hourly charge-out rate based on an hour of their time.

My own current charge-out rate is £[   ] per hour. The current charge-out rate for my assistant solicitors is £[   ] and the rate for my trainee solicitor is £[   ] per hour. I will let you know the charge-out rates of any other individual members of the firm dealing with your case whenever you request. The charge-out rates are exclusive of VAT.

Figures given to you for charge-out rates of any individuals in the firm are of

course subject to periodic review (for example to take into account inflation or any increase in the level of qualification or responsibility of any member of the firm dealing with the case).

Charge-out rates may also be increased if any of the factors mentioned at the beginning of this section apply.

Charge-out rates will apply to all the work done on your case including time spent on the telephone, reading incoming post or emails, writing or dictating outgoing letters or emails, preparing file notes of meetings, considering and drafting documents, reviewing your file, considering your case, preparing instructions and briefs to barristers, researching law where necessary, attending conferences with barristers, attending court, meetings with you, meetings with the lawyers acting for the other person in your case or other people connected with the case, taking statements from witnesses and so on.

As well as the charges made by this firm, incidental expenses such as the fees of any barristers or experts and court fees will be added to the bill.

Our charges are not contingent upon the result of your case. They are payable 'win or lose'. You are primarily liable for the charges. Even if the court orders someone else to pay your costs, you will have to pay in the first instance and may then be reimbursed when funds clear from the person ordered to pay your costs.

In cases involving court proceedings it is always difficult to forecast the amount of time that will be spent since much will depend on the attitude of the other person in your case and their solicitors, the volume and complexity of the documents disclosed and the time required for preparation and in court.

In general, costs are likely to be as follows.

- If a case is resolved by agreement, it could cost as little as £[2,000], but sometimes it will be necessary to consider a great volume of documents such as solicitors' files and correspondence before it is possible to provide you with the advice that is necessary for you to be able to make an informed decision about proposals for settlement. Therefore, even if the matter is resolved by agreement, the costs can be higher and could be £[5,000] or more.

- If the case is not resolved by agreement and the case proceeds to a final hearing, the costs could be up to £[20,000] or more. A complex case may cost £[30,000–50,000] or even more.

I enclose a costs schedule forecasting the costs up to a stage where it will be possible for me to advise you where your case may be going. I should be able to give you a forecast for the costs after that stage then. Please note that the schedule is not a quote, but simply my best guess of what your costs are likely to be. Your costs may be higher or lower and will depend on the factors set out above. If you require a new forecast for your own case at any time, please ask and I will do my best to give one.

I will always try to give you my best estimate of the likely costs of your case, but the estimates are not fixed. Sometimes I may only be able to give you my best estimate of the costs of the next stage of your case. I will give you an estimate at least every six months.

Unfortunately, because of delays in the court system, court proceedings can often take a long time to conclude. If we did not require payment until the end of a case, our staff and overhead costs involved in financing your case would become prohibitive. It is for this reason that it is our standard practice both to require money on account and to deliver regular interim bills on account where appropriate. Because of the nature of family work, however, it is likely that at certain times during the case we will give you (without any further notification) varying amounts of credit which reflects on-going work which has not yet been billed.

[The interim bills on account are based on an estimate of the costs incurred to the date of that bill. These will be a guide to the total cost to that date, although they may require some adjustment at the end of a case.

or

All interim bills are based on the time spent and recorded over a period, and are final for the period stated on the bill. This may include incidental expenses not yet paid, but will not always include all incidental expenses for that period (for example if we have not yet received a bill from someone). We will send you a breakdown of the time spent with the bill.]

You must pay all bills within 14 days. Unless the work on your file is complete, you will also have to pay (or replenish) money we hold on account for you. Sometimes we will need to ask you for more money on account, for example if there is a court hearing coming up. For any bills that are not paid within 1 month from the date of the bill you will have to pay interest at the rate of 8% per year on the outstanding sum.

You have a right to ask for your overall costs to be limited to a maximum. Since it is difficult to predict the work involved in family cases, I do not recommend you to do so. It could mean that I would have to stop acting for you half way through the case.

The final total costs will depend on all the circumstances, in particular the total amount of time involved on the matter, which cannot be foreseen with any certainty, although I will keep you informed as to the costs incurred as the case progresses.

You may be ordered to pay the costs of someone else. In such a case, you must provide this firm with funds within seven days.

4.   Recovering costs from the other person in your case

If you decide not to proceed with your case before court proceedings are issued, or if the case is settled before then, there is no rule of law requiring another person in your case to make any payment towards your legal costs, although this may of course be part of an overall agreement reached.

As soon as court proceedings have been commenced, the general rule is that the unsuccessful party is ordered by the court to pay the winner's costs. If you are successful the court will usually order the other party to pay most of your costs.

If there is no order for costs, each person will pay their own costs. You may have been paying costs as the case goes on, in which case you will not have any money returned to you unless there is surplus money on account.

The court may order you to pay some or all of the costs of another person in your case either as a fixed sum or to be assessed by the court. If you are ordered to pay costs to another person in court proceedings at any stage in your case you must do so within 14 days from the order. I will not pay other people's costs on your behalf.

You might be able to find 'after-the-event insurance' which would pay the costs of the other person in your case if you lost. Although this is quite common in areas like personal injury litigation, I am not aware of any insurers actually offering such policies for your type of case. You would have to do your own research for policies in this area.

You are primarily liable for the fees charged by this firm and any incidental expenses, no matter what the result and even if someone else is ordered to pay your costs in court proceedings.

Even if you are successful, there can be additional problems with orders for costs for example:

- If you have pursued a number of different arguments and have only been successful on some of them, the court may look at the costs relating to the different points. The court may not order the other person in your case to pay all your costs if the judge feels that some of the arguments ought not to have been pursued. If you have lost certain arguments you may be ordered to pay the other party's costs of arguing that point. If you are concerned about particular parts of your claim and the way in which they are being pursued you must raise this with me at the time.

- If the court considers that parts of your claim were exaggerated, or highly speculative or very costly to prove.

- If the court considers that some fees or incidental expenses were disproportionate to the value of your claim. The court must look at the proportionality between the costs and the benefit for each part of each claim. I will always do my best to keep costs in proportion. However, your instructions, or the circumstances of the case, may mean that at the end of your case the costs are considered disproportionate and, although you remain liable for all our reasonable costs and expenses, your opponent may only have to pay some of these costs.

- If during your case you lost interim hearings and did not pay the other party's costs at the time, these may be deducted from money due to you or any costs someone else is ordered to pay to you.

- The person who has been ordered to pay the costs may not do so. If they do not pay, you will have to try to enforce the costs order (for example by sending in the bailiffs or obtaining a charge over property owned by them) and this itself costs more money and takes time.

- The other person in your case may have very little or no money and the court may not order them to pay your costs for this reason.

- The person who has been ordered to pay the costs may then turn out to have no money or they may disappear.

In any event, no matter how successful you are at the final hearing of your case and no matter that the other person is good for all the money which they are ordered to pay, they will only have to pay those costs which the court assesses as reasonable and proportionate. This will vary from case to case, but may only amount to as little as 60% of your costs or less. You will still remain liable to pay the remainder of the costs and incidental expenses.

In certain circumstances, particularly if you have tried to settle the case at an early stage for a reasonable sum, it may be possible to get all your costs from the other person in your case. I will discuss with you the tactics, and the advantages and disadvantages, of making and accepting offers to settle. These are important matters which the court takes into account when deciding on who should pay costs and how much they should pay.

5. Proceeds of Crime Act

Under the Proceeds of Crime Act we have to take full proof of ID from you. We usually do this at the first meeting. However, if we have not yet done so for whatever reason, we will ask you to make an appointment for this as soon as possible.

As part of court proceedings about property you may be obliged to give disclosure of your financial and personal circumstances. The Proceeds of Crime Act 2002 in certain circumstances makes it a criminal offence for you to enter into a financial settlement with someone if you know that any income or capital of whatever nature which you or the other person uses for the settlement represents the proceeds of crime. The proceeds of crime are any money which has arisen as a result of any crime and include, for example, money saved as a result of tax evasion or undeclared cash taken out of a business. If you are aware of such money in your circumstances, you should tell me about it as soon as possible. We can then discuss what steps need to be taken.

6.   Ending instructing me

You may terminate your instructions to me in writing at any time, but I will be entitled to keep all your papers and documents while there is money owing to the firm for our charges and expenses. I may decide to stop acting for you only with good reason, for example:

1.   if you do not pay a bill;
2.   if you fail to comply with a request for payment of money on account;
3.   if you do not give me clear or proper instructions;
4.   if I cannot continue to act without being in breach of rules of professional conduct; or
5.   if there has been an irretrievable breakdown in trust and confidence.

If this happens and court proceedings are ongoing, this firm will have to come off the court record. [*To avoid having to attend court for this reason, we require all clients to sign a 'Notice of Acting in Person' which we can then send to the court and all other parties. We will let you know in advance if we ever have to make use of this.*]

7.   At the end of your case

My firm will keep your file of papers (except for any papers that you ask to be returned to you) for at least six years from the date of the last bill. My firm will keep the file on the understanding that we have the authority to destroy it after this period. My firm will not destroy documents that you ask us to deposit in safe custody.

If you require the file during the period while it is in storage, we can provide this to you on payment of our reasonable fees for delivery, locating any specific documents and making any copies for you. As you will appreciate, we hold a number of files in storage and it may take some time to retrieve your particular papers.

8.   Procedure for resolving problems

If a problem arises at any time, please contact me so that we can talk about your concerns. If that does not provide the solution, please contact my client care partner, [   ], who can supply you with this firm's written complaints procedure if you require this.

All solicitors must attempt to resolve problems that may arise with their services. It is therefore important that you immediately raise with me any concerns you may have. I would be disappointed if you thought that you had reason to be unhappy with the service that I am providing.

In the unlikely event that a mistake is made by my firm, we have professional indemnity insurance in the sum of £[   ] per claim. We do require that you limit any claim you may have in respect of professional negligence against this firm to the amount of that sum.

If you continue to instruct me, this will mean that you accept the terms of business set out in this letter.

Yours sincerely

Enc. costs schedule

CC7S Terms of business for private client envisaging Trust of Land Act or Inheritance Act claim: solicitor acting

1. Introduction

I am a solicitor and I will have the overall management and responsibility for your case. A trainee solicitor under my supervision may help me and deal with some of the day-to-day work. The partner with overall responsibility for your case is [   ]. I set out in this letter the terms of business for clients of this firm as they apply to you.

2. Standards

Every solicitor in our offices endeavours to maintain certain minimum standards of case management. If you find that the standards set out below are not maintained, please speak to me.

I will try to return your telephone calls as soon as possible. I have a personal voicemail facility, so if for any reason I am not at my desk, please leave a message on my voicemail.

3. Charges

Our charges, like those of all solicitors, are based on a number of different factors.

Factors which will be taken into account are:

1.   the time spent;
2.   the skills, specialised knowledge and responsibility required of the members of the firm handling the matter;
3.   the complexities and difficulty or novelty of the questions involved;
4.   the circumstances in which the business involved is transacted (for instance if, due to the urgency, evening or weekend work is required or if an unusually large amount of documentation needs to be considered).

The most important of these factors is the amount of time spent by members of the firm in dealing with your case. We have a computer-based time recording system on which each member of the firm records the time spent on your case. Each individual has an hourly charge-out rate based on an hour of their time.

My own current charge-out rate is £[   ] per hour. The current charge-out rate for my trainee solicitor is £[   ] per hour and the rate for the partner responsible for your case is £[   ] per hour. I will let you know the charge-out rates of any other individual members of the firm dealing with your case whenever you request. The charge-out rates are exclusive of VAT.

Figures given to you for charge-out rates of any individuals in the firm are of course subject to periodic review (for example to take into account inflation or any increase in the level of qualification or responsibility of any member of the firm dealing with the case).

Charge-out rates may also be increased if any of the factors mentioned at the beginning of this section apply.

Charge-out rates will apply to all the work done on your case including time spent on the telephone, reading incoming post or emails, writing or dictating outgoing letters or emails, preparing file notes of meetings, considering and drafting documents, reviewing your file, considering your case, preparing instructions and briefs to barristers, researching law where necessary, attending conferences with barristers, attending court, meetings with you, meetings with the lawyers acting for the other person in your case or other people connected with the case, taking statements from witnesses and so on.

As well as the charges made by this firm, incidental expenses such as the fees of any barristers or experts and court fees will be added to the bill.

Our charges are not contingent upon the result of your case. They are payable 'win or lose'. You are primarily liable for the charges. Even if the court orders someone else to pay your costs, you will have to pay in the first instance and may then be reimbursed when funds clear from the person ordered to pay your costs.

In cases involving court proceedings it is always difficult to forecast the amount of time that will be spent since much will depend on the attitude of the other person in your case and their solicitors, the volume and complexity of the documents disclosed and the time required for preparation and in court.

In general, costs are likely to be as follows.

- If a case is resolved by agreement, it could cost as little as £[2,000], but sometimes it will be necessary to consider a great volume of documents such as solicitors' files and correspondence before it is possible to provide you with the advice that is necessary for you to be able to make an informed decision about proposals for settlement. Therefore, even if the matter is resolved by agreement, the costs can be higher and could be £[5,000] or more.

- If the case is not resolved by agreement and the case proceeds to a final hearing, the costs could be up to £[20,000] or more. A complex case may cost £[30,000–50,000] or even more.

I enclose a costs schedule forecasting the costs up to a stage where it will be possible for me to advise you where your case may be going. I should be able to give you a forecast for the costs after that stage then. Please note that the schedule is not a quote, but simply my best guess of what your costs are likely to be. Your costs may be higher or lower and will depend on the factors set out above. If you require a new forecast for your own case at any time, please ask and I will do my best to give one.

I will always try to give you my best estimate of the likely costs of your case, but the estimates are not fixed. Sometimes I may only be able to give you my best estimate of the costs of the next stage of your case. I will give you an estimate at least every six months.

Unfortunately, because of delays in the court system, court proceedings can often take a long time to conclude. If we did not require payment until the end of a case, our staff and overhead costs involved in financing your case would become prohibitive. It is for this reason that it is our standard practice both to require money on account and to deliver regular interim bills on account where appropriate. Because of the nature of family work, however, it is likely that at certain times during the case we will give you (without any further notification) varying amounts of credit which reflects on-going work which has not yet been billed.

[The interim bills on account are based on an estimate of the costs incurred to the date of that bill. These will be a guide to the total cost to that date, although they may require some adjustment at the end of a case.

or

All interim bills are based on the time spent and recorded over a period, and are final for the period stated on the bill. This may include incidental expenses not yet paid, but will not always include all incidental expenses for that period (for example if we have not yet received a bill from someone). We will send you a breakdown of the time spent with the bill.]

You must pay all bills within 14 days. Unless the work on your file is complete, you will also have to pay (or replenish) money we hold on account for you. Sometimes we will need to ask you for more money on account, for example if there is a court hearing coming up. For any bills that are not paid within 1 month from the date of the bill you will have to pay interest at the rate of 8% per year on the outstanding sum.

You have a right to ask for your overall costs to be limited to a maximum. Since it is difficult to predict the work involved in family cases, I do not recommend you to do so. It could mean that I would have to stop acting for you half way through the case.

The final total costs will depend on all the circumstances, in particular the total amount of time involved on the matter, which cannot be foreseen with any certainty, although I will keep you informed as to the costs incurred as the case progresses.

You may be ordered to pay the costs of someone else. In such a case, you must provide this firm with funds within seven days.

4.   Recovering costs from the other person in your case

If you decide not to proceed with your case before court proceedings are issued, or if the case is settled before then, there is no rule of law requiring another person in your case to make any payment towards your legal costs, although this may of course be part of an overall agreement reached.

As soon as court proceedings have been commenced, the general rule is that the unsuccessful party is ordered by the court to pay the winner's costs. If you are successful the court will usually order the other party to pay most of your costs.

If there is no order for costs, each person will pay their own costs. You may have been paying costs as the case goes on, in which case you will not have any money returned to you unless there is surplus money on account.

The court may order you to pay some or all of the costs of another person in your case either as a fixed sum or to be assessed by the court. If you are ordered to pay costs to another person in court proceedings at any stage in your case you must do so within 14 days from the order. I will not pay other people's costs on your behalf.

You might be able to find 'after-the-event insurance' which would pay the costs of the other person in your case if you lost. Although this is quite common in areas like personal injury litigation, I am not aware of any insurers actually offering such policies for your type of case. You would have to do your own research for policies in this area.

You are primarily liable for the fees charged by this firm and any incidental expenses, no matter what the result and even if someone else is ordered to pay your costs in court proceedings.

Even if you are successful, there can be additional problems with orders for costs for example:

- If you have pursued a number of different arguments and have only been successful on some of them, the court may look at the costs relating to the different points. The court may not order the other person in your case to pay all your costs if the judge feels that some of the arguments ought not to have been pursued. If you have lost certain arguments you may be ordered to pay the other party's costs of arguing that point. If you are concerned about particular parts of your claim and the way in which they are being pursued you must raise this with me at the time.

- If the court considers that parts of your claim were exaggerated, or highly speculative or very costly to prove.

- If the court considers that some fees or incidental expenses were disproportionate to the value of your claim. The court must look at the proportionality between the costs and the benefit for each part of each claim. I will always do my best to keep costs in proportion. However, your instructions, or the circumstances of the case, may mean that at the end of your case the costs are considered disproportionate and, although you remain liable for all our reasonable costs and expenses, your opponent may only have to pay some of these costs.

- If during your case you lost interim hearings and did not pay the other party's costs at the time, these may be deducted from money due to you or any costs someone else is ordered to pay to you.

- The person who has been ordered to pay the costs may not do so. If they do not pay, you will have to try to enforce the costs order (for example by sending in the bailiffs or obtaining a charge over property owned by them) and this itself costs more money and takes time.

- The other person in your case may have very little or no money and the court may not order them to pay your costs for this reason.

- The person who has been ordered to pay the costs may then turn out to have no money or they may disappear.

In any event, no matter how successful you are at the final hearing of your case and no matter that the other person is good for all the money which they are ordered to pay, they will only have to pay those costs which the court assesses as reasonable and proportionate. This will vary from case to case, but may only amount to as little as 60% of your costs or less. You will still remain liable to pay the remainder of the costs and incidental expenses.

In certain circumstances, particularly if you have tried to settle the case at an early stage for a reasonable sum, it may be possible to get all your costs from the other person in your case. I will discuss with you the tactics, and the advantages and disadvantages, of making and accepting offers to settle. These are important matters which the court takes into account when deciding on who should pay costs and how much they should pay.

5.   Proceeds of Crime Act

Under the Proceeds of Crime Act we have to take full proof of ID from you. We usually do this at the first meeting. However, if we have not yet done so for whatever reason, we will ask you to make an appointment for this as soon as possible.

As part of court proceedings about property you may be obliged to give disclosure of your financial and personal circumstances. The Proceeds of Crime Act 2002 in certain circumstances makes it a criminal offence for you to enter into a financial settlement with someone if you know that any income or capital of whatever nature which you or the other person uses for the settlement represents the proceeds of crime. The proceeds of crime are any money which has arisen as a result of any crime and include, for example, money saved as a result of tax evasion or undeclared cash taken out of a business. If you are aware of such money in your circumstances, you should tell me about it as soon as possible. We can then discuss what steps need to be taken.

6. Ending instructing me

You may terminate your instructions to me in writing at any time, but I will be entitled to keep all your papers and documents while there is money owing to the firm for our charges and expenses. I may decide to stop acting for you only with good reason, for example:

1. if you do not pay a bill;
2. if you fail to comply with a request for payment of money on account;
3. if you do not give me clear or proper instructions;
4. if I cannot continue to act without being in breach of rules of professional conduct; or
5. if there has been an irretrievable breakdown in trust and confidence.

If this happens and court proceedings are ongoing, this firm will have to come off the court record. [*To avoid having to attend court for this reason, we require all clients to sign a 'Notice of Acting in Person' which we can then send to the court and all other parties. We will let you know in advance if we ever have to make use of this.*]

7. At the end of your case

My firm will keep your file of papers (except for any papers that you ask to be returned to you) for at least six years from the date of the last bill. My firm will keep the file on the understanding that we have the authority to destroy it after this period. My firm will not destroy documents that you ask us to deposit in safe custody.

If you require the file during the period while it is in storage, we can provide this to you on payment of our reasonable fees for delivery, locating any specific documents and making any copies for you. As you will appreciate, we hold a number of files in storage and it may take some time to retrieve your particular papers.

8. Procedure for resolving problems

If a problem arises at any time, please contact me or my supervising partner so that we can talk about your concerns. If that does not provide the solution, please contact my client care partner, [   ], who can supply you with this firm's written complaints procedure if you require this.

All solicitors must attempt to resolve problems that may arise with their services. It is therefore important that you immediately raise with me any concerns you may have. I would be disappointed if you thought that you had reason to be unhappy with the service that I am providing.

In the unlikely event that a mistake is made by my firm, we have professional indemnity insurance in the sum of £[   ] per claim. We do require that you limit any claim you may have in respect of professional negligence against this firm to the amount of that sum.

If you continue to instruct me, this will mean that you accept the terms of business set out in this letter.

Yours sincerely

Enc. costs schedule

CC7T Terms of business for private client envisaging Trust of Land Act or Inheritance Act claim: trainee solicitor acting

Dear [*client*]

1. Introduction

I refer to your recent meeting with my trainee solicitor [   ] who took your instructions. I am writing to you to confirm your instructions as the [partner/solicitor] responsible for supervising the conduct of your case. [*The partner with overall responsibility for your case is [   ].*]

I set out in this letter the terms of business for clients of this firm as they apply to you.

2. Standards

Every solicitor in our offices endeavours to maintain certain minimum standards of case management. If you find that the standards set out below are not maintained, please speak to me.

I will try to return your telephone calls as soon as possible. I have a personal voicemail facility, so if for any reason I am not at my desk, please leave a message on my voicemail.

3. Charges

Our charges, like those of all solicitors, are based on a number of different factors.

Factors which will be taken into account are:

1. the time spent;
2. the skills, specialised knowledge and responsibility required of the members of the firm handling the matter;
3. the complexities and difficulty or novelty of the questions involved;
4. the circumstances in which the business involved is transacted (for instance if, due to the urgency, evening or weekend work is required or if an unusually large amount of documentation needs to be considered).

The most important of these factors is the amount of time spent by members of the firm in dealing with your case. We have a computer-based time recording system on which each member of the firm records the time spent on your case. Each individual has an hourly charge-out rate based on an hour of their time.

[   ]'s current charge-out rate is £[   ] per hour. My own current charge-out rate is £[   ] per hour [*and the rate for the partner responsible for your case is £[   ] per hour*]. I will let you know the charge-out rates of any other individual members of the firm dealing with your case whenever you request. The charge-out rates are exclusive of VAT.

Figures given to you for charge-out rates of any individuals in the firm are of course subject to periodic review (for example to take into account inflation or any increase in the level of qualification or responsibility of any member of the firm dealing with the case).

Charge-out rates may also be increased if any of the factors mentioned at the beginning of this section apply.

Charge-out rates will apply to all the work done on your case including time spent on the telephone, reading incoming post or emails, writing or dictating outgoing letters or emails, preparing file notes of meetings, considering and drafting documents, reviewing your file, considering your case, preparing instructions and briefs to barristers, researching law where necessary, attending conferences with barristers, attending court, meetings with you, meetings with the lawyers acting for the other person in your case or other people connected with the case, taking statements from witnesses and so on.

As well as the charges made by this firm, incidental expenses such as the fees of any barristers or experts and court fees will be added to the bill.

Our charges are not contingent upon the result of your case. They are payable 'win or lose'. You are primarily liable for the charges. Even if the court orders someone else to pay your costs, you will have to pay in the first instance and may then be reimbursed when funds clear from the person ordered to pay your costs.

In cases involving court proceedings it is always difficult to forecast the amount of time that will be spent since much will depend on the attitude of the other person in your case and their solicitors, the volume and complexity of the documents disclosed and the time required for preparation and in court.

In general, costs are likely to be as follows.

- If a case is resolved by agreement, it could cost as little as £[2,000], but sometimes it will be necessary to consider a great volume of documents such as solicitors' files and correspondence before it is possible to provide you with the advice that is necessary for you to be able to make an informed decision about proposals for settlement. Therefore, even if the matter is resolved by agreement, the costs can be higher and could be £[5,000] or more.

- If the case is not resolved by agreement and the case proceeds to a final hearing, the costs could be up to £[20,000] or more. A complex case may cost £[30,000–50,000] or even more.

I enclose a costs schedule forecasting the costs up to a stage where it will be possible for me to advise you where your case may be going. I should be able to give you a forecast for the costs after that stage then. Please note that the schedule is not a quote, but simply my best guess of what your costs are likely to be. Your costs may be higher or lower and will depend on the factors set out above. If you require a new forecast for your own case at any time, please ask and I will do my best to give one.

I will always try to give you my best estimate of the likely costs of your case, but the estimates are not fixed. Sometimes I may only be able to give you my best estimate of the costs of the next stage of your case. I will give you an estimate at least every six months.

Unfortunately, because of delays in the court system, court proceedings can often take a long time to conclude. If we did not require payment until the end of a case, our staff and overhead costs involved in financing your case would become prohibitive. It is for this reason that it is our standard practice both to require money on account and to deliver regular interim bills on account where appropriate. Because of the nature of family work, however, it is likely that at certain times during the case we will give you (without any further notification) varying amounts of credit which reflects on-going work which has not yet been billed.

[The interim bills on account are based on an estimate of the costs incurred to the date of that bill. These will be a guide to the total cost to that date, although they may require some adjustment at the end of a case.

or

All interim bills are based on the time spent and recorded over a period, and are final for the period stated on the bill. This may include incidental expenses not yet paid, but will not always include all incidental expenses for that period (for example if we have not yet received a bill from someone). We will send you a breakdown of the time spent with the bill.]

You must pay all bills within 14 days. Unless the work on your file is complete, you will also have to pay (or replenish) money we hold on account for you. Sometimes we will need to ask you for more money on account, for example if there is a court hearing coming up. For any bills that are not paid within 1 month from the date of the bill you will have to pay interest at the rate of 8% per year on the outstanding sum.

You have a right to ask for your overall costs to be limited to a maximum. Since it is difficult to predict the work involved in family cases, I do not recommend you to do so. It could mean that I would have to stop acting for you half way through the case.

The final total costs will depend on all the circumstances, in particular the total amount of time involved on the matter, which cannot be foreseen with any certainty, although I will keep you informed as to the costs incurred as the case progresses.

You may be ordered to pay the costs of someone else. In such a case, you must provide this firm with funds within seven days.

4.　Recovering costs from the other person in your case

If you decide not to proceed with your case before court proceedings are issued, or if the case is settled before then, there is no rule of law requiring another person in your case to make any payment towards your legal costs, although this may of course be part of an overall agreement reached.

As soon as court proceedings have been commenced, the general rule is that the unsuccessful party is ordered by the court to pay the winner's costs. If you are successful the court will usually order the other party to pay most of your costs.

If there is no order for costs, each person will pay their own costs. You may have been paying costs as the case goes on, in which case you will not have any money returned to you unless there is surplus money on account.

The court may order you to pay some or all of the costs of another person in your case either as a fixed sum or to be assessed by the court. If you are ordered to pay costs to another person in court proceedings at any stage in your case you must do so within 14 days from the order. I will not pay other people's costs on your behalf.

You might be able to find 'after-the-event insurance' which would pay the costs of the other person in your case if you lost. Although this is quite common in areas like personal injury litigation, I am not aware of any insurers actually offering such policies for your type of case. You would have to do your own research for policies in this area.

You are primarily liable for the fees charged by this firm and any incidental expenses, no matter what the result and even if someone else is ordered to pay your costs in court proceedings.

Even if you are successful, there can be additional problems with orders for costs for example:

- If you have pursued a number of different arguments and have only been successful on some of them, the court may look at the costs relating to the different points. The court may not order the other person in your case to pay all your costs if the judge feels that some of the arguments ought not to have been pursued. If you have lost certain arguments you may be ordered to pay the other party's costs of arguing that point. If you are concerned about particular parts of your claim and the way in which they are being pursued you must raise this with me at the time.

- If the court considers that parts of your claim were exaggerated, or highly speculative or very costly to prove.

- If the court considers that some fees or incidental expenses were disproportionate to the value of your claim. The court must look at the proportionality between the costs and the benefit for each part of each claim. I will always do my best to keep costs in proportion. However, your instructions, or the circumstances of the case, may mean that at the end of your case the costs are considered disproportionate and, although you remain liable for all our reasonable costs and expenses, your opponent may only have to pay some of these costs.

- If during your case you lost interim hearings and did not pay the other party's costs at the time, these may be deducted from money due to you or any costs someone else is ordered to pay to you.

- The person who has been ordered to pay the costs may not do so. If they do not pay, you will have to try to enforce the costs order (for example by sending in the bailiffs or obtaining a charge over property owned by them) and this itself costs more money and takes time.

- The other person in your case may have very little or no money and the court may not order them to pay your costs for this reason.

- The person who has been ordered to pay the costs may then turn out to have no money or they may disappear.

In any event, no matter how successful you are at the final hearing of your case and no matter that the other person is good for all the money which they are ordered to pay, they will only have to pay those costs which the court assesses as reasonable and proportionate. This will vary from case to case, but may only amount to as little as 60% of your costs or less. You will still remain liable to pay the remainder of the costs and incidental expenses.

In certain circumstances, particularly if you have tried to settle the case at an early stage for a reasonable sum, it may be possible to get all your costs from the other person in your case. I will discuss with you the tactics, and the advantages and disadvantages, of making and accepting offers to settle. These are important matters which the court takes into account when deciding on who should pay costs and how much they should pay.

5. Proceeds of Crime Act

Under the Proceeds of Crime Act we have to take full proof of ID from you. We usually do this at the first meeting. However, if we have not yet done so for whatever reason, we will ask you to make an appointment for this as soon as possible.

As part of court proceedings about property you may be obliged to give disclosure of your financial and personal circumstances. The Proceeds of Crime Act 2002 in certain circumstances makes it a criminal offence for you to enter into a financial settlement with someone if you know that any income or capital of whatever nature which you or the other person uses for the settlement represents the proceeds of crime. The proceeds of crime are any money which has arisen as a result of any crime and include, for example, money saved as a result of tax evasion or undisclosed cash taken out of a business. If you are aware of such money in your circumstances, you should tell me about it as soon as possible. We can then discuss what steps need to be taken.

6.   Ending instructing me

You may terminate your instructions to me in writing at any time, but I will be entitled to keep all your papers and documents while there is money owing to the firm for our charges and expenses. I may decide to stop acting for you only with good reason, for example:

1.   if you do not pay a bill;
2.   if you fail to comply with a request for payment of money on account;
3.   if you do not give me clear or proper instructions;
4.   if I cannot continue to act without being in breach of rules of professional conduct; or
5.   if there has been an irretrievable breakdown in trust and confidence.

If this happens and court proceedings are ongoing, this firm will have to come off the court record. [*To avoid having to attend court for this reason, we require all clients to sign a 'Notice of Acting in Person' which we can then send to the court and all other parties. We will let you know in advance if we ever have to make use of this.*]

7.   At the end of your case

My firm will keep your file of papers (except for any papers that you ask to be returned to you) for at least six years from the date of the last bill. My firm will keep the file on the understanding that we have the authority to destroy it after this period. My firm will not destroy documents that you ask us to deposit in safe custody.

If you require the file during the period while it is in storage, we can provide this to you on payment of our reasonable fees for delivery, locating any specific documents and making any copies for you. As you will appreciate, we hold a number of files in storage and it may take some time to retrieve your particular papers.

8.   Procedure for resolving problems

If a problem arises at any time, please contact me so that we can talk about your concerns. If that does not provide the solution, please contact my client care partner, [   ], who can supply you with this firm's written complaints procedure if you require this.

All solicitors must attempt to resolve problems that may arise with their services. It is therefore important that you immediately raise with me any concerns you may have. I would be disappointed if you thought that you had reason to be unhappy with the service that we are providing.

In the unlikely event that a mistake is made by my firm, we have professional indemnity insurance in the sum of £[   ] per claim. We do require that you limit any claim you may have in respect of professional negligence against this firm to the amount of that sum.

If you continue to instruct me, this will mean that you accept the terms of business set out in this letter.

Yours sincerely

Enc. costs schedule

Model Letters for Family Lawyers

CC8   Costs schedule

Work	Time spent in hours	Incidental expenses	VAT
Total			

For the total time of [   ] hours, at my current charging rate of £[   ] this would amount to £[   ] plus VAT of £[   ]. If any work is done by another lawyer, the charges may vary.

SECTION 2

DIVORCE

Andrea Woelke

Divorce

Acting for Respondent

section **2** DIVORCE

D1 Preliminary letter explaining divorce procedure

Dear [*petitioner*]

Divorce

There is only one ground for divorce and that is that the marriage has broken down irretrievably. The person who starts the divorce proceedings is known as 'the petitioner' and their spouse is called 'the respondent'.

To satisfy the court that there has been an irretrievable breakdown the petitioner must prove one of the following five facts:

(a)   The respondent has committed adultery and the petitioner finds it intolerable to live with the respondent.

(b)   The respondent has behaved in such a way that the petitioner cannot reasonably be expected to live with the respondent.

(c)   The respondent has deserted the petitioner for a continuous period of at least two years immediately before the start of the divorce.

(d)   You have lived apart for a continuous period of at least two years immediately before the start of the divorce and the respondent consents to a decree being granted.

(e)   You have lived apart for a continuous period of at least five years immediately before the start of the divorce.

Most divorces are based on facts (a) 'adultery' or (b) 'behaviour'. 'Adultery' is an act of sexual intercourse with a person of the opposite sex. To be able to rely on this in the divorce the adultery must have happened in the six months before separation or at any time after separation. There is no need to name the person with whom the adultery took place or indeed to involve them in the court proceedings.

The test for 'behaviour' is subjective and it does not need to consist of extensive violence, drug or alcohol addiction or other extreme behaviour. A combination of less obvious behaviour can be sufficient. Often issues like working too much (or not working enough), showing too much (or too little) affection, combined with a number of other similar factors are used.

Regularising your separation

If you would prefer to regularise your separation without actually divorcing there are two options available:

1.   judicial separation;
2.   separation agreement.

section **2** DIVORCE

Judicial separation

This involves a court procedure which is virtually identical to that which applies to a divorce. The essential difference is that the court pronounces a decree of judicial separation rather than a divorce and therefore you and your spouse would remain married. The main reason people choose judicial separation over divorce is for religious reasons or if valuable pension benefits are lost on divorce. However, since the court can now share pensions, this is no longer so important.

Separation agreement

Many couples prefer to reach an agreement about financial matters arising out of their separation without involving the court at all. The way this can be achieved is for them to sign a written document which incorporates the agreement they have reached. Commonly, such agreements deal with confirmation that the parties to the marriage are to live apart and the manner in which any maintenance and property issues are to be dealt with. Whilst there are no restrictions on what can or cannot be included in such an agreement, it is important to bear in mind that if either person makes a subsequent financial application to the court, the court is not bound by the financial arrangements in the separation agreement.

I hope that this outline is helpful and if you want me to give you further information, please let me know.

Yours sincerely

Enc.

D2H   Letter to husband petitioner enclosing petition

Dear [*petitioner*]

I have now prepared the documents to start divorce proceedings on your behalf. The only document which you need to approve is the divorce petition and so I enclose a copy. Please check that the details are correct and meet with your agreement.

[*Please send me your original marriage certificate because I must send it to the court together with the petition. If you cannot find your marriage certificate, please let me know as soon as possible so that I can arrange for a new one to be issued by the register office. There is only a small fee for this, but it will take a week or so to obtain a new certificate. Alternatively, you can order the marriage certificate yourself either by calling 0845 603 7788 with your credit card details or online at* www.gro.gov.uk. *In either case, please ask for it to be send to me direct, quoting the reference at the top of this letter.*]

The petition

Paragraphs 1 to 10 are standard and paragraph 11 sets out the fact on which you are relying to establish that the marriage has broken down irretrievably.

The petition ends with a section which begins 'the petitioner therefore prays'. This incorporates a request for all of the financial claims which are available. This is standard practice and does not necessarily mean that you want to pursue these claims. I have also included a claim for your costs of the divorce to be paid by your wife [in case she defends the divorce./You can decide at a later date whether you do still want to ask for an order for costs on the divorce]. This deals only with your costs in connection with the divorce procedure. Any costs in relation to other matters, such as finances are dealt with separately.

Please let me know whether you approve the petition and, if there is anything which is not correct, please let me know as soon as possible so that I can make any necessary alterations to it.

Filing the petition

Once you have approved the petition, I can sign it on your behalf and send it to the court together with the other requisite documents and the court fee of £[300]. Once the court office staff have processed your petition, it will be sent to your wife together with an acknowledgement of service form. She should complete this form indicating whether she wants to defend the divorce and return it to the court within eight days. If she does not return the form, it may eventually be necessary for us to arrange for another set of the documents to be served on her, unless we can prove in some other way that she has received the petition and accompanying documents from the court. This may for example be done by a process server giving it to her personally.

Once I receive the acknowledgement of service form from the court, or once you can prove that your wife has received the petition, I can prepare your application for the conditional divorce order, the decree nisi. This is the point at which the district judge looks at your petition and decides whether you are entitled to a divorce. The court will then set a date for the formal pronouncement of the decree nisi, which may be a week to a month or so after the district judge has approved your divorce. This is only the first divorce order and you remain married until the final order, the decree absolute. You can apply for the decree absolute six weeks after the date of the pronouncement of the decree nisi. The court should process the application within a week or so, but it often takes longer.

In all, the divorce can take as little as four to six months from start to finish. However, it can take a lot longer if either or both of you delay in taking particular steps during the proceedings, or if there are problems with the court.

I look forward to hearing from you.

Yours sincerely

Enc.

D2W Letter to wife petitioner enclosing petition

Dear [*petitioner*]

I have now prepared the documents to start divorce proceedings on your behalf. The only document which you need to approve is the divorce petition and so I enclose a copy. Please check that the details are correct and meet with your agreement.

[Please send me your original marriage certificate because I must send it to the court together with the petition. If you cannot find your marriage certificate, please let me know as soon as possible so that I can arrange for a new one to be issued by the register office. There is only a small fee for this, but it will take a week or so to obtain a new certificate. Alternatively, you can order the marriage certificate yourself either by calling 0845 603 7788 with your credit card details or online at www.gro.gov.uk. In either case, please ask for it to be send to me direct, quoting the reference at the top of this letter.]

The petition

Paragraphs 1 to 10 are standard and paragraph 11 sets out the fact on which you are relying to establish that the marriage has broken down irretrievably.

The petition ends with a section which begins 'the petitioner therefore prays'. This incorporates a request for all of the financial claims which are available. This is standard practice and does not necessarily mean that you want to pursue these claims. I have also included a claim for your costs of the divorce to be paid by your husband [in case he defends the divorce./You can decide at a later date whether you do still want to ask for an order for costs on the divorce]. This deals only with your costs in connection with the divorce procedure. Any costs in relation to other matters, such as finances are dealt with separately.

Please let me know whether you approve the petition and, if there is anything which is not correct, please let me know as soon as possible so that I can make any necessary alterations to it.

Filing the petition

Once you have approved the petition, I can sign it on your behalf and send it to the court together with the other requisite documents and the court fee of £[300]. Once the court office staff have processed your petition, it will be sent to your husband together with an acknowledgement of service form. He should complete this form indicating whether he wants to defend the divorce and return it to the court within eight days. If he does not return the form, it may eventually be necessary for us to arrange for another set of the documents to be served on him, unless we can prove in some other way that he has received the petition and accompanying documents from the court. This may for example be done by a process server giving it to him personally.

Once I receive the acknowledgement of service form from the court, or once you can prove that your husband has received the petition, I can prepare your application for the conditional divorce order, the decree nisi. This is the point at which the district judge looks at your petition and decides whether you are entitled to a divorce. The court will then set a date for the formal pronouncement of the decree nisi, which may be a week to a month or so after the district judge has approved your divorce. This is only the first divorce order and you remain married until the final order, the decree absolute. You can apply for the decree absolute six weeks after the date of the pronouncement of the decree nisi. The court should process the application within a week or so, but it often takes longer.

In all, the divorce can take as little as four to six months from start to finish. However, it can take a lot longer if either or both of you delay in taking particular steps during the proceedings, or if there are problems with the court.

I look forward to hearing from you.

Yours sincerely

Enc.

D3HLH   Letter to husband petitioner on Legal Help enclosing petition (with application for exemption of fee)

Dear [*petitioner*]

I have now prepared the documents to start divorce proceedings on your behalf. The only document which you need to approve is the divorce petition and so I enclose a copy. Please check that the details are correct and meet with your agreement.

[Please send me your original marriage certificate because I must send it to the court together with the petition. If you cannot find your marriage certificate, please let me know as soon as possible so that I can arrange for a new one to be issued by the register office. There is only a small fee for this, but it will take a week or so to obtain a new certificate. Alternatively, you can order the marriage certificate yourself either by calling 0845 603 7788 with your credit card details or online at www.gro.gov.uk. In either case, please ask for it to be send to me direct, quoting the reference at the top of this letter.]

The petition

Paragraphs 1 to 10 are standard and paragraph 11 sets out the fact on which you are relying to establish that the marriage has broken down irretrievably.

The petition ends with a section which begins 'the petitioner therefore prays'. This incorporates a request for all of the financial claims which are available. This is standard practice and does not necessarily mean that you want to pursue these claims. I have also included a claim for your costs of the divorce to be paid by your wife [in case she defends the divorce./You can decide at a later date whether you do still want to ask for an order for costs on the divorce]. This deals only with your costs in connection with the divorce procedure. Any costs in relation to other matters, such as finances are dealt with separately.

Please let me know whether you approve the petition and, if there is anything which is not correct, please let me know as soon as possible so that I can make any necessary alterations to it. If nothing needs to be changed, please sign it where indicated on the last page and return it to me.

Application for a fee exemption or remission

Please check and sign this form and return it to me.

Filing the petition

Once you have approved and signed the petition and returned it to me, I can send it to the court together with the other requisite documents and the court fee of £[300] or your application for a fee exemption or remission form. Once the court office staff have processed your petition it will be sent to your wife together with an acknowledgement of service form. She should complete this form indicating whether she wants to defend the divorce and return it to the court within eight days. If she does not return the form, it may eventually be necessary for us to arrange for another set of the documents to be served on her, unless we can prove in some other way that she has received the petition and accompanying documents from the court. This may for example be done by a process server giving it to her personally.

Once I receive the acknowledgement of service form from the court, or once you can prove that your wife has received the petition, I can prepare your application for the conditional divorce order, the decree nisi. This is the point at which the district judge looks at your petition and decides whether you are entitled to a divorce. The court will then set a date for the formal pronouncement of the decree nisi, which may be a week to a month or so after the district judge has approved your divorce. This is only the first divorce order and you remain married until the final order, the decree absolute. You can apply for the decree absolute six weeks after the date of the pronouncement of the decree nisi. The court should process the application within a week or so, but it often takes longer.

In all, the divorce can take as little as four to six months from start to finish. However, it can take a lot longer if either or both of you delay in taking particular steps during the proceedings, or if there are problems with the court.

I look forward to hearing from you.

Yours sincerely

Enc.

D3WLH   Letter to wife petitioner on Legal Help enclosing petition (with application for exemption of fee)

Dear [*petitioner*]

I have now prepared the documents to start divorce proceedings on your behalf. The only document which you need to approve is the divorce petition and so I enclose a copy. Please check that the details are correct and meet with your agreement.

[Please send me your original marriage certificate because I must send it to the court together with the petition. If you cannot find your marriage certificate, please let me know as soon as possible so that I can arrange for a new one to be issued by the register office. There is only a small fee for this, but it will take a week or so to obtain a new certificate. Alternatively, you can order the marriage certificate yourself either by calling 0845 603 7788 with your credit card details or online at www.gro.gov.uk. *In either case, please ask for it to be send to me direct, quoting the reference at the top of this letter.]*

section 2 DIVORCE

The petition

Paragraphs 1 to 10 are standard and paragraph 11 sets out the fact on which you are relying to establish that the marriage has broken down irretrievably.

The petition ends with a section which begins 'the petitioner therefore prays'. This incorporates a request for all of the financial claims which are available. This is standard practice and does not necessarily mean that you want to pursue these claims. I have also included a claim for your costs of the divorce to be paid by your husband [in case he defends the divorce./You can decide at a later date whether you do still want to ask for an order for costs on the divorce]. This deals only with your costs in connection with the divorce procedure. Any costs in relation to other matters, such as finances are dealt with separately.

Please let me know whether you approve the petition and, if there is anything which is not correct, please let me know as soon as possible so that I can make any necessary alterations to it.

Application for a fee exemption or remission

Please check and sign this form and return it to me.

Filing the petition

Once you have approved and signed the petition and returned it to me, I can send it to the court together with the other requisite documents and the court fee of £[300] or your application for a fee exemption or remission form. Once the court office staff have processed your petition, it will be sent to your husband together with an acknowledgement of service form. He should complete this form indicating whether he wants to defend the divorce and return it to the court within eight days. If he does not return the form, it may eventually be necessary for us to arrange for another set of the documents to be served on him, unless we can prove in some other way that he has received the petition and accompanying documents from the court. This may for example be done by a process server giving it to him personally.

Once I receive the acknowledgement of service form from the court, or once you can prove that your husband has received the petition, I can prepare your application for the conditional divorce order, the decree nisi. This is the point at which the district judge looks at your petition and decides whether you are entitled to a divorce. The court will then set a date for the formal pronouncement of the decree nisi, which may be a week to a month or so after the district judge has approved your divorce. This is only the first divorce order and you remain married until the final order, the decree absolute. You can apply for the decree absolute six weeks after the date of the pronouncement of the decree nisi. The court should process the application within a week or so, but it often takes longer.

In all, the divorce can take as little as four to six months from start to finish. However, it can take a lot longer if either or both of you delay in taking particular steps during the proceedings, or if there are problems with the court.

I look forward to hearing from you.

Yours sincerely

Enc.

D4H Letter to husband petitioner enclosing petition and statement of arrangements for children

Dear [*petitioner*]

Further to our recent meeting, I have now prepared the documents to start divorce proceedings including the petition and statement of arrangements for children. I enclose copies of these documents for your approval.

[Please send me your original marriage certificate because I must send it to the court together with the petition. If you cannot find your marriage certificate, please let me know as soon as possible so that I can arrange for a new one to be issued by the register office. There is only a small fee for this, but it will take a week or so to obtain a new certificate. Alternatively, you can order the marriage certificate yourself either by calling 0845 603 7788 with your credit card details or online at www.gro.gov.uk. *In either case, please ask for it to be send to me direct, quoting the reference at the top of this letter.]*

The petition

Paragraphs 1 to 10 are standard and paragraph 11 sets out the fact on which you are relying to establish that the marriage has broken down irretrievably.

The petition ends with a section which begins 'the petitioner therefore prays'. This incorporates a request for all of the financial claims which are available. This is standard practice and does not necessarily mean that you want to pursue these claims. I have also included a claim for your costs of the divorce to be paid by your wife [in case she defends the divorce./You can decide at a later date whether you do still want to ask for an order for costs on the divorce]. This deals only with your costs in connection with the divorce procedure. Any costs in relation to other matters, such as finances or children are dealt with separately.

Please let me know whether you approve the petition and, if there is anything which is not correct, please let me know as soon as possible so that I can make any necessary alterations to it.

Statement of arrangements for children

Again, please read it carefully to check that you agree the contents. If you do, please sign it where indicated on the last page and return it to me. If it is not accurate, please let me know so that I can make the necessary amendments.

Filing the petition

Once you have approved the petition and returned the statement of arrangements to me, I can sign the petition on your behalf and send it to the court together with the other documents necessary and the court fee of £[300]. Once the court office staff have processed your petition, it will be sent to your

section 2 DIVORCE

wife together with an acknowledgement of service form. She should complete this form indicating whether she wants to defend the divorce and return it to the court within eight days. If she does not return the form, it may eventually be necessary for us to arrange for another set of the documents to be served on her, unless we can prove in some other way that she has received the petition and accompanying documents from the court. This may for example be done by a process server giving it to her personally.

Once I receive the acknowledgement of service form from the court, or once you can prove that your wife has received the petition, I can prepare your application for the conditional divorce order, the decree nisi. This is the point at which the district judge looks at your petition and decides whether you are entitled to a divorce. The court will then set a date for the formal pronouncement of the decree nisi, which may be a week to a month or so after the district judge has approved your divorce. This is only the first divorce order and you remain married until the final order, the decree absolute. You can apply for the decree absolute six weeks after the date of the pronouncement of the decree nisi. The court should process the application within a week or so, but it often takes longer.

In all, the divorce can take as little as four to six months from start to finish. However, it can take a lot longer if either or both of you delay in taking particular steps during the proceedings, or if there are problems with the court.

I look forward to hearing from you.

Yours sincerely

Enc.

D4W Letter to wife petitioner enclosing petition and statement of arrangements for children

Dear [*petitioner*]

Further to our recent meeting, I have now prepared the documents to start divorce proceedings including the petition and statement of arrangements for children. I enclose copies of these documents for your approval.

[Please send me your original marriage certificate because I must send it to the court together with the petition. If you cannot find your marriage certificate, please let me know as soon as possible so that I can arrange for a new one to be issued by the register office. There is only a small fee for this, but it will take a week or so to obtain a new certificate. Alternatively, you can order the marriage certificate yourself either by calling 0845 603 7788 with your credit card details or online at www.gro.gov.uk. In either case, please ask for it to be send to me direct, quoting the reference at the top of this letter.]

The petition

Paragraphs 1 to 10 are standard and paragraph 11 sets out the fact on which you are relying to establish that the marriage has broken down irretrievably.

The petition ends with a section which begins 'the petitioner therefore prays'. This incorporates a request for all of the financial claims which are available. This is standard practice and does not necessarily mean that you want to pursue these claims. I have also included a claim for your costs of the divorce to be paid by your husband [in case he defends the divorce./You can decide at a later date whether you do still want to ask for an order for costs on the divorce]. This deals only with your costs in connection with the divorce procedure. Any costs in relation to other matters, such as finances or children are dealt with separately.

Please let me know whether you approve the petition and, if there is anything which is not correct, please let me know as soon as possible so that I can make any necessary alterations to it.

Statement of arrangements for children

Again, please read it carefully to check that you agree the contents. If you do, please sign it where indicated on the last page and return it to me. If it is not accurate, please let me know so that I can make the necessary amendments.

Filing the petition

Once you have approved the petition and returned the statement of arrangements to me, I can sign the petition on your behalf and send it to the court together with the other documents necessary and the court fee of £[300]. Once the court office staff have processed your petition, it will be sent to your husband together with an acknowledgement of service form. He should complete this form indicating whether he wants to defend the divorce and return it to the court within eight days. If he does not return the form, it may eventually be necessary for us to arrange for another set of the documents to be served on him, unless we can prove in some other way that he has received the petition and accompanying documents from the court. This may for example be done by a process server giving it to him personally.

Once I receive the acknowledgement of service form from the court, or once you can prove that your husband has received the petition, I can prepare your application for the conditional divorce order, the decree nisi. This is the point at which the district judge looks at your petition and decides whether you are entitled to a divorce. The court will then set a date for the formal pronouncement of the decree nisi, which may be a week to a month or so after the district judge has approved your divorce. This is only the first divorce order and you remain married until the final order, the decree absolute. You can apply for the decree absolute six weeks after the date of the pronouncement of the decree nisi. The court should process the application within a week or so, but it often takes longer.

In all, the divorce can take as little as four to six months from start to finish. However, it can take a lot longer if either or both of you delay in taking particular steps during the proceedings, or if there are problems with the court.

I look forward to hearing from you.

Yours sincerely

Enc.

D5HLH   Letter to husband petitioner on Legal Help enclosing petition (with application for exemption of fee) and statement of arrangements for children

Dear [*petitioner*]

Further to our recent meeting, I have now prepared the documents to start divorce proceedings including the petition and statement of arrangements for children. I enclose copies of these documents for your approval.

[Please send me your original marriage certificate because I must send it to the court together with the petition. If you cannot find your marriage certificate, please let me know as soon as possible so that I can arrange for a new one to be issued by the register office. There is only a small fee for this, but it will take a week or so to obtain a new certificate. Alternatively, you can order the marriage certificate yourself either by calling 0845 603 7788 with your credit card details or online at www.gro.gov.uk. *In either case, please ask for it to be send to me direct, quoting the reference at the top of this letter.]*

The petition

Paragraphs 1 to 10 are standard and paragraph 11 sets out the fact on which you are relying to establish that the marriage has broken down irretrievably.

The petition ends with a section which begins 'the petitioner therefore prays'. This incorporates a request for all of the financial claims which are available. This is standard practice and does not necessarily mean that you want to pursue these claims. I have also included a claim for your costs of the divorce to be paid by your wife [in case she defends the divorce./You can decide at a later date whether you do still want to ask for an order for costs on the divorce]. This deals only with your costs in connection with the divorce procedure. Any costs in relation to other matters, such as finances or children are dealt with separately.

Please let me know whether you approve the petition and, if there is anything which is not correct, please let me know as soon as possible so that I can make any necessary alterations to it. If nothing needs to be changed, please sign it where indicated on the last page and return it to me.

Application for a fee exemption or remission

Please check and sign this form and return it to me.

Statement of arrangements for children

Again, please read it carefully to check that you agree the contents. If you do, please sign it where indicated on the last page and return it to me. If it is not accurate, please let me know so that I can make the necessary amendments.

Filing the petition

Once you have approved and signed the petition and returned it and the statement of arrangements to me, I can send it to the court together with the other documents necessary and the court fee of £[300] or your application for a fee exemption or remission form. Once the court office staff have processed your petition, it will be sent to your wife together with an acknowledgement of service form. She should complete this form indicating whether she wants to defend the divorce and return it to the court within eight days. If she does not return the form, it may eventually be necessary for us to arrange for another set of the documents to be served on her, unless we can prove in some other way that she has received the petition and accompanying documents from the court. This may for example be done by a process server giving it to her personally.

Once I receive the acknowledgement of service form from the court, or once you can prove that your wife has received the petition, I can prepare your application for the conditional divorce order, the decree nisi. This is the point at which the district judge looks at your petition and decides whether you are entitled to a divorce. The court will then set a date for the formal pronouncement of the decree nisi, which may be a week to a month or so after the district judge has approved your divorce. This is only the first divorce order and you remain married until the final order, the decree absolute. You can apply for the decree absolute six weeks after the date of the pronouncement of the decree nisi. The court should process the application within a week or so, but it often takes longer.

In all, the divorce can take as little as four to six months from start to finish. However, it can take a lot longer if either or both of you delay in taking particular steps during the proceedings, or if there are problems with the court.

I look forward to hearing from you.

Yours sincerely

Enc.

D5WLH Letter to wife petitioner on Legal Help enclosing petition (with application for exemption of fee) and statement of arrangements for children

Dear [*petitioner*]

Further to our recent meeting, I have now prepared the documents to start divorce proceedings including the petition and statement of arrangements for children. I enclose copies of these documents for your approval.

[Please send me your original marriage certificate because I must send it to the court together with the petition. If you cannot find your marriage certificate, please let me know as soon as possible so that I can arrange for a new one to be issued by the register office. There is only a small fee for this, but it will take a week or so to obtain a new certificate. Alternatively, you can order the marriage certificate yourself either by calling 0845 603 7788 with your credit card details or online at www.gro.gov.uk. *In either case, please ask for it to be send to me direct, quoting the reference at the top of this letter.]*

The petition

Paragraphs 1 to 10 are standard and paragraph 11 sets out the fact on which you are relying to establish that the marriage has broken down irretrievably.

The petition ends with a section which begins 'the petitioner therefore prays'. This incorporates a request for all of the financial claims which are available. This is standard practice and does not necessarily mean that you want to pursue these claims. I have also included a claim for your costs of the divorce to be paid by your husband [in case he defends the divorce./You can decide at a later date whether you do still want to ask for an order for costs on the divorce]. This deals only with your costs in connection with the divorce procedure. Any costs in relation to other matters, such as finances or children are dealt with separately.

Please let me know whether you approve the petition and, if there is anything which is not correct, please let me know as soon as possible so that I can make any necessary alterations to it.

Application for a fee exemption or remission

Please check and sign this form and return it to me.

Statement of arrangements for children

Again, please read it carefully to check that you agree the contents. If you do, please sign it where indicated on the last page and return it to me. If it is not accurate, please let me know so that I can make the necessary amendments.

section **2** DIVORCE

Filing the petition

Once you have approved and signed the petition and returned it and the statement of arrangements to me, I can send it to the court together with the other documents necessary and the court fee of £[300] or your application for a fee exemption or remission form. Once the court office staff have processed your petition, it will be sent to your husband together with an acknowledgement of service form. He should complete this form indicating whether he wants to defend the divorce and return it to the court within eight days. If he does not return the form, it may eventually be necessary for us to arrange for another set of the documents to be served on him, unless we can prove in some other way that he has received the petition and accompanying documents from the court. This may for example be done by a process server giving it to him personally.

Once I receive the acknowledgement of service form from the court, or once you can prove that your husband has received the petition, I can prepare your application for the conditional divorce order, the decree nisi. This is the point at which the district judge looks at your petition and decides whether you are entitled to a divorce. The court will then set a date for the formal pronouncement of the decree nisi, which may be a week to a month or so after the district judge has approved your divorce. This is only the first divorce order and you remain married until the final order, the decree absolute. You can apply for the decree absolute six weeks after the date of the pronouncement of the decree nisi. The court should process the application within a week or so, but it often takes longer.

In all, the divorce can take as little as four to six months from start to finish. However, it can take a lot longer if either or both of you delay in taking particular steps during the proceedings, or if there are problems with the court.

I look forward to hearing from you.

Yours sincerely

Enc.

D6H Paragraph in letter to husband petitioner explaining the prayer

The petition ends with a section which begins 'the petitioner therefore prays'. This incorporates a request for all of the financial claims which are available. This is standard practice and does not necessarily mean that you want to pursue these claims. I have also included a claim for your costs of the divorce to be paid by your wife [in case she defends the divorce./You can decide at a later date whether you do still want to ask for an order for costs on the divorce]. This deals only with your costs in connection with the divorce procedure. Any costs in relation to other matters, such as finances or children are dealt with separately.

D6W Paragraph in letter to wife petitioner explaining the prayer

The petition ends with a section which begins 'the petitioner therefore prays'. This incorporates a request for all of the financial claims which are available. This is standard practice and does not necessarily mean that you want to pursue these claims. I have also included a claim for your costs of the divorce to be paid by your husband [in case he defends the divorce./You can decide at a later date whether you do still want to ask for an order for costs on the divorce]. This deals only with your costs in connection with the divorce procedure. Any costs in relation to other matters, such as finances or children are dealt with separately.

D7 Application for a fee exemption or remission for clients not on Legal Help

I enclose the application for a fee exemption or remission form EX160 together with the guide EX160A. If you qualify, you will not have to pay a court fee. If you think you do, please complete the form. Please also let me have the evidence that is required depending on your specific circumstances. I can take copies and send the originals straight back to you if necessary. You could also ring to make a short appointment so you can come here to have your papers copied while you wait. Please ensure that you complete all sections that apply to you. If you have any difficulties in completing the form, please let me know. Please then sign the form where indicated and return it to me.

D8   Letter filing petition with fee

Dear Sir or Madam

Solicitor service

We act for our above-named client and now enclose:

1.   petition with copy for service.

[2.   *statement of arrangements for children with copy for service.*]

3.   Marriage certificate.

4.   Certificate about reconciliation.

5.   Cheque in the sum of £[300].

Please return the issued proceedings to us for us to effect service on the respondent.

We look forward to hearing from you in due course.

Yours faithfully

Enc.

D9   Letter filing petition (with application for a fee exemption or remission)

Dear Sir or Madam

We are advising and assisting our above-named client under the Legal Help scheme and now enclose:

1.   petition with copy for service.

[2.   *statement of arrangements for children with copy for service.*]

3.   Marriage certificate.

4.   Application for a fee exemption or remission.

We look forward to hearing from you in due course with confirmation that the petition has been served on the respondent.

Yours faithfully

Enc.

D10H   Conciliatory letter to husband respondent preliminary to divorce based on behaviour

Dear [*respondent*]

We have been consulted by your wife about the difficulties the two of you are currently having in your relationship. She has reluctantly decided, after much thought, that it would be best for there to be a divorce.

Both we and your wife would like to emphasise that she hopes that a divorce and the other arrangements that will also need to be made can be reached in a constructive and non-confrontational way by agreement.

We have explained to your wife that the only ground in this country for obtaining a divorce is irretrievable breakdown of the marriage. We have advised her that, in order to prove this, she has to establish one of five facts. Three of those facts depend on periods of separation of two years or more. As you have not been separated for two years or more, a divorce will have to be based on either of the two remaining facts. These are 'adultery' or 'behaviour'.

We understand from your wife that adultery is not relevant, and so the only fact on which she could rely to start a divorce now is your alleged 'behaviour'. Your wife hopes that it is possible to achieve a divorce by agreement and that both of you can agree the particulars of behaviour in the petition, which we enclose.

We recommend that you obtain independent legal advice about the contents of this letter. We recommend that you contact a member of Resolution in your area. You will find details of them on www.resolution.org.uk or by calling 01689 820272. Resolution members are normally specialists in family law and subscribe to a code of practice which is geared towards encouraging a constructive and non-confrontational approach in all family matters.

Your wife is anxious to resolve matters quickly and therefore we look forward to hearing from you, or solicitors instructed by you, within the next 21 days.

Yours faithfully

D10W   Conciliatory letter to wife respondent preliminary to divorce based on unreasonable behaviour

Dear [*respondent*]

We have been consulted by your husband about the difficulties the two of you are currently having in your relationship. He has reluctantly decided, after much thought, that it would be best for there to be a divorce.

Both we and your husband would like to emphasise that he hopes that a divorce and the other arrangements that will also need to be made can be reached in a constructive and non-confrontational way by agreement.

We have explained to your husband that the only ground in this country for obtaining a divorce is irretrievable breakdown of the marriage. We have advised him that, in order to prove this, he has to establish one of five facts. Three of those facts depend on periods of separation of two years or more. As you have not been separated for two years or more, a divorce will have to be based on either of the two remaining facts. These are 'adultery' or 'behaviour'.

We understand from your husband that adultery is not relevant, and so the only fact on which he could rely to start a divorce now is your alleged 'behaviour'. Your husband hopes that it is possible to achieve a divorce by agreement and that both of you can agree the particulars of behaviour in the petition, which we enclose.

We recommend that you obtain independent legal advice about the contents of this letter. We recommend that you contact a member of Resolution in your area. You will find details of them on www.resolution.org.uk or by calling 01689 820272. Resolution members are normally specialists in family law and subscribe to a code of practice which is geared towards encouraging a constructive and non-confrontational approach in all family matters.

Your husband is anxious to resolve matters quickly and therefore we look forward to hearing from you, or solicitors instructed by you, within the next 21 days.

Yours faithfully

D11H   First letter to husband respondent – no children

Dear [*respondent*]

We have been consulted by your wife who has come to the conclusion that your marriage is sadly at an end and we have been instructed to start a divorce.

Both we and your wife hope that a divorce and the other arrangements that will also need to be made can be reached in a constructive and non-confrontational way by agreement.

[paragraph relating to fact in petition]

Your wife hopes that the two of you can reach an agreement about finances without the need to start court proceedings. In order to be able to advise your wife on a financial settlement, we need to have a clear and full picture of the financial situation of both of you. We are currently collecting the relevant information and preparing a financial disclosure statement for your wife. Please prepare your own disclosure and let us have this as soon as possible. We enclose a blank Form E, which is the form that both of you would have to complete if there were court proceedings. At this stage we suggest that there is no need to complete sections 4 and 5 other than section 4.1 and 4.6. You might find it a helpful guide as to what information is required. If your finances are straightforward, it may not be necessary to complete the entire Form E.

We recommend that you obtain independent legal advice about the contents of this letter. We recommend that you contact a member of Resolution in your area. You will find details of them on www.resolution.org.uk or by calling 01689 820272. Resolution members are normally specialists in family law and subscribe to a code of practice which is geared towards encouraging a constructive and non-confrontational approach in all family matters.

Your wife is anxious to resolve matters quickly and therefore we look forward to hearing from you, or solicitors instructed by you, within the next 21 days.

Yours faithfully

Enc.

D11W   First letter to wife respondent – no children

Dear [*respondent*]

We have been consulted by your husband who has come to the conclusion that your marriage is sadly at an end and we have been instructed to start a divorce.

Both we and your husband hope that a divorce and the other arrangements that will also need to be made can be reached in a constructive and non-confrontational way by agreement.

[*paragraph relating to fact in petition*]

Your husband hopes that the two of you can reach an agreement about finances without the need to start court proceedings. In order to be able to advise your husband on a financial settlement, we need to have a clear and full picture of the financial situation of both of you. We are currently collecting the relevant information and preparing a financial disclosure statement for your husband. Please prepare your own disclosure and let us have this as soon as possible. We enclose a blank Form E, which is the form that both of you would have to complete if there were court proceedings. At this stage we suggest that there is no need to complete sections 4 and 5 other than section 4.1 and 4.6. You might find it a helpful guide as to what information is required. If your finances are straightforward, it may not be necessary to complete the entire Form E.

We recommend that you obtain independent legal advice about the contents of this letter. We recommend that you contact a member of Resolution in your area. You will find details of them on www.resolution.org.uk or by calling 01689 820272. Resolution members are normally specialists in family law and subscribe to a code of practice which is geared towards encouraging a constructive and non-confrontational approach in all family matters.

Your husband is anxious to resolve matters quickly and therefore we look forward to hearing from you, or solicitors instructed by you, within the next 21 days.

Yours faithfully

Enc.

D11HC   First letter to husband respondent enclosing statement of arrangements for children

Dear [*respondent*]

We have been consulted by your wife who has come to the conclusion that your marriage is sadly at an end and we have been instructed to start a divorce.

Both we and your wife hope that a divorce and the other arrangements that will also need to be made can be reached in a constructive and non-confrontational way by agreement.

[*paragraph relating to fact in petition*]

One of the documents required to start a divorce is a statement of arrangements for children, summarising what arrangements there are at the moment for any child who is under 16, or under 18 and still in full-time education. It includes such information as where any child is to live and what arrangements are to be made for contact. We enclose a copy of the statement which we have prepared because, where possible, the courts prefer it if both parents agree the arrangements. The statement only sets out the present arrangements and anything written there does not mean that this is a final arrangement for the children. The courts hardly ever raise an issue on them. The fact that the court processes it does not mean that the arrangements are somehow endorsed by the court.

If you agree the statement, please sign it on the last page and return it to us in the accompanying envelope. If you do not agree, please let us know whether there are some amendments that we could make and that your wife may agree. She can start the divorce even if you do not agree and return the signed statement.

Your wife hopes that the two of you can reach an agreement about finances without the need to start court proceedings. In order to be able to advise your wife on a financial settlement, we need to have a clear and full picture of the financial situation of both of you. We are currently collecting the relevant information and preparing a financial disclosure statement for your wife. Please prepare your own disclosure and let us have this as soon as possible. We enclose a blank Form E, which is the form that both of you would have to complete if there were court proceedings. At this stage we suggest that there is no need to complete sections 4 and 5 other than section 4.1 and 4.6. You might find it a helpful guide as to what information is required. If your finances are straightforward, it may not be necessary to complete the entire Form E.

We recommend that you obtain independent legal advice about the contents of this letter. We recommend that you contact a member of Resolution in your area. You will find details of them on www.resolution.org.uk or by calling 01689 820272. Resolution members are normally specialists in family law and subscribe to a code of practice which is geared towards encouraging a constructive and non-confrontational approach in all family matters.

Your wife is anxious to resolve matters quickly and therefore we look forward to hearing from you, or solicitors instructed by you, within the next 21 days.

Yours faithfully

Enc.

D11WC First letter to wife respondent enclosing statement of arrangements for children

Dear [*respondent*]

We have been consulted by your husband who has come to the conclusion that your marriage is sadly at an end and we have been instructed to start a divorce.

Both we and your husband hope that a divorce and the other arrangements that will also need to be made can be reached in a constructive and non-confrontational way by agreement.

[paragraph relating to fact in petition]

One of the documents required to start a divorce is a statement of arrangements for children, summarising what arrangements there are at the moment for any child who is under 16, or under 18 and still in full-time education. It includes such information as where any child is to live and what arrangements are to be made for contact. We enclose a copy of the statement which we have prepared because, where possible, the courts prefer it if both parents agree the arrangements. The statement only sets out the present arrangements and anything written there does not mean that this is a final arrangement for the children. The courts hardly ever raise an issue on them. The fact that the court processes it does not mean that the arrangements are somehow endorsed by the court.

If you agree the statement, please sign it on the last page and return it to us in the accompanying envelope. If you do not agree, please let us know whether there are some amendments that we could make and that your husband may agree. He can start the divorce even if you do not agree and return the signed statement.

Your husband hopes that the two of you can reach an agreement about finances without the need to start court proceedings. In order to be able to advise your husband on a financial settlement, we need to have a clear and full picture of the financial situation of both of you. We are currently collecting the relevant information and preparing a financial disclosure statement for your husband. Please prepare your own disclosure and let us have this as soon as possible. We enclose a blank Form E, which is the form that both of you would have to complete if there were court proceedings. At this stage we suggest that there is no need to complete sections 4 and 5 other than section 4.1 and 4.6. You might find it a helpful guide as to what information is required. If your finances are straightforward, it may not be necessary to complete the entire Form E.

We recommend that you obtain independent legal advice about the contents of this letter. We recommend that you contact a member of Resolution in your area. You will find details of them on www.resolution.org.uk or by calling 01689 820272. Resolution members are normally specialists in family law and subscribe to a code of practice which is geared towards encouraging a constructive and non-confrontational approach in all family matters.

Your husband is anxious to resolve matters quickly and therefore we look forward to hearing from you, or solicitors instructed by you, within the next 21 days.

Yours faithfully

Enc.

D12AH   Paragraph of letter to husband respondent – basis of divorce: adultery

We are instructed to start a divorce based on your relationship with another woman. It will not be necessary for us to name her in the divorce papers.

Please confirm in a short letter to us that you agree to a divorce on this basis.

D12AW   Paragraph of letter to wife respondent – basis of divorce: adultery

We are instructed to start a divorce based on your relationship with another man. It will not be necessary for us to name him in the divorce papers.

Please confirm in a short letter to us that you agree to a divorce on this basis.

D12BH   Paragraph of letter to husband respondent – basis of divorce: behaviour

We have advised your wife that the only basis on which she can start a divorce at this time is either adultery or your behaviour. Since your wife believes that adultery is not relevant, we are instructed to start a divorce based on your behaviour. Therefore, we enclose a draft divorce petition for your approval. Please let us know if you would like to propose amendments to the petition.

Please confirm that you will agree to a divorce on this basis[, in which case your wife will not claim the costs of the divorce].

D12BW   Paragraph of letter to wife respondent – basis of divorce: unreasonable behaviour

We have advised your husband that the only basis on which he can start a divorce at this time is either adultery or your behaviour. Since your husband believes that adultery is not relevant, we are instructed to start a divorce based on your behaviour. Therefore, we enclose a draft divorce petition for your approval. Please let us know if you would like to propose amendments to the petition.

Please confirm that you will agree to a divorce on this basis[, in which case your husband will not claim the costs of the divorce].

D12DH   Paragraph of letter to husband respondent – basis of divorce: two years' separation

We understand that you have been separated for two years. Do you agree to a divorce based on this fact? If so, your wife will not claim the costs of the divorce.

D12DW   Paragraph of letter to wife respondent – basis of divorce: two years' separation

We understand that you have been separated for two years. Do you agree to a divorce based on this fact? If so, your husband will not claim the costs of the divorce.

D12EH   Paragraph of letter to husband respondent – basis of divorce: five years' separation

We understand from your wife that you have been separated for five years. Please confirm that you agree to a divorce based on five years' separation. If so, your wife will not claim the costs of the divorce.

D12EW   Paragraph of letter to wife respondent – basis of divorce: five years' separation

We understand from your husband that you have been separated for five years. Please confirm that you agree to a divorce based on five years' separation. If so, your husband will not claim the costs of the divorce.

D13   First letter to respondent's solicitors

Dear Sirs

Surname

We are pleased that you have been instructed.

We note that your client agrees to the divorce as proposed. Please confirm whether you will accept service on your client's behalf.

Yours faithfully

D14   Letter to respondent's solicitors serving petition

Dear Sirs

Surname

We enclose by way of service our client's petition[, *statement of arrangements for children*] and acknowledgement of service form. Please acknowledge receipt.

Please send us a copy of the completed acknowledgement of service form when you file it at court.

Yours faithfully

Enc.

D15H   Letter to respondent husband serving petition

Dear [*respondent*]

Your wife's petition asking that your marriage be brought to an end has now been processed by the court and we enclose by way of service the petition [, *statement of arrangements for children*] and the acknowledgement of service form.

You will need to complete the acknowledgement of service form and return it to the court within eight days of receiving this letter saying whether you agree to the divorce. Please let us know once you have done this and send us a copy of the completed form.

We recommend that you obtain independent legal advice about the contents of this letter. We recommend that you contact a member of Resolution in your area. You will find details of them on www.resolution.org.uk or by calling 01689 820272. Resolution members are normally specialists in family law and subscribe to a code of practice which is geared towards encouraging a constructive and non-confrontational approach in all family matters.

We look forward to hearing from you, or solicitors instructed by you.

Yours sincerely

Enc.

D15W   Letter to respondent wife serving petition

Dear [*respondent*]

Your husband's petition asking that your marriage be brought to an end has now been processed by the court and we enclose by way of service the petition [, *statement of arrangements for children*] and the acknowledgement of service form.

You will need to complete the acknowledgement of service form and return it to the court within eight days of receiving this letter saying whether you agree to the divorce. Please let us know once you have done this and send us a copy of the completed form.

We recommend that you obtain independent legal advice about the contents of this letter. We recommend that you contact a member of Resolution in your area. You will find details of them on www.resolution.org.uk or by calling 01689 820272. Resolution members are normally specialists in family law and subscribe to a code of practice which is geared towards encouraging a constructive and non-confrontational approach in all family matters.

We look forward to hearing from you, or solicitors instructed by you.

Yours sincerely

Enc.

section 2 DIVORCE

D16HPC Letter to husband petitioner enclosing affidavit in support of petition (private client)

Dear [*petitioner*]

I have now received from the court and enclose a copy of the acknowledgement of service form which your wife has filed. You will see that she does not intend to defend the divorce. You will also see that she [agrees/ does not agree] to pay the costs of the divorce.

The next stage in the proceedings is for you to swear a statement, an affidavit, in support of your petition. I need to file this at court to apply for the district judge to approve your petition and direct that the conditional divorce order, the decree nisi, is pronounced.

I now enclose your affidavit which you should read through carefully. If any amendments need to be made to it, please let me know as soon as possible. If it is correct, you should take it to another firm of solicitors and ask if you may swear it there. There will be a fee of £7.

Alternatively, you may go to a county court office where you can swear the affidavit free of charge.

Once you have done this, please return this document to me as soon as possible so that I may send it to court. Provided the district judge considers that you have proved your case, I will receive notification of the date when the decree nisi will be pronounced and can let you know. This may take four weeks or even longer. Remember that you cannot apply for the divorce to be finalised until six weeks after the date on which the decree nisi is pronounced.

I look forward to hearing from you.

Yours sincerely

Enc.

D16WPC Letter to wife petitioner enclosing affidavit in support of petition (private client)

Dear [*petitioner*]

I have now received from the court and enclose a copy of the acknowledgement of service form which your husband has filed. You will see that he does not intend to defend the divorce. You will also see that he [agrees/does not agree] to pay the costs of the divorce.

The next stage in the proceedings is for you to swear a statement, an affidavit, in support of your petition. I need to file this at court to apply for the district judge to approve your petition and direct that the conditional divorce order, the decree nisi, is pronounced.

I now enclose your affidavit which you should read through carefully. If any amendments need to be made to it, please let me know as soon as possible. If it is correct, you should take it to another firm of solicitors and ask if you may swear it there. There will be a fee of £7.

Alternatively, you may go to a county court office where you can swear the affidavit free of charge.

Once you have done this, please return this document to me as soon as possible so that I may send it to court. Provided the district judge considers that you have proved your case, I will receive notification of the date when the decree nisi will be pronounced and can let you know. This may take four weeks or even longer. Remember that you cannot apply for the divorce to be finalised until six weeks after the date on which the decree nisi is pronounced.

I look forward to hearing from you.

Yours sincerely

Enc.

D17   Letter to client following receipt of sworn affidavit

Dear [*petitioner*]

Thank you for returning your sworn affidavit. I confirm that I have sent it to the court.

As you will remember, the next stage is for a district judge to check the papers to ensure that you have proved your case and for the court to fix a date for the pronouncement of decree nisi. The time between sending the affidavit to the court and receiving the district judge's certificate, which tells us the date for decree nisi, varies from case to case but the average time can be up to [six] weeks. The papers have to pass through several departments in the court and in my experience it is almost impossible to speed up the process.

I will write to you again when I receive the district judge's certificate.

Yours sincerely

D18   Letter to court requesting district judge's Certificate

Dear Sir or Madam

We act for the petitioner and accordingly enclose:

1.   Request for Directions for Trial.

2.   Affidavit in support of the petition.

We look forward to receiving the district judge's certificate in due course.

Yours faithfully

Enc.

D19HPC Letter to husband petitioner explaining service problems and options (private client)

Dear [*petitioner*]

I am writing to advise you that your wife has still not sent the completed acknowledgement of service form to the court. Her time for responding to the petition for divorce has now run out. However, until she returns the acknowledgement of service form to the court or you can prove that she has received the divorce papers, the divorce cannot proceed.

Your options to get an order that your wife has received the papers are:

1. Swear a statement that you have seen them in her possession or that she has told you that she has received them if that applies.

2. Instruct a process server to give them to her.

3. Ask someone else to give them to her and swear a statement for the court that they have done so.

4. Apply to the court for the papers to be served in some other way.

Statement

If you know that your wife has received the divorce papers, because she has told you so or you have seen them in her possession, we could use that as evidence that she has received them. Please let me know if this is the case. I could draft a short affidavit about this for you to swear. The affidavit will then be used as an application for an order that service of the petition can be presumed to have taken place.

Process server

If you do not have such evidence, the next step will be to arrange for the papers to be handed to your wife personally. I could arrange for a professional process server to give your wife the papers in person. This will involve extra costs for the process server of about £100. You may get these costs back if you succeed in your claim that your wife should meet your costs of the divorce herself and those costs are paid. If you have a photograph of your wife, please let me have that so that the process server can identify her. Please also let me have a short description of her.

Personal service by someone else

Alternatively, you may know of someone who could serve the papers for you which would keep the costs down.

Unfortunately you cannot hand the papers to your wife yourself.

Alternative service

As a last resort, it is sometimes possible to get an order from the court that service should take place by the papers being sent to someone other than your wife. However, the courts generally need to be persuaded that it is impossible to carry out service in any other way.

Please let me know if you have any evidence that your wife has received the divorce papers so that I can decide with you the best way to ensure that the divorce proceeds with the minimum delay.

Yours sincerely

D19WPC Letter to wife petitioner explaining service problems and options (private client)

Dear [*petitioner*]

I am writing to advise you that your husband has still not sent the completed acknowledgement of service form to the court. His time for responding to the petition for divorce has now run out. However, until he returns the acknowledgement of service form to the court or you can prove that he has received the divorce papers, the divorce cannot proceed.

Your options to get an order that your husband has received the papers are:

1. Swear a statement that you have seen them in his possession or that he has told you that he has received them if that applies.

2. Instruct a process server to give them to him.

3. Ask someone else to give them to him and swear a statement for the court that they have done so.

4. Apply to the court for the papers to be served in some other way.

Statement

If you know that your husband has received the divorce papers, because he has told you so or you have seen them in his possession, we could use that as evidence that he has received them. Please let me know if this is the case. I could draft a short affidavit about this for you to swear. The affidavit will then be used as an application for an order that service of the petition can be presumed to have taken place.

Process server

If you do not have such evidence, the next step will be to arrange for the papers to be handed to your husband personally. I could arrange for a professional process server to give your husband the papers in person. This will involve extra costs for the process server of about £100. You may get these costs back if you succeed in your claim that your husband should meet your costs of the divorce himself and those costs are paid. If you have a photograph of your husband, please let me have that so that the process server can identify him. Please also let me have a short description of him.

Personal service by someone else

Alternatively, you may know of someone who could serve the papers for you which would keep the costs down.

Unfortunately you cannot hand the papers to your husband yourself.

Alternative service

As a last resort, it is sometimes possible to get an order from the court that service should take place by the papers being sent to someone other than your husband. However, the courts generally need to be persuaded that it is impossible to carry out service in any other way.

Please let me know if you have any evidence that your husband has received the divorce papers so that I can decide with you the best way to ensure that the divorce proceeds with the minimum delay.

Yours sincerely

D20HLH Letter to husband petitioner explaining service problems and options (Legal Help)

Dear [*petitioner*]

Your wife has still not sent the completed acknowledgement of service form to the court. Her time for defending the petition has now run out. However, until she returns the acknowledgement of service form to the court, or it is proven that she has received your petition and has failed to comply with the time-limit for defending it, the divorce cannot proceed.

If you know that your wife has received the divorce papers, because she has told you so, or if you have seen them in her possession, we could use that as evidence that she has received them. Please let me know if this is the case. I could draft a short affidavit for you to swear in support of an application for an order that service of the petition be deemed to have taken place.

If, on the other hand, you do not have such evidence, the next step will be to arrange for the papers to be handed to her personally. To arrange that, I would ask the court bailiffs to serve it personally. Unfortunately, court bailiffs have a heavy workload so this method can be very slow.

I am afraid that you cannot hand the papers to your wife yourself.

As a last resort, it is sometimes possible to get an order from the court that service should take place by the papers being served on someone other than your wife. However, the courts generally need to be persuaded that it is impossible to ensure that service can be proved in some other way.

Please let me know if you have any evidence that your wife has received the divorce papers so that I can decide with you the best way to ensure that the divorce proceeds.

Yours sincerely

section **2** DIVORCE

D20WLH Letter to wife petitioner explaining service problems and options (Legal Help)

Dear [*petitioner*]

Your husband has still not sent the completed acknowledgement of service form to the court. His time for defending the petition has now run out. However, until he returns the acknowledgement of service form to the court, or it is proven that he has received your petition and has failed to comply with the time-limit for defending it, the divorce cannot proceed.

If you know that your husband has received the divorce papers, because he has told you so, or if you have seen them in his possession, we could use that as evidence that he has received them. Please let me know if this is the case. I could draft a short affidavit for you to swear in support of an application for an order that service of the petition be deemed to have taken place.

If, on the other hand, you do not have such evidence, the next step will be to arrange for the papers to be handed to him personally. To arrange that, I would ask the court bailiffs to serve it personally. Unfortunately, court bailiffs have a heavy workload so this method can be very slow.

I am afraid that you cannot hand the papers to your husband yourself.

As a last resort, it is sometimes possible to get an order from the court that service should take place by the papers being served on someone other than your husband. However, the courts generally need to be persuaded that it is impossible to ensure that service can be proved in some other way.

Please let me know if you have any evidence that your husband has received the divorce papers so that I can decide with you the best way to ensure that the divorce proceeds.

Yours sincerely

D21 Letter to client petitioner enclosing application for bailiff service (Legal Help)

Dear [*petitioner*]

I enclose two copies of from D89, the application for bailiff service. Please sign the forms and return them to me together with a photograph and a physical description of your spouse.

Application for a fee exemption or remission

There is normally a court fee of £[30]. I enclose the application for a fee exemption or remission form EX160 together with the guide EX160A. You must complete the form so that you do not have to pay the court fee when the application is sent to the court. Please check that everything in the form is correct. Please also let me have the evidence that is required depending on your specific circumstances. I can take copies and send the originals straight back to you if necessary. You could also ring to make a short appointment so you can come here to have your papers copied while you wait. Please ensure that you complete all sections that apply to you. If you have any difficulties in completing the form, please let me know. Please then sign the form where indicated and return it to me.

When you have returned these forms to me, I can send them to the court.

Unfortunately, because of delays at court it could be two to three months before I hear from the bailiffs.

Yours sincerely

Enc.

D22H   Letter to husband petitioner explaining order dispensing with service

Dear [*petitioner*]

It is now necessary to consider applying to the court for an order that the divorce petition does not need to be served on your wife. If the judge agrees, the divorce can proceed even though you cannot prove that your wife has received the divorce papers.

The court requires that every effort has been made to ensure that your wife has received the papers. I enclose a copy of a draft statement, which you will need to swear. Please make any amendments or corrections that are necessary setting out all attempts you have made to find your wife and for the divorce papers to reach her.

I look forward to hearing from you.

Yours sincerely

Enc.

D22W   Letter to wife petitioner explaining order dispensing with service

Dear [*petitioner*]

It is now necessary to consider applying to the court for an order that the divorce petition does not need to be served on your husband. If the judge agrees, the divorce can proceed even though you cannot prove that your husband has received the divorce papers.

The court requires that every effort has been made to ensure that your husband has received the papers. I enclose a copy of a draft statement, which you will need to swear. Please make any amendments or corrections that are necessary setting out all attempts you have made to find your husband and for the divorce papers to reach him.

I look forward to hearing from you.

Yours sincerely

Enc.

D23H Letter to husband petitioner enclosing enquiries as to respondent's whereabouts

Dear [*petitioner*]

For you to get a divorce, it is usually necessary to prove that your wife has received a copy of the divorce papers, unless you can show that you have taken all reasonable steps to trace her without success.

Please let me have your written replies to the following questions so I can advise you on whether it is possible to find her:

1. On what date and at what address did you and your wife last live together?

2. Where did your wife live after you separated?

3. When was your wife last seen or heard of?

4. What relatives or friends of your wife are known to you? Do you know the name and address of any other person your wife might still be in touch with, such as a doctor, dentist, solicitor or accountant?

5. Do you have an email address for your wife?

6. Have you made an online search to find her?

7. Do you have any telephone number for her or any of her relatives?

8. Was your wife working in employment at or after the date when you separated?

9. Did your wife, to your knowledge, have any bank, building society or credit card accounts? If possible, please supply full details.

10. Was your wife a member of any trade union or professional organisation? Did she have any store cards or was she a member of any reward point schemes?

11. Is there a Child Support Agency assessment for child maintenance in force?

12. What other enquiries have you made, or what information do you have concerning the whereabouts of your wife?

13. Do you know of any other enquiry which could be made which might lead to your wife being traced?

I look forward to hearing from you.

Yours sincerely

section 2 DIVORCE

D23W   Letter to wife petitioner enclosing enquiries as to respondent's whereabouts

Dear [*petitioner*]

For you to get a divorce, it is usually necessary to prove that your husband has received a copy of the divorce papers, unless you can show that you have taken all reasonable steps to trace him without success.

Please let me have your written replies to the following questions so I can advise you on whether it is possible to find him:

1.   On what date and at what address did you and your husband last live together?

2.   Where did your husband live after you separated?

3.   When was your husband last seen or heard of?

4.   What relatives or friends of your husband are known to you? Do you know the name and address of any other person your husband might still be in touch with, such as a doctor, dentist, solicitor or accountant?

5.   Do you have an email address for your husband?

6.   Have you made an online search to find him?

7.   Do you have any telephone number for him or any of his relatives?

8.   Was your husband working in employment at or after the date when you separated?

9.   Did your husband, to your knowledge, have any bank, building society or credit card accounts? If possible, please supply full details.

10.   Was your husband a member of any trade union or professional organisation? Did he have any store cards or was he a member of any reward point schemes?

11.   Is there a Child Support Agency assessment for child maintenance in force?

12.   What other enquiries have you made, or what information do you have concerning the whereabouts of your husband?

13.   Do you know of any other enquiry which could be made which might lead to your husband being traced?

I look forward to hearing from you.

Yours sincerely

D24 Letter to client petitioner advising date of decree nisi – no children

Dear [*petitioner*]

I am writing to let you know that a date has been fixed for pronouncement of the conditional divorce order, the decree nisi, on [   ]. The district judge has now looked at your petition and decided that you are entitled to a divorce. I enclose a copy of the district judge's certificate stating this, for your information.

[The district judge made no order as to the costs of the divorce itself, meaning that you have to pay your own costs.]

There will be no need for you to go to court for this. A copy of the decree nisi and any orders will be sent to me by the court after the date it is pronounced and I can then forward you a copy.

Yours sincerely

Enc.

D25 Letter to client petitioner advising date of decree nisi – district judge satisfied with arrangements for children

Dear [*petitioner*]

I am writing to let you know that a date has been fixed for pronouncement of the conditional divorce order, the decree nisi, on [   ]. The district judge has now looked at your petition and decided that you are entitled to a divorce. I enclose a copy of the district judge's certificate stating this, for your information.

The district judge has certified that arrangements for the children summarised in the statement of arrangements for children are satisfactory. You will recall that this form was prepared with the divorce petition, giving information on such matters as the children's accommodation, schooling, and contact. This does not mean that the court has endorsed the arrangements or made an order for them. The judge has simply decided that there is no reason to intervene at this stage.

[The district judge made no order as to the costs of the divorce itself, meaning that you have to pay your own costs.]

There will be no need for you to go to court for this. A copy of the decree nisi and any orders will be sent to me by the court after the date it is pronounced and I can then forward you a copy.

Yours sincerely

Enc.

section 2 DIVORCE

D26HPC Letter to husband petitioner about appointment with district judge to consider arrangements for children (private client)

Dear [*petitioner*]

You will see that the district judge is concerned about the arrangements for the children summarised in the statement of arrangements for children. You will recall that this was the form sent to the court with the divorce petition, giving information on such matters as the children's accommodation, schooling, and contact.

The district judge will want to see you to discuss the arrangements for the children at [   ] on [   ] in Room [   ] at [the Principal Registry of the Family Division, First Avenue House, 42–49 High Holborn, London WC1V 6NP]. The district judge will base any questions on the information in the statement of arrangements for children form. Your wife should also attend. I enclose a further copy of the statement for your information.

The hearing is designed to be informal and you could attend on your own. If you want me to attend, I can, of course, do so. However, this will increase your costs. If you are prepared to go on your own, you should arrange to be at the court ten minutes early and make yourself known to the district judge's clerk or the usher, who will be near the room where the district judge is sitting. The district judge should be addressed as 'Sir' or 'Madam'.

A hearing such as this, where you are not legally represented, is meant to be informal and you should not feel intimidated by the district judge. There will be no wigs and gowns and the hearing is likely to take place in a small room. You will not have to stand up to talk. Simply answer the questions as best as you can.

Please telephone me when you get this letter to let me know whether you want me to go to court or whether you are going on your own.

Yours sincerely

Enc. statement of arrangements for children

D26WPC Letter to wife petitioner about appointment with district judge to consider arrangements for children (private client)

Dear [*petitioner*]

You will see that the district judge is concerned about the arrangements for the children summarised in the statement of arrangements for children. You will recall that this was the form sent to the court with the divorce petition, giving information on such matters as the children's accommodation, schooling, and contact.

The district judge will want to see you to discuss the arrangements for the children at [   ] on [   ] in Room [   ] at [the Principal Registry of the Family Division, First Avenue House, 42–49 High Holborn, London WC1V 6NP]. The district judge will base any questions on the information in the statement of arrangements for children form. Your husband should also attend. I enclose a further copy of the statement for your information.

The hearing is designed to be informal and you could attend on your own. If you want me to attend, I can, of course, do so. However, this will increase your costs. If you are prepared to go on your own, you should arrange to be at the court ten minutes early and make yourself known to the district judge's clerk or the usher, who will be near the room where the district judge is sitting. The district judge should be addressed as 'Sir' or 'Madam'.

A hearing such as this, where you are not legally represented, is meant to be informal and you should not feel intimidated by the district judge. There will be no wigs and gowns and the hearing is likely to take place in a small room. You will not have to stand up to talk. Simply answer the questions as best as you can.

Please telephone me when you get this letter to let me know whether you want me to go to court or whether you are going on your own.

Yours sincerely

Enc. statement of arrangements for children

D26HLH Letter to husband petitioner about appointment with district judge to consider arrangements for children (Legal Help)

Dear [*petitioner*]

You will see that the district judge is concerned about the arrangements for the children summarised in the statement of arrangements for children. You will recall that this was the form sent to the court with the divorce petition, giving information on such matters as the children's accommodation, schooling, and contact.

The district judge will want to see you to discuss the arrangements for the children at [   ] on [   ] in Room [   ] at [the Principal Registry of the Family Division, First Avenue House, 42–49 High Holborn, London WC1V 6NP]. The district judge will base any questions on the information in the statement of arrangements for children form. Your wife should also attend. I enclose a further copy of the statement for your information.

As I am advising and assisting you under the Legal Help scheme, I cannot attend court on your behalf and you must to go to the court hearing yourself. You should arrange to be at the court at least ten minutes early and make yourself known to the district judge's clerk or the usher, who will be near the room where the district judge is sitting. The district judge should be addressed as 'Sir' or 'Madam'.

A hearing such as this, where you are not legally represented, is meant to be informal and you should not feel intimidated by the district judge. There will be no wigs and gowns and the hearing is likely to take place in a small room. You will not have to stand up to talk. Simply answer the questions as best as you can.

Please telephone me when you get this letter to confirm that you will be going to the court hearing.

Yours sincerely

Enc. statement of arrangements for children

D26WLH Letter to wife petitioner about appointment with district judge to consider arrangements for children (Legal Help)

Dear [*petitioner*]

You will see that the district judge is concerned about the arrangements for the children summarised in the statement of arrangements for children. You will recall that this was the form sent to the court with the divorce petition, giving information on such matters as the children's accommodation, schooling, and contact.

The district judge will want to see you to discuss the arrangements for the children at [   ] on [   ] in Room [   ] at [the Principal Registry of the Family Division, First Avenue House, 42–49 High Holborn, London WC1V 6NP]. The district judge will base any questions on the information in the statement of arrangements for children form. Your husband should also attend. I enclose a further copy of the statement for your information.

As I am advising and assisting you under the Legal Help scheme, I cannot attend court on your behalf and you must to go to the court hearing yourself. You should arrange to be at the court at least ten minutes early and make yourself known to the district judge's clerk or the usher, who will be near the room where the district judge is sitting. The district judge should be addressed as 'Sir' or 'Madam'.

A hearing such as this, where you are not legally represented, is meant to be informal and you should not feel intimidated by the district judge. There will be no wigs and gowns and the hearing is likely to take place in a small room. You will not have to stand up to talk. Simply answer the questions as best as you can.

Please telephone me when you get this letter to confirm that you will be going to the court hearing.

Yours sincerely

Enc. statement of arrangements for children

section 2 DIVORCE

D27H   Paragraph in letter to husband petitioner confirming award of costs

The district judge has made an order for your wife to pay your costs of the divorce itself. This should not be confused with the costs of any court proceedings about finances. If your wife does not agree the amount, the court will have to assess these costs at a separate hearing.

D27W   Paragraph in letter to wife petitioner confirming award of costs

The district judge has made an order for your husband to pay your costs of the divorce itself. This should not be confused with the costs of any court proceedings about finances. If your husband does not agree the amount, the court will have to assess these costs at a separate hearing.

D28   Letter to client petitioner about costs appointment

Dear [*petitioner*]

The district judge has not made a decision about your application that your spouse meet your costs of the divorce itself. There will be a short hearing at which the district judge will decide whether or not your spouse should do so. This will take place in Room [   ] at [   ] on [   ] at the [Principal Registry of the Family Division, First Avenue House, 42–49 High Holborn, London WC1V 6NP].

It is essential that you or someone on your behalf goes to the court hearing. Generally speaking, it will not be cost-effective for me to go and I suggest you go on your own. Please telephone me to let me know what you want to do. If you decide to go to court on your own, you should arrange to be at the court ten minutes early and make yourself known to the district judge's clerk, who will be in or near the room where the district judge is sitting. The district judge should be addressed as 'Sir' or 'Madam'.

A hearing such as this, where you are not legally represented, is meant to be informal and you should not feel intimidated by the district judge. Simply answer the questions as best as you can.

Yours sincerely

section 2 DIVORCE

D29HPC Letter with decree nisi to husband petitioner (private client)

Dear [*petitioner*]

I refer to the pronouncement of the conditional order for divorce, the decree nisi, on [   ]. I have now received it from the court and enclose a copy.

I confirm I will be in a position to apply for your divorce to be made final, the decree absolute, six weeks after the date of decree nisi which I calculate to be [   ]. You can let me know nearer the time whether you want me to make the application then or wait. If you have not reached a financial settlement, you may want to wait before making the application. You need to consider the following:

1. If your wife died before the financial arrangements are finalised, you may be better off being her widower because if she has not made a will, you would inherit a part of her estate automatically and in any event there would be no inheritance tax on anything that goes to you from her estate. There may also be pension rights or life policies which you would lose on decree absolute.

2. There may be tactical reasons why you do not want to make the application now. If your wife wants the decree nisi to be made absolute and if you say that you will not make the application until the financial arrangements are finalised, this may make your wife more reasonable or more generous in the hope that you will agree to finalise the divorce more quickly. However, your wife can make an application to the court for the decree absolute three months after the date that you can first apply for it. The court will not automatically grant it, however. The court will have to consider whether it is reasonable to finalise the divorce.

[3. *As your home is in your wife's sole name, you will lose the right to occupy the property once decree absolute has been made. It is possible to extend your rights of occupation beyond decree absolute, but the application must be made before the court makes the decree absolute.*]

If you wish to discuss this further, please let me know. Otherwise, let me know whether or not you want me to make the application as soon as I can.

Yours sincerely

Enc. decree nisi

D29WPC Letter with decree nisi to wife petitioner (private client)

Dear [*petitioner*]

I refer to the pronouncement of the conditional order for divorce, the decree nisi, on [   ]. I have now received it from the court and enclose a copy.

I confirm I will be in a position to apply for your divorce to be made final, the decree absolute, six weeks after the date of decree nisi which I calculate to be [   ]. You can let me know nearer the time whether you want me to make the application then or wait. If you have not reached a financial settlement, you may want to wait before making the application. You need to consider the following:

1. If your husband died before the financial arrangements are finalised, you may be better off being his widow because if he has not made a will, you would inherit a part of his estate automatically and in any event there would be no inheritance tax on anything that goes to you from his estate. There may also be pension rights or life policies which you would lose on decree absolute.

2. There may be tactical reasons why you do not want to make the application now. If your husband wants the decree nisi to be made absolute and if you say that you will not make the application until the financial arrangements are finalised, this may make your husband more reasonable or more generous in the hope that you will agree to finalise the divorce more quickly. However, your husband can make an application to the court for the decree absolute three months after the date that you can first apply for it. The court will not automatically grant it, however. The court will have to consider whether it is reasonable to finalise the divorce.

[3. *As your home is in your husband's sole name, you will lose the right to occupy the property once decree absolute has been made. It is possible to extend your rights of occupation beyond decree absolute, but the application must be made before the court makes the decree absolute.*]

If you wish to discuss this further, please let me know. Otherwise, let me know whether or not you want me to make the application as soon as I can.

Yours sincerely

Enc. decree nisi

D30HLH Letter with decree nisi to husband petitioner (Legal Help)

Dear [*petitioner*]

I refer to the pronouncement of the conditional order for divorce, the decree nisi, on [   ]. I have now received it from the court and enclose a copy.

I confirm I will be in a position to apply for your divorce to be made final, the decree absolute, six weeks after the date of decree nisi which I calculate to be [   ].

I enclose the form applying for the decree nisi to be made absolute. Please sign this where indicated, but do not date it, and return it to me. I will keep the form until the time comes to make the application.

Application for a fee exemption or remission

Please check and sign this form and return it to me.

You can let me know nearer the time whether you want me to make the application then or wait. If you have not reached a financial settlement, you may want to wait before making the application. You need to consider the following:

1. If your wife died before the financial arrangements are finalised, you may be better off being her widower because if she has not made a will, you would inherit a part of her estate automatically and in any event there would be no inheritance tax on anything that goes to you from her estate. There may also be pension rights or life policies which you would lose on decree absolute.

2. There may be tactical reasons why you do not want to make the application now. If your wife wants the decree nisi to be made absolute and if you say that you will not make the application until the financial arrangements are finalised, this may make your wife more reasonable or more generous in the hope that you will agree to finalise the divorce more quickly. However, your wife can make an application to the court for the decree absolute three months after the date that you can first apply for it. The court will not automatically grant it, however. The court will have to consider whether it is reasonable to finalise the divorce.

[3. *As your home is in your wife's sole name, you will lose the right to occupy the property once decree absolute has been made. It is possible to extend your rights of occupation beyond decree absolute, but the application must be made before the court makes the decree absolute.*]

If you wish to discuss this further, please let me know. Otherwise, let me know whether or not you want me to make the application as soon as I can.

Yours sincerely

Enc. decree nisi
    application for decree absolute
    EX160
    EX160A

D30WLH Letter with decree nisi to wife petitioner (Legal Help)

Dear [*petitioner*]

I refer to the pronouncement of the conditional order for divorce, the decree nisi, on [   ]. I have now received it from the court and enclose a copy.

I confirm I will be in a position to apply for your divorce to be made final, the decree absolute, six weeks after the date of decree nisi which I calculate to be [   ].

I enclose the form applying for the decree nisi to be made absolute. Please sign this where indicated, but do not date it, and return it to me. I will keep the form until the time comes to make the application.

Application for a fee exemption or remission

Please check and sign this form and return it to me.

You can let me know nearer the time whether you want me to make the application then or wait. If you have not reached a financial settlement, you may want to wait before making the application. You need to consider the following:

1. If your husband died before the financial arrangements are finalised, you may be better off being his widow because if he has not made a will, you would inherit a part of his estate automatically and in any event there would be no inheritance tax on anything that goes to you from his estate. There may also be pension rights or life policies which you would lose on decree absolute.

2. There may be tactical reasons why you do not want to make the application now. If your husband wants the decree nisi to be made absolute and if you say that you will not make the application until the financial arrangements are finalised, this may make your husband more reasonable or more generous in the hope that you will agree to finalise the divorce more quickly. However, your husband can make an application to the court for the decree absolute three months after the date that you can first apply for it. The court will not automatically grant it, however. The court will have to consider whether it is reasonable to finalise the divorce.

[3. *As your home is in your husband's sole name, you will lose the right to occupy the property once decree absolute has been made. It is possible to extend your rights of occupation beyond decree absolute, but the application must be made before the court makes the decree absolute.*]

If you wish to discuss this further, please let me know. Otherwise, let me know whether or not you want me to make the application as soon as I can.

Yours sincerely

Enc. decree nisi
    application for decree absolute
    EX160
    EX160A

section **2** DIVORCE

D31 Paragraph in letter with decree nisi about agreeing costs

I also enclose the order that your spouse pay your costs of the divorce. I will try to agree the amount of your costs with your [spouse/spouse's solicitors]. If we cannot agree the amount, the court will have to assess it.

D32PC Letter to court enclosing application for decree absolute (private client)

Dear Sirs

We act for the petitioner and enclose an application for decree nisi to be made absolute together with our cheque in the sum of £[40].

We look forward to receiving the decree absolute.

Yours faithfully

Enc.

D32LH Letter to court enclosing application for decree absolute (Legal Help)

Dear Sirs

We are assisting the petitioner under the Legal Help Scheme and enclose an application for decree nisi to be made absolute [*together with the application for fee exemption or remission*].

We look forward to receiving the decree absolute.

Yours faithfully

Enc.

D33H   Letter advising husband of decree absolute

Dear [*petitioner*]

I now enclose your decree absolute dated [   ] which you should retain in a safe place as this document replaces your marriage certificate.

Please note that divorce affects pension rights. You will probably no longer be entitled to a widower's pension under an occupational or private pension scheme. Now that you are divorced you should check your National Insurance Contributions position. This is particularly important for your basic state pension. You can get information about your National Insurance Contribution record from the Pension Service by calling them during office hours on 0845 3000 168. You will find further information about the state retirement pension on www.pensionservice.gov.uk. If you have not yet reached retirement age, you can select to use all your former wife's National Insurance Contribution record instead of your own if this would entitle you to a higher state pension. If you are already retired and you are receiving a state pension, you will continue to do so at the same level at which you are receiving it now.

The Pension Service can work out whether it is beneficial to you to use your former wife's National Insurance Contribution record for your basic state pension. However, if you marry again or you register a civil partnership before you reach 65, you will lose your entitlement to use that record and your basic state pension will instead be based on your own contributions record or on the contributions of your new wife or civil partner. If your new wife or (if you retire after 2015) civil partner does not have a full National Insurance Contribution record, you would lose out. You would also lose out if you register a civil partnership before 2015. Therefore, if you are thinking about marrying again or registering a civil partnership shortly before you reach retirement age and you want to keep your right to receive your basic state pension based on your former wife's National Insurance Contribution records, you should consider delaying the wedding or registration until after you have retired. Please let me know if you want me to explain this further.

I also advise you that divorce affects inheritance. If you do not have a will, you should make one now. If you have a will, you should review it.

[My firm can draft a new will for you. I enclose a will questionnaire for you to complete and return if you want us to advise you on your will. Please let me know if you would like me to [*ask the partner in this firm who deals with wills to*] contact you about making a new will. The charges for preparing the will are based on the time spent and the usual fee for preparation of a straightforward will is about £[150 plus VAT].]

[Please let me know if you want me to refer you to a specialist in wills and estate planning.]

Please note that if you marry again or form a civil partnership, any existing will is automatically cancelled and of no effect and if you die your estate will then pass in accordance with the laws of intestacy.

Yours sincerely

Enc. decree absolute

D33W   Letter advising wife of decree absolute

Dear [*petitioner*]

I now enclose your decree absolute dated [   ] which you should retain in a safe place as this document replaces your marriage certificate.

Now you are divorced you should check your National Insurance position. From now on various benefits will depend on your own contributions. If you have so far paid lower National Insurance Contributions as a married woman, you should consider whether to pay the full rate of National Insurance Contributions. These benefits include Maternity Allowance, Contribution-based Job Seeker's Allowance and Incapacity Benefit. I suggest that you check the position with Her Majesty's Revenue and Customs by calling them during office hours on 0845 302 1479 and make any amendments which are necessary.

Please note that divorce affects pension rights. You will probably no longer be entitled to a widow's pension under an occupational or private pension scheme. Your National Insurance Contributions are also particularly important for your basic state pension. You will find further information about the state retirement pension on www.pensionservice.gov.uk. If you have not yet reached retirement age, you can select to use all your former husband's National Insurance Contribution record instead of your own if this would entitle you to a higher state pension. If you are already retired and you are receiving a state pension, you will continue to do so at the same level at which you are receiving it now.

The Pension Service can work out whether it is beneficial to you to use your former husband's National Insurance Contribution record for your basic state pension. However, if you marry again or you register a civil partnership before you reach state retirement age, you will lose your entitlement to use that record and your basic state pension will instead be based on your own contributions record or on the contributions of your new husband or (if you retire after 2010) civil partner. Your state retirement age is between 60 and 65 depending on your date of birth. If you do not know the date, you can work it out from the calculator on *www.pensionservice.gov.uk/resourcecentre/home/statepensioncalc.asp* or ring the pension service on 0845 3000 168. If your new husband or civil partner does not have a full National Insurance Contribution record, you would lose out. You will also lose out if you register a civil partnership before 2010. Therefore, if you are thinking about marrying again or registering a civil partnership shortly before you reach retirement age and you want to keep your right to receive your basic state pension based on your former husband's National Insurance Contribution records, you should consider delaying the wedding or registration until after you have retired. Please let me know if you want me to explain this further.

section **2** DIVORCE

Model Letters for Family Lawyers

I also advise you that divorce affects inheritance. If you do not have a will, you should make one now. If you have a will, you should review it.

[My firm can draft a new will for you. I enclose a will questionnaire for you to complete and return if you want us to advise you on your will. Please let me know if you would like me to [*ask the partner in this firm who deals with wills to*] contact you about making a new will. The charges for preparing the will are based on the time spent and the usual fee for preparation of a straightforward will is about £[150 plus VAT].]

[Please let me know if you want me to refer you to a specialist in wills and estate planning.]

Please note that if you marry again or form a civil partnership any, existing will is automatically cancelled and of no effect and if you die your estate will then pass in accordance with the laws of intestacy.

Yours sincerely

Enc. decree absolute

D34 Paragraph in letter with decree absolute to client petitioner if no financial proceedings have been issued

You have not yet started court proceedings for your claims for maintenance or a lump sum order or transfer of property order. You should be aware that any delay of longer than, say, three years after the date of the decree absolute before you start financial court proceedings would prejudice your claim. Therefore, it is important that you proceed with your claims as soon as possible.

D35 Paragraph in letter with decree absolute to client respondent if no financial proceedings have been issued

You have not yet started court proceedings for your claims for maintenance or a lump sum order or transfer of property order. If you intend to do so, you must start a financial claim at the court before you marry again or form a civil partnership. After that date you can no longer make an application for financial provision.

In addition any delay of longer than about three years after the date of the decree absolute before you start financial court proceedings would prejudice your claim. Therefore, it is important that you make your claim as soon as possible.

D36H   Letter to husband respondent with draft petition

Dear [*respondent*]

I enclose a copy of a letter from your wife's solicitors.

You will see that your wife proposes to start a divorce based on [your adultery/ your behaviour/two years' separation and your consent/five years' separation.] I also enclose the draft petition.

*[Insert paragraph **D40A**, **D40B**, **D40C** or **D40D**]*

When you look at the divorce petition, you will see that at the end of the petition in a part starting with 'The petitioner therefore prays', your wife asks for the marriage to be dissolved. She may also ask for you to pay her costs of the divorce. These are not the costs of any proceedings dealing with finances or children, but only the charges for the time spent by her solicitors in dealing with the divorce itself and the court fees for the divorce. She will also almost certainly ask for a whole range of financial provisions. It is customary to include these as a matter of course and this does not mean that your wife will pursue these applications in the future. The reason for their inclusion in the petition is that, if they were not included, your wife might not be able to make an application for financial provision in the future.

If your wife has made a claim for costs, the court will consider her claim when she applies for decree nisi. If her petition is based on your adultery or behaviour, I expect that you will be ordered to pay her costs. If it is based on two or five years' separation, the court would not normally order that you should pay her costs. I could ask your wife to agree to you not paying her costs as a trade-off for your agreeing not to contest her petition. Since your wife is the petitioner, her solicitors have done nearly all the work involved in obtaining the divorce. You might find that a fair compromise would be to offer to pay half of her costs, so that both of you share the divorce costs roughly equally.

Please let me know your views on the proposed divorce.

*[as in **D38H**]*

I am a member of Resolution and enclose a copy of their Code of Practice. You will see that the underlying aim is to further a non-confrontational approach towards a resolution of the issues surrounding your separation.

I look forward to hearing from you.

Yours sincerely

Enc. copy letter from your wife's solicitors
     draft petition
     Resolution Code of Practice

D36W Letter to wife respondent with draft petition

Dear [*respondent*]

I enclose a copy of a letter from your husband's solicitors.

You will see that your husband proposes to start a divorce based on [your adultery/your behaviour/two years' separation and your consent/five years' separation.] I also enclose the draft petition.

[Insert paragraph D40A, D40B, D40C or D40D]

When you look at the divorce petition, you will see that at the end of the petition in a part starting with 'The petitioner therefore prays', your husband asks for the marriage to be dissolved. He may also ask for you to pay his costs of the divorce. These are not the costs of any proceedings dealing with finances or children, but only the charges for the time spent by his solicitors in dealing with the divorce itself and the court fees for the divorce. He will also almost certainly ask for a whole range of financial provisions. It is customary to include these as a matter of course and this does not mean that your husband will pursue these applications in the future. The reason for their inclusion in the petition is that, if they were not included, your husband might not be able to make an application for financial provision in the future.

If your husband has made a claim for costs, the court will consider his claim when he applies for decree nisi. If his petition is based on your adultery or behaviour, I expect that you will be ordered to pay his costs. If it is based on two or five years' separation, the court would not normally order that you should pay his costs. I could ask your husband to agree to you not paying his costs as a trade-off for your agreeing not to contest his petition. Since your husband is the petitioner, his solicitors have done nearly all the work involved in obtaining the divorce. You might find that a fair compromise would be to offer to pay half of his costs, so that both of you share the divorce costs roughly equally.

Please let me know your views on the proposed divorce.

[as in D38W]

I am a member of Resolution and enclose a copy of their Code of Practice. You will see that the underlying aim is to further a non-confrontational approach towards a resolution of the issues surrounding your separation.

I look forward to hearing from you.

Yours sincerely

Enc. copy letter from your husband's solicitors
    draft petition
    Resolution Code of Practice

section 2 DIVORCE

D36HC Letter to husband respondent with draft petition and draft statement of arrangements for children

Dear [*respondent*]

I enclose a copy of a letter from your wife's solicitors.

Divorce

You will see that your wife proposes to start a divorce based on [your adultery/ your behaviour/two years' separation and your consent/five years' separation.] I also enclose the draft petition.

[*Insert paragraph **D40A, D40B, D40C** or **D40D***]

When you look at the divorce petition, you will see that at the end of the petition in a part starting with 'The petitioner therefore prays', your wife asks for the marriage to be dissolved. She may also ask for you to pay her costs of the divorce. These are not the costs of any proceedings dealing with finances or children, but only the charges for the time spent by her solicitors in dealing with the divorce itself and the court fees for the divorce. She will also almost certainly ask for a whole range of financial provisions. It is customary to include these as a matter of course and this does not mean that your wife will pursue these applications in the future. The reason for their inclusion in the petition is that, if they were not included, your wife might not be able to make an application for financial provision in the future.

If your wife has made a claim for costs, the court will consider her claim when she applies for decree nisi. If her petition is based on your adultery or behaviour, I expect that you will be ordered to pay her costs. If it is based on two or five years' separation, the court would not normally order that you should pay her costs. I could ask your wife to agree to you not paying her costs as a trade-off for your agreeing not to contest her petition. Since your wife is the petitioner, her solicitors have done nearly all the work involved in obtaining the divorce. You might find that a fair compromise would be to offer to pay half of her costs, so that both of you share the divorce costs roughly equally.

Children

I also enclose the statement of arrangements for children, which is also required to start the divorce. This summarises what arrangements there are at the moment for any child who is under 16, or under 18 and still in full-time education. It includes such information as where any child is to live and what arrangements are to be made for contact. The statement only sets out the present arrangements and anything written there does not mean that this is a final arrangement for the children. The courts hardly ever raise an issue on them. The fact that the court processes it does not mean that the arrangements are somehow endorsed by the court.

If you agree the statement, please sign it on the last page and return it to me.

If there are issues you do not agree with, please let me know and I can then advise you on how best to deal with it. It would be best if you could make a list of the issues you do not agree with cross-referring to the paragraph numbers in the statement, if there are more than one or two.

Please let me know your views on the proposed divorce.

[*as in* **D39H**]

I am a member of Resolution and enclose a copy of their Code of Practice. You will see that the underlying aim is to further a non-confrontational approach towards a resolution of the issues surrounding your separation.

I look forward to hearing from you.

Yours sincerely

Enc. copy letter from your wife's solicitors
    draft petition
    Resolution Code of Practice

D36WC   Letter to wife respondent with draft petition and draft statement of arrangements for children

Dear [*respondent*]

I enclose a copy of a letter from your husband's solicitors.

Divorce

You will see that your husband proposes to start a divorce based on [your adultery/your behaviour/two years' separation and your consent/five years' separation.] I also enclose the draft petition.

*[Insert paragraph **D40A**, **D40B**, **D40C** or **D40D**]*

When you look at the divorce petition, you will see that at the end of the petition in a part starting with 'The petitioner therefore prays', your husband asks for the marriage to be dissolved. He may also ask for you to pay his costs of the divorce. These are not the costs of any proceedings dealing with finances or children, but only the charges for the time spent by his solicitors in dealing with the divorce itself and the court fees for the divorce. He will also almost certainly ask for a whole range of financial provisions. It is customary to include these as a matter of course and this does not mean that your husband will pursue these applications in the future. The reason for their inclusion in the petition is that, if they were not included, your husband might not be able to make an application for financial provision in the future.

If your husband has made a claim for costs, the court will consider his claim when he applies for decree nisi. If his petition is based on your adultery or behaviour, I expect that you will be ordered to pay his costs. If it is based on two or five years' separation, the court would not normally order that you should pay his costs. I could ask your husband to agree to you not paying his costs as a trade-off for your agreeing not to contest his petition. Since your husband is the petitioner, his solicitors have done nearly all the work involved in obtaining the divorce. You might find that a fair compromise would be to offer to pay half of his costs, so that both of you share the divorce costs roughly equally.

Children

I also enclose the statement of arrangements for children, which is also required to start the divorce. This summarises what arrangements there are at the moment for any child who is under 16, or under 18 and still in full-time education. It includes such information as where any child is to live and what arrangements are to be made for contact. The statement only sets out the present arrangements and anything written there does not mean that this is a final arrangement for the children. The courts hardly ever raise an issue on them. The fact that the court processes it does not mean that the arrangements are somehow endorsed by the court.

If you agree the statement, please sign it on the last page and return it to me.

If there are issues you do not agree with, please let me know and I can then advise you on how best to deal with it. It would be best if you could make a list of the issues you do not agree with cross-referring to the paragraph numbers in the statement, if there are more than one or two.

Please let me know your views on the proposed divorce.

[*as in D39W*]

I am a member of Resolution and enclose a copy of their Code of Practice. You will see that the underlying aim is to further a non-confrontational approach towards a resolution of the issues surrounding your separation.

I look forward to hearing from you.

Yours sincerely

Enc. copy letter from your husband's solicitors
    draft petition
    Resolution Code of Practice

section **2** DIVORCE

D37H   Letter to husband respondent without draft petition

Dear [*respondent*]

I enclose a copy of a letter from your wife's solicitors.

You will see that your wife proposes to start a divorce based on [your adultery/ your behaviour/two years' separation and your consent/five years' separation.]

*[Insert paragraph **D40A**, **D40B**, **D40C** or **D40D**]*

Your wife's solicitors will soon be sending the divorce papers to the court and the court will then send a set of the papers to you by post. Please consider the divorce papers and let me know any comments you have.

When you look at the divorce petition, you will see that at the end of the petition in a part starting with 'The petitioner therefore prays', your wife asks for the marriage to be dissolved. She may also ask for you to pay her costs of the divorce. These are not the costs of any proceedings dealing with finances or children, but only the time spent by her solicitors in dealing with the divorce itself and the court fees for the divorce. She will also almost certainly ask for a whole range of financial provisions. It is customary to include these as a matter of course and this does not mean that your wife will pursue these applications in the future. The reason for their inclusion in the petition is that, if they were not included, your wife might not be able to make an application for financial provision in the future.

*[as in **D38H** or **D39H**]*

I am a member of Resolution and enclose a copy of their Code of Practice. You will see that the underlying aim is to further a non-confrontational approach towards a resolution of the issues surrounding your separation.

Yours sincerely

Enc. copy letter from your wife's solicitors
    Resolution Code of Practice

D37W   Letter to wife respondent without draft petition

Dear [*respondent*]

I enclose a copy of a letter from your husband's solicitors.

You will see that your husband proposes to start a divorce based on [your adultery/your behaviour/two years' separation and your consent/five years' separation.]

*[Insert paragraph **D40A**, **D40B**, **D40C** or **D40D**]*

Your husband's solicitors will soon be sending the divorce papers to the court and the court will then send a set of the papers to you by post. Please consider the divorce papers and let me know any comments you have.

When you look at the divorce petition, you will see that at the end of the petition in a part starting with 'The petitioner therefore prays', your husband asks for the marriage to be dissolved. He may also ask for you to pay his costs of the divorce. These are not the costs of any proceedings dealing with finances or children, but only the time spent by his solicitors in dealing with the divorce itself and the court fees for the divorce. He will also almost certainly ask for a whole range of financial provisions. It is customary to include these as a matter of course and this does not mean that your husband will pursue these applications in the future. The reason for their inclusion in the petition is that, if they were not included, your husband might not be able to make an application for financial provision in the future.

*[as in **D38W** or **D39W**]*

I am a member of Resolution and enclose a copy of their Code of Practice. You will see that the underlying aim is to further a non-confrontational approach towards a resolution of the issues surrounding your separation.

Yours sincerely

Enc. copy letter from your husband's solicitors
        Resolution Code of Practice

D38H   Section explaining divorce procedure in letter to husband respondent – no children

When you receive the divorce papers from the court, please note the date on which you receive the papers on the front of the acknowledgement of service form and then sign the form at the top of the back page. Please then keep a photocopy of the papers and send the originals to me immediately. I will need to return the acknowledgement of service form to the court within eight days from the date you received the papers. However, a short delay is not going to make a significant difference and often if there are any issues, both sides agree to an extension of time. Nevertheless, the quicker this can be done, the better.

Once the court receives the completed form from me, it will stamp it and send a copy to your wife's solicitors. Your wife may then make her application for the conditional divorce order, the decree nisi. When the court gets the application, the district judge will consider whether or not your wife has proved the contents of the petition and is entitled to a divorce. In the vast majority of cases the courts simply approve the petition.

In that case, a date will be fixed for a formal pronouncement of the decree nisi. This is unlikely to be less than one month from when she makes her application and depends mainly on the timetable at court. Neither of you has to go to court for that hearing. Usually the judge reads out the names of all couples who are divorcing formally in open court to pronounce their decrees nisi without anyone attending court.

If your wife has made a claim for costs, the judge will also consider this. If her petition is based on your adultery or behaviour, I expect that you will be ordered to pay her costs. If it is based on two or five years' separation, the court would not normally order that you should pay her costs. I could ask your wife to agree to you not paying her costs as a trade-off for your agreeing not to contest her petition. Since your wife is the petitioner, her solicitors have done nearly all the work involved in obtaining the divorce. You might find that a fair compromise would be to offer to pay half of her costs, so that both of you share the divorce costs roughly equally.

Very rarely a short court hearing may take place if the district judge has any questions to ask you and your wife.

The divorce is not final until the decree nisi has been made absolute. Your wife can apply to the court for the decree nisi to be made absolute six weeks after pronouncement of decree nisi. This would be processed by the court staff without a hearing.

If she fails to apply within three months of that date, that means roughly four and a half months from the date of decree nisi, you can apply for the decree nisi to be made absolute yourself. However, if you do have to make this application you will not be granted the decree absolute automatically. A short hearing will be fixed before a district judge who will consider whether it is reasonable for the divorce to be finalised.

Therefore, the whole process can take as little as three to four months, but can take six months or more. The timing will depend to a large extent on how quickly your wife wants the divorce to proceed.

D38W   Section explaining divorce procedure in letter to wife respondent – no children

When you receive the divorce papers from the court, please note the date on which you receive the papers on the front of the acknowledgement of service form and then sign the form at the top of the back page. Please then keep a photocopy of the papers and send the originals to me immediately. I will need to return the acknowledgement of service form to the court within eight days from the date you received the papers. However, a short delay is not going to make a significant difference and often if there are any issues, both sides agree to an extension of time. Nevertheless, the quicker this can be done, the better.

Once the court receives the completed form from me, it will stamp it and send a copy to your husband's solicitors. Your husband may then make his application for the conditional divorce order, the decree nisi. When the court gets the application, the district judge will consider whether or not your husband has proved the contents of the petition and is entitled to a divorce. In the vast majority of cases the courts simply approve the petition.

In that case, a date will be fixed for a formal pronouncement of the decree nisi. This is unlikely to be less than one month from when he makes his application and depends mainly on the timetable at court. Neither of you has to go to court for that hearing. Usually the judge reads out the names of all couples who are divorcing formally in open court to pronounce their decrees nisi without anyone attending court.

If your husband has made a claim for costs, the judge will also consider this. If his petition is based on your adultery or behaviour, I expect that you will be ordered to pay his costs. If it is based on two or five years' separation, the court would not normally order that you should pay his costs. I could ask your husband to agree to you not paying his costs as a trade-off for your agreeing not to contest his petition. Since your husband is the petitioner, his solicitors have done nearly all the work involved in obtaining the divorce. You might find that a fair compromise would be to offer to pay half of his costs, so that both of you share the divorce costs roughly equally.

Very rarely a short court hearing may take place if the district judge has any questions to ask you and your husband.

The divorce is not final until the decree nisi has been made absolute. Your husband can apply to the court for the decree nisi to be made absolute six weeks after pronouncement of decree nisi. This would be processed by the court staff without a hearing.

If he fails to apply within three months of that date, that means roughly four and a half months from the date of decree nisi, you can apply for the decree nisi to be made absolute yourself. However, if you do have to make this application you will not be granted the decree absolute automatically. A short hearing will be fixed before a district judge who will consider whether it is reasonable for the divorce to be finalised.

Therefore, the whole process can take as little as three to four months, but can take six months or more. The timing will depend to a large extent on how quickly your husband wants the divorce to proceed.

D39H Section explaining divorce procedure in letter to husband respondent – children

When you receive the divorce papers from the court, please note the date on which you receive the papers on the front of the acknowledgement of service form and then sign the form at the top of the back page. Please then keep a photocopy of the papers and send the originals to me immediately. I will need to return the acknowledgement of service form to the court within eight days from the date you received the papers. However, a short delay is not going to make a significant difference and often if there are any issues, both sides agree to an extension of time. Nevertheless, the quicker this can be done, the better.

You will also be sent a copy of the statement of arrangements for children, which is also required to start the divorce. This summarises what arrangements there are at the moment for any child who is under 16, or under 18 and still in full-time education. It includes such information as where any child is to live and what arrangements are to be made for contact. The statement only sets out the present arrangements and anything written there does not mean that this is a final arrangement for the children. The courts hardly ever raise an issue on them. The fact that the court processes it does not mean that the arrangements are somehow endorsed by the court.

If you agree the statement, please let me know and make sure you sign the acknowledgement of service form that comes with the petition.

If there are issues you do not agree with, please let me know and I can then advise you on how best to deal with it. It would be best, if you could make a list of the issues you do not agree with cross-referring to the paragraph numbers in the statement if there are more than one or two.

Once the court receives the completed form from me, it will stamp it and send a copy to your wife's solicitors. Your wife may then make her application for the conditional divorce order, the decree nisi. When the court gets the application, the district judge will consider whether or not your wife has proved the contents of the petition and is entitled to a divorce. In the vast majority of cases the courts simply approve the petition.

At the same time, the district judge will consider whether the arrangements for the children of the family are satisfactory and, until the district judge is satisfied that they are, the decree nisi cannot be made absolute. In rare cases the district judge may decide that he wants to see you and your wife to discuss the arrangements.

If the judge approves the petition, a date will be fixed for a formal pronouncement of the decree nisi. This is unlikely to be less than one month from when she makes her application and depends mainly on the timetable at court. Neither of you has to go to court for that hearing. Usually the judge reads out the names of all couples who are divorcing formally in open court to pronounce their decrees nisi without anyone attending court.

If your wife has made a claim for costs, the judge will also consider this. If her petition is based on your adultery or behaviour, I expect that you will be ordered to pay her costs. If it is based on two or five years' separation, the court would not normally order that you should pay her costs. I could ask your wife to agree to you not paying her costs as a trade-off for your agreeing not to contest her petition. Since your wife is the petitioner, her solicitors have done nearly all the work involved in obtaining the divorce. You might find that a fair compromise would be to offer to pay half of her costs, so that both of you share the divorce costs roughly equally.

Very rarely a short court hearing may take place if the district judge has any questions to ask you and your wife.

The divorce is not final until the decree nisi has been made absolute. Your wife can apply to the court for the decree nisi to be made absolute six weeks after pronouncement of decree nisi. This would be processed by the court staff without a hearing.

If she fails to apply within three months of that date, that means roughly four and a half months from the date of decree nisi, you can apply for the decree nisi to be made absolute yourself. However, if you do have to make this application you will not be granted the decree absolute automatically. A short hearing will be fixed before a district judge who will consider whether it is reasonable for the divorce to be finalised.

Therefore, the whole process can take as little as three to four months, but can take six months or more. The timing will depend to a large extent on how quickly your wife wants the divorce to proceed.

section 2 DIVORCE

D39W   **Section explaining divorce procedure in letter to wife respondent – children**

When you receive the divorce papers from the court, please note the date on which you receive the papers on the front of the acknowledgement of service form and then sign the form at the top of the back page. Please then keep a photocopy of the papers and send the originals to me immediately. I will need to return the acknowledgement of service form to the court within eight days from the date you received the papers. However, a short delay is not going to make a significant difference and often if there are any issues, both sides agree to an extension of time. Nevertheless, the quicker this can be done, the better.

You will also be sent a copy of the statement of arrangements for children, which is also required to start the divorce. This summarises what arrangements there are at the moment for any child who is under 16, or under 18 and still in full-time education. It includes such information as where any child is to live and what arrangements are to be made for contact. The statement only sets out the present arrangements and anything written there does not mean that this is a final arrangement for the children. The courts hardly ever raise an issue on them. The fact that the court processes it does not mean that the arrangements are somehow endorsed by the court.

If you agree the statement, please let me know and make sure you sign the acknowledgement of service form that comes with the petition.

If there are issues you do not agree with, please let me know and I can then advise you on how best to deal with it. It would be best, if you could make a list of the issues you do not agree with cross-referring to the paragraph numbers in the statement if there are more than one or two.

Once the court receives the completed form from me, it will stamp it and send a copy to your husband's solicitors. Your husband may then make his application for the conditional divorce order, the decree nisi. When the court gets the application, the district judge will consider whether or not your husband has proved the contents of the petition and is entitled to a divorce. In the vast majority of cases the courts simply approve the petition.

At the same time, the district judge will consider whether the arrangements for the children of the family are satisfactory and, until the district judge is satisfied that they are, the decree nisi cannot be made absolute. In rare cases the district judge may decide that he wants to see you and your husband to discuss the arrangements.

If the judge approves the petition, a date will be fixed for a formal pronouncement of the decree nisi. This is unlikely to be less than one month from when he makes his application and depends mainly on the timetable at court. Neither of you has to go to court for that hearing. Usually the judge reads out the names of all couples who are divorcing formally in open court to pronounce their decrees nisi without anyone attending court.

If your husband has made a claim for costs, the judge will also consider this. If his petition is based on your adultery or behaviour, I expect that you will be ordered to pay his costs. If it is based on two or five years' separation, the court would not normally order that you should pay his costs. I could ask your husband to agree to you not paying his costs as a trade-off for your agreeing not to contest his petition. Since your husband is the petitioner, his solicitors have done nearly all the work involved in obtaining the divorce. You might find that a fair compromise would be to offer to pay half of his costs, so that both of you share the divorce costs roughly equally.

Very rarely a short court hearing may take place if the district judge has any questions to ask you and your husband.

The divorce is not final until the decree nisi has been made absolute. Your husband can apply to the court for the decree nisi to be made absolute six weeks after pronouncement of decree nisi. This would be processed by the court staff without a hearing.

If he fails to apply within three months of that date, that means roughly four and a half months from the date of decree nisi, you can apply for the decree nisi to be made absolute yourself. However, if you do have to make this application you will not be granted the decree absolute automatically. A short hearing will be fixed before a district judge who will consider whether it is reasonable for the divorce to be finalised.

Therefore, the whole process can take as little as three to four months, but can take six months or more. The timing will depend to a large extent on how quickly your husband wants the divorce to proceed.

D40A   Paragraph explaining adultery petition

It is not necessary to name the other person, the 'third party', in a petition based on adultery and it is now very uncommon. If a third party is named and you object to this, you could ask me to negotiate and say that you would not contest the petition if the third party was not named.

Please note that the fact that you may not contest a petition based on adultery does not necessarily mean that you will be disadvantaged in any financial proceedings. It is possible to say in a letter and/or in the acknowledgment of service form that you do not think that this is the real reason why the marriage has broken down, but that you agree it has now irretrievably broken down and that therefore you will not contest the divorce. Please let me know if this is the case.

The only alternative would be to contest the divorce. This would involve court proceedings very much like a civil trial with a final hearing in open court with witnesses as to the allegation. Costs for such a hearing could be tens of thousands of pounds or more.

D40B   Paragraph explaining behaviour petition

You may find some of the allegations of behaviour objectionable and you may also think that they are simply not true. It is not necessary to use very serious allegations of behaviour. The test is whether the behaviour is such that the person starting the divorce cannot reasonably be expected to continue to live with the other person.

If there are allegations which you find particularly upsetting, please let me know. I could try to negotiate on your behalf for the petition to be amended. If any of those relate to incidents that happened more than six months before the petition was issued at court or before you separated (if earlier), they should be left out anyway as they are probably irrelevant.

Please note that the fact that you may not contest a petition based on your behaviour does not necessarily mean that you will be disadvantaged in any financial proceedings. I would state that you do not admit the allegations as stated, but because you agree that the marriage has irretrievably broken down and in order to save costs, you will not contest the petition. That way it could not be said that you have admitted the allegations if the issue arises in later financial proceedings.

The only alternative would be to contest the divorce. This would involve court proceedings very much like a civil trial with a final hearing in open court with witnesses as to the allegation. Costs for such a hearing could be tens of thousands of pounds or more.

D40D   Paragraph explaining petition based on two years' separation

For the divorce to proceed on this basis, you will have to give your consent. If you do not consent to the divorce, it cannot proceed on this basis. Without your consent, a divorce based on separation can only be started five years after separation.

That does not mean that a divorce could not be based on your behaviour or adultery (if applicable). You might find that you would rather agree to a divorce based on two years' separation than having to contest a divorce based on your behaviour or adultery at great financial and emotional expense.

D40E Paragraph explaining petition based on five years' separation

The only way to object to a divorce based on five years' separation is to show that you have not been separated for that long.

section **2** DIVORCE

D41PC   Letter for respondent to court filing acknowledgement (private client)

Dear Sir or Madam

We act for the respondent in these proceedings and enclose the acknowledgement of service form. Please ensure that this form is put on the court's record.

Yours faithfully

Enc. acknowledgement of service form

D41LH   Letter for respondent to court filing acknowledgement (Legal Help)

Dear Sirs

We are advising and assisting the respondent in these proceedings under the legal help scheme and we enclose the acknowledgement of service form.

Please note that the respondent's address for service is care of this firm.

Yours faithfully

Enc. acknowledgement of service form

D42H   Letter to husband respondent confirming acknowledgement of service

Dear [*respondent*]

In accordance with your instructions, I confirm that I have filed the acknowledgement of service form at court.

I refer you to my earlier letter when I set out the court's procedure. The court will send a copy of the acknowledgement to your wife's solicitors. She will then be able to make the application for the conditional divorce order, the decree nisi, as I have explained to you.

I will let you know when I receive the district judge's certificate, which will state whether or not your wife has proved the contents of her petition, and will give a date for pronouncement of decree nisi. This is unlikely to be in less than four weeks and may even be longer, depending on delays at court.

[*The certificate will say whether the district judge is satisfied with the arrangements for the children outlined in the statement of arrangements for children which your wife completed and sent to the court with her petition.*]

[*The certificate will also deal with your wife's claim for you to meet her costs of the divorce itself.*]

Yours sincerely

D42W   Letter to wife respondent confirming acknowledgement of service

Dear [*respondent*]

In accordance with your instructions, I confirm that I have filed the acknowledgement of service form at court.

I refer you to my earlier letter when I set out the court's procedure. The court will send a copy of the acknowledgement to your husband's solicitors. He will then be able to make the application for the conditional divorce order, decree nisi, as I have explained to you.

I will let you know when I receive the district judge's certificate, which will state whether or not your husband has proved the contents of his petition, and will give a date for pronouncement of decree nisi. This is unlikely to be in less than four weeks and may even be longer, depending on delays at court.

[*The certificate will say whether the district judge is satisfied with the arrangements for the children outlined in the statement of arrangements for children which your husband completed and sent to the court with his petition.*]

[*The certificate will also deal with your husband's claim for you to meet his costs of the divorce itself.*]

Yours sincerely

D43H   Letter advising husband respondent of date of decree nisi – no children

Dear [*respondent*]

I am writing to let you know that a date has been fixed for pronouncement of decree nisi, the conditional divorce order, on [   ]. The district judge has now looked at your wife's petition and decided that she is entitled to a divorce.

I enclose a copy of the district judge's certificate stating this, for your information.

[The district judge made no order as to the costs of the divorce itself. This means that you and your wife each have to pay your own costs./The district judge ordered you to pay your wife's costs of the divorce. The amount you will have to pay will have to be agreed or assessed at a later stage. Sometimes it is possible to agree that as part of an overall financial settlement they are not enforced.]

There will be no need for you to go to the court hearing when the decree nisi is pronounced. A copy of the decree nisi and any orders will be sent to me by the court afterwards and I can send you a copy when I receive them. There is often a long delay of several weeks, however.

Your wife can apply for the divorce to become final six weeks after the date on which decree nisi is formally pronounced.

Yours sincerely

Enc. district judge's certificate

D43W   Letter advising wife respondent of date of decree nisi – no children

Dear [*respondent*]

I am writing to let you know that a date has been fixed for pronouncement of decree nisi, the conditional divorce order, on [   ]. The district judge has now looked at your husband's petition and decided that he is entitled to a divorce.

I enclose a copy of the district judge's certificate stating this, for your information.

[The district judge made no order as to the costs of the divorce itself. This means that you and your husband each have to pay your own costs./The district judge ordered you to pay your husband's costs of the divorce. The amount you will have to pay will have to be agreed or assessed at a later stage. Sometimes it is possible to agree that as part of an overall financial settlement they are not enforced.]

There will be no need for you to go to the court hearing when the decree nisi is pronounced. A copy of the decree nisi and any orders will be sent to me by the court afterwards and I can send you a copy when I receive them. There is often a long delay of several weeks, however.

Your husband can apply for the divorce to become final six weeks after the date on which decree nisi is formally pronounced.

Yours sincerely

Enc. district judge's certificate

D44H   Letter advising husband respondent of date of decree nisi – children

Dear [*respondent*]

I am writing to let you know that a date has been fixed for pronouncement of decree nisi, the conditional divorce order, on [   ]. The district judge has now looked at your wife's petition and decided that she is entitled to a divorce.

I enclose a copy of the district judge's certificate stating this, for your information.

The district judge is satisfied with the arrangements for the children summarised in the statement of arrangements for children. This is the form which was sent to the court with the divorce petition and which set out the present arrangements about things like accommodation, schooling, and contact for any children.

[The district judge made no order as to the costs of the divorce itself. This means that you and your wife each have to pay your own costs./The district judge ordered you to pay your wife's costs of the divorce. The amount you will have to pay will have to be agreed or assessed at a later stage. Sometimes it is possible to agree that as part of an overall financial settlement they are not enforced.]

There will be no need for you to go to the court hearing when the decree nisi is pronounced. A copy of the decree nisi and any orders will be sent to me by the court afterwards and I can send you a copy when I receive them. There is often a long delay of several weeks, however.

Your wife can apply for the divorce to become final six weeks after the date on which decree nisi is formally pronounced.

Yours sincerely

Enc. district judge's certificate

section 2 DIVORCE

D44W   Letter advising wife respondent of date of decree nisi – children

Dear [*respondent*]

I am writing to let you know that a date has been fixed for pronouncement of decree nisi, the conditional divorce order, on [   ]. The district judge has now looked at your husband's petition and decided that he is entitled to a divorce.

I enclose a copy of the district judge's certificate stating this, for your information.

The district judge is satisfied with the arrangements for the children summarised in the statement of arrangements for children. This is the form which was sent to the court with the divorce petition and which set out the present arrangements about things like accommodation, schooling, and contact for any children.

[The district judge made no order as to the costs of the divorce itself. This means that you and your husband each have to pay your own costs./The district judge ordered you to pay your husband's costs of the divorce. The amount you will have to pay will have to be agreed or assessed at a later stage. Sometimes it is possible to agree that as part of an overall financial settlement they are not enforced.]

There will be no need for you to go to the court hearing when the decree nisi is pronounced. A copy of the decree nisi and any orders will be sent to me by the court afterwards and I can send you a copy when I receive them. There is often a long delay of several weeks, however.

Your husband can apply for the divorce to become final six weeks after the date on which decree nisi is formally pronounced.

Yours sincerely

Enc. district judge's certificate

D45HPC Letter to husband respondent about children appointment (private client)

Dear [*respondent*]

You will see that the district judge is concerned about the arrangements for the children summarised in the statement of arrangements for children. This is the form which was sent to the court with your wife's divorce petition and which set out the present arrangements about things like accommodation, schooling, and contact for any children.

The district judge wants to see you to discuss the arrangements for the children at [   ] on [   ] in Room [   ] at [the Principal Registry of the Family Division, First Avenue House, 42–49 High Holborn, London WC1V 6NP.]

The district judge will base any questions on the information in the statement of arrangements. Your wife should also go to the court hearing. I enclose a further copy of the statement of arrangements for children for your information.

The hearing is designed to be informal and you could attend on your own. If you want me to attend, I can, of course, do so. However, this will increase your costs. If you are prepared to go on your own, you should arrange to be at the court ten minutes early and make yourself known to the district judge's clerk or the usher, who will be near the room where the district judge is sitting. The district judge should be addressed as 'Sir' or 'Madam'.

A hearing such as this, where you are not legally represented, is meant to be informal and you should not feel intimidated by the district judge. There will be no wigs and gowns and the hearing is likely to take place in a small room. You will not have to stand up to talk. Simply answer the questions as best as you can.

Please telephone me when you get this letter to let me know whether you want me to go to court or whether you are going on your own.

Yours sincerely

Enc. statement of arrangements for children

D45WPC Letter to wife respondent about children appointment (private client)

Dear [*respondent*]

You will see that the district judge is concerned about the arrangements for the children summarised in the statement of arrangements for children. This is the form which was sent to the court with your husband's divorce petition and which set out the present arrangements about things like accommodation, schooling, and contact for any children.

The district judge wants to see you to discuss the arrangements for the children at [   ] on [   ] in Room [   ] at [the Principal Registry of the Family Division, First Avenue House, 42–49 High Holborn, London WC1V 6NP.]

The district judge will base any questions on the information in the statement of arrangements. Your husband should also go to the court hearing. I enclose a further copy of the statement of arrangements for children for your information.

The hearing is designed to be informal and you could attend on your own. If you want me to attend, I can, of course, do so. However, this will increase your costs. If you are prepared to go on your own, you should arrange to be at the court ten minutes early and make yourself known to the district judge's clerk or the usher, who will be near the room where the district judge is sitting. The district judge should be addressed as 'Sir' or 'Madam'.

A hearing such as this, where you are not legally represented, is meant to be informal and you should not feel intimidated by the district judge. There will be no wigs and gowns and the hearing is likely to take place in a small room. You will not have to stand up to talk. Simply answer the questions as best as you can.

Please telephone me when you get this letter to let me know whether you want me to go to court or whether you are going on your own.

Yours sincerely

Enc. statement of arrangements for children

D45HLH Letter to husband respondent about children appointment (Legal Help)

Dear [*respondent*]

You will see that the district judge is concerned about the arrangements for the children summarised in the statement of arrangements for children. This is the form which was sent to the court with your wife's divorce petition and which set out the present arrangements about things like accommodation, schooling, and contact for any children.

The district judge wants to see you to discuss the arrangements for the children at [   ] on [   ] in Room [   ] at [the Principal Registry of the Family Division, First Avenue House, 42–49 High Holborn, London WC1V 6NP.]

The district judge will base any questions on the information in the statement of arrangements. Your wife should also go to the court hearing. I enclose a further copy of the statement of arrangements for children for your information.

As I am advising and assisting you under the Legal Help scheme, I cannot attend court on your behalf and you must to go to the court hearing yourself. You should arrange to be at the court at least ten minutes early and make yourself known to the district judge's clerk or the usher, who will be near the room where the district judge is sitting. The district judge should be addressed as 'Sir' or 'Madam'.

A hearing such as this, where you are not legally represented, is meant to be informal and you should not feel intimidated by the district judge. There will be no wigs and gowns and the hearing is likely to take place in a small room. You will not have to stand up to talk. Simply answer the questions as best as you can.

Please telephone me when you get this letter to confirm that you will be going to the court hearing.

Yours sincerely

Enc. statement of arrangements for children

section 2 DIVORCE

D45WLH Letter to wife respondent about children appointment (Legal Help)

Dear [*respondent*]

You will see that the district judge is concerned about the arrangements for the children summarised in the statement of arrangements for children. This is the form which was sent to the court with your husband's divorce petition and which set out the present arrangements about things like accommodation, schooling, and contact for any children.

The district judge wants to see you to discuss the arrangements for the children at [   ] on [   ] in Room [   ] at [the Principal Registry of the Family Division, First Avenue House, 42–49 High Holborn, London WC1V 6NP.]

The district judge will base any questions on the information in the statement of arrangements. Your husband should also go to the court hearing. I enclose a further copy of the statement of arrangements for children for your information.

As I am advising and assisting you under the Legal Help scheme, I cannot attend court on your behalf and you must to go to the court hearing yourself. You should arrange to be at the court at least ten minutes early and make yourself known to the district judge's clerk or the usher, who will be near the room where the district judge is sitting. The district judge should be addressed as 'Sir' or 'Madam'.

A hearing such as this, where you are not legally represented, is meant to be informal and you should not feel intimidated by the district judge. There will be no wigs and gowns and the hearing is likely to take place in a small room. You will not have to stand up to talk. Simply answer the questions as best as you can.

Please telephone me when you get this letter to confirm that you will be going to the court hearing.

Yours sincerely

Enc. statement of arrangements for children

D46H   Letter advising husband respondent of decree nisi

Dear [*respondent*]

I refer to the pronouncement of decree nisi on [   ]. I have now
received the decree nisi from the court and I enclose a copy.

I confirm your wife will be in a position to apply for the divorce to be
finalised, the decree absolute, six weeks after the date of the decree nisi,
which I calculate to be on [   ]. She may choose not to do so for a
variety of reasons, most commonly because there has not been a final financial
settlement.

If your wife does not apply for the decree absolute at that time, you can apply
to the court for the decree absolute yourself three months later, or four-and-
a-half months after decree nisi. I can discuss with you nearer the time if it is
necessary for you to make that application.

Yours sincerely

Enc. copy decree nisi

D46W   Letter advising wife respondent of decree nisi

Dear [*respondent*]

I refer to the pronouncement of decree nisi on [   ]. I have now
received the decree nisi from the court and I enclose a copy.

I confirm your husband will be in a position to apply for the divorce to be
finalised, the decree absolute, six weeks after the date of the decree nisi,
which I calculate to be on [   ]. He may choose not to do so for a
variety of reasons, most commonly because there has not been a final financial
settlement.

If your husband does not apply for the decree absolute at that time, you can
apply to the court for the decree absolute yourself three months later, or four-
and-a-half months after decree nisi. I can discuss with you nearer the time if it
is necessary for you to make that application.

Yours sincerely

Enc. copy decree nisi

D47H Letter advising husband respondent of decree nisi – costs order

Dear [*respondent*]

I refer to the pronouncement of decree nisi on [   ]. I have now received the decree nisi from the court and I enclose a copy.

[Unless you want me to, I will not raise the question of the costs you have to pay until your wife's solicitors do so. Please note, however, that once the amount of the costs has been agreed or assessed by the court, you have to pay the costs within 14 days from that date. In the meantime interest is accruing at [8]%.

or

You will see that the district judge has assessed the costs at £[   ]. You will have to pay these costs within 14 days. Please let me have a cheque made payable to your wife for that amount immediately.]

I confirm your wife will be in a position to apply for the divorce to be finalised, the decree absolute, six weeks after the date of decree nisi, which I calculate to be on [   ]. She may choose not to do so for a variety of reasons, most commonly because there has not been a final financial settlement.

If your wife does not apply for the decree absolute at that time, you can apply to the court for the decree absolute yourself three months later, or four-and-a-half months after decree nisi. I can discuss with you nearer the time if it is necessary for you to make that application.

Yours sincerely

Enc. copy decree nisi
    copy costs order

D47W   Letter advising wife respondent of decree nisi – costs order

Dear [*respondent*]

I refer to the pronouncement of decree nisi on [   ]. I have now received the decree nisi from the court and I enclose a copy.

[Unless you want me to, I will not raise the question of the costs you have to pay until your husband's solicitors do so. Please note, however, that once the amount of the costs has been agreed or assessed by the court, you have to pay the costs within 14 days from that date. In the meantime interest is accruing at [8]%.

or

You will see that the district judge has assessed the costs at £[   ]. You will have to pay these costs within 14 days. Please let me have a cheque made payable to your husband for that amount immediately.]

I confirm your husband will be in a position to apply for the divorce to be finalised, the decree absolute, six weeks after the date of decree nisi, which I calculate to be on [   ]. He may choose not to do so for a variety of reasons, most commonly because there has not been a final financial settlement.

If your husband does not apply for the decree absolute at that time, you can apply to the court for the decree absolute yourself three months later, or four-and-a-half months after decree nisi. I can discuss with you nearer the time if it is necessary for you to make that application.

Yours sincerely

Enc. copy decree nisi
     copy costs order

D48H   Letter advising husband respondent of costs hearing

Dear [*respondent*]

The district judge has not made a decision about your wife's application that you pay for the costs of the divorce itself. There will be a short hearing at which the district judge will decide whether or not you should do so. This will take place in Room [   ] at [   ] on [   ] at [the Principal Registry of the Family Division, First Avenue House, 42–49 High Holborn, London WC1V 6NP].

It is essential that you or I go to the court hearing on that date. I have already explained to you that it is unlikely that the court will not order you to pay your wife's costs of the divorce.

Your wife or her solicitor should send me a schedule of her costs a day before the hearing. If you are ordered to pay your wife's costs, the district judge will make a decision on the amount you have to pay there and then. Generally, you should query the amount of work involved if it is more than four hours of work.

Generally speaking, it will not be cost-effective for me to attend on your behalf. If you wish to argue your case on costs you should make arrangements to go to the court hearing.

If you decide to attend court on your own, you should arrange to be at the court ten minutes early and make yourself known to the district judge's clerk or the usher, who will be in or nearby the room where the district judge is sitting. The district judge should be addressed as 'Sir' or 'Madam'.

A hearing such as this, where you are not legally represented, is meant to be informal and you should not feel intimidated by the district judge. There will be no wigs and gowns and the hearing is likely to take place in a small room. You will not have to stand up to talk. Simply answer the questions as best as you can.

Please telephone me on receipt of this letter to let me know whether you will be going to the court hearing yourself.

As an alternative, you could make an offer for costs now. It is equally not economic for your wife's solicitor to go to court to argue about the costs and she may well agree to you paying only some of the costs provided you agree the amount. We can discuss this further when I get the schedule of the work and the costs from her solicitors.

Yours sincerely

D48W   Letter advising wife respondent of costs hearing

Dear [*respondent*]

The district judge has not made a decision about your husband's application that you pay for the costs of the divorce itself. There will be a short hearing at which the district judge will decide whether or not you should do so. This will take place in Room [   ] at [   ] on [   ] at [the Principal Registry of the Family Division, First Avenue House, 42–49 High Holborn, London WC1V 6NP].

It is essential that you or I go to the court hearing on that date. I have already explained to you that it is unlikely that the court will not order you to pay your husband's costs of the divorce.

Your husband or his solicitor should send me a schedule of his costs a day before the hearing. If you are ordered to pay your husband's costs, the district judge will make a decision on the amount you have to pay there and then. Generally, you should query the amount of work involved if it is more than four hours of work.

Generally speaking, it will not be cost-effective for me to attend on your behalf. If you wish to argue your case on costs you should make arrangements to go to the court hearing.

If you decide to attend court on your own, you should arrange to be at the court ten minutes early and make yourself known to the district judge's clerk or the usher, who will be in or nearby the room where the district judge is sitting. The district judge should be addressed as 'Sir' or 'Madam'.

A hearing such as this, where you are not legally represented, is meant to be informal and you should not feel intimidated by the district judge. There will be no wigs and gowns and the hearing is likely to take place in a small room. You will not have to stand up to talk. Simply answer the questions as best as you can.

Please telephone me on receipt of this letter to let me know whether you will be going to the court hearing yourself.

As an alternative, you could make an offer for costs now. It is equally not economic for your husband's solicitor to go to court to argue about the costs and he may well agree to you paying only some of the costs provided you agree the amount. We can discuss this further when I get the schedule of the work and the costs from his solicitors.

Yours sincerely

D49   Letter to client explaining alternatives to divorce

Dear [*client*]

If you decide to separate without getting divorced at this stage, there are four other options:

1.   You live separate and apart without reaching a formal agreement about finances or any other matters.

2.   You live separate and apart and questions about finances or other matters are agreed in correspondence between solicitors.

3.   You live separate and apart and questions about finances or other matters are agreed in correspondence between solicitors. In addition, you sign a formal separation agreement setting out the terms of your separation. Obviously, this is only possible if you both agree.

4.   You apply to the court for a decree of judicial separation. The process for this is almost exactly the same as that for a divorce and you will need to rely on one of the five facts that apply for divorce. The court can then make an order about finances, but this is not a final order.

In any case if one of your started a divorce later on, either of you could apply to the court for financial provision. The judge will then consider all the circumstances and make an order that the they think is fair. The judge does not have to stick to an agreement you have reached, even if it is by way of a formal separation agreement or a financial order as part of a judicial separation. However, any agreement that you reach now would be taken into account as one of the factors by the judge. We can discuss this in more detail and I could illustrate this when we know what kind of agreement you may reach now.

Yours sincerely

D50H   Letter to client husband explaining effect of Talaq

Dear [*client*]

A bare Talaq (where there is no court procedure at the time you pronounced the Talaq) will be recognised in this country if:

1.   It has been authenticated by a relevant foreign court.

2.   It is recognised under the law of the country in which it was obtained.

3.   At the time the Talaq was obtained, you were both domiciled in that country or, if only one of you was domiciled there, the other one was domiciled in a country where you can also divorce by way of bare Talaq.

If the Talaq was made with the involvement of the court (rather than a registration at the Sharia court after it was pronounced), the requirements are not quite as stringent.

Even if the Talaq is recognised, you or your wife may still be able to apply to the English court for financial provision. Please let me have full details about the Talaq so that we can discuss this in more detail.

Yours sincerely

D50W   Letter to client wife explaining effect of Talaq

Dear [*client*]

A bare Talaq (where there is no court procedure at the time your husband pronounced the Talaq) will be recognised in this country if:

1.   It has been authenticated by a relevant foreign court.

2.   It is recognised under the law of the country in which it was obtained.

3.   At the time the Talaq was obtained, you were both domiciled in that country or if only one of you was domiciled there, the other one was domiciled in a country where you can also divorce by way of bare Talaq.

If the Talaq was made with the involvement of the court (rather than a registration at the Sharia court after it was pronounced), the requirements are not quite as stringent.

Even if the Talaq is recognised, you or your husband may still be able to apply to the English court for financial provision. Please let me have full details about the Talaq so that we can discuss this in more detail.

Yours sincerely

D51H   Letter to husband about Get

Dear [*husband*]

I understand that it is important for Jewish wives to obtain a Get from their husband as part of the divorce.

The English courts cannot order you to grant your wife a Get, which would of course be done before the Beth Din. However, your wife can ask the court to make an order that your divorce is not made final and the decree is not made absolute unless both of you declare that you have taken all steps to obtain the Get. This would mean that:

1.   neither of you could legally marry again or form a civil partnership until the divorce is finalised.
2.   any financial settlement or order has no final effect and either of you could apply to the court for a variation of that order if circumstances change in the meantime.

It is therefore a good idea to make arrangements to obtain the Get as early as possible.

Yours sincerely

D51W Letter to wife about Get

Dear [*wife*]

I understand that it is important for Jewish wives to obtain a Get from their husband as part of the divorce.

The English courts cannot order your husband to grant you a Get, which would of course be done before the Beth Din. However, you can ask the court to make an order that your divorce is not made final and the decree is not made absolute unless both of you declare that your husband have taken all steps to obtain the Get. This would mean that:

1.   neither of you could legally marry again or form a civil partnership until the divorce is finalised.
2.   any financial settlement or order has no final effect and either of you could apply to the court for a variation of that order if circumstances change in the meantime.

This is meant to encourage husbands to grant Gets as most husbands would want to finalise the divorce at some stage. I hope that your husband will therefore make arrangements to obtain the Get as early as possible. If you think that he may be difficult, we need to make the application to the court before he is able to apply for the divorce to be finalised, that means the decree to be made absolute.

Yours sincerely

D52H   Letter for husband to central index of Decrees Absolute

The Principal Registry of the Family Division
Decree Absolute Search Section
DX 396 London

Dear Sirs

We act for [   ]. He has not seen his wife for [   ] years.

Please carry out a search of the central index to see whether his wife has, at any time, filed divorce proceedings and obtained decree absolute. Please search between [19xx] and [20xx].

[We enclose our cheque in the sum of £[20 for every 10 year period] in respect of your fee./We enclose the application for a fee exemption or remission form.]

The relevant available information is:

1.   Full name of wife (possible petitioner):

2.   Date of marriage:

3.   Date of separation:

4.   Full name of co-respondent (if any):

5.   Date or year the petition was filed:

6.   Registry or court in which the petition was filed:

7.   Date or year in which decree nisi was pronounced:

8.   The court in which decree nisi was pronounced:

9.   Date or year in which the decree nisi was made absolute:

We look forward to hearing from you.

Yours faithfully

Enc.   cheque

D52W   Letter for wife to central index of Decrees Absolute

The Principal Registry of the Family Division
Decree Absolute Search Section
DX 396 London

Dear Sirs

We act for [   ]. She has not seen her husband for [   ] years.

Please carry out a search of the central index to see whether her husband has, at any time, filed divorce proceedings and obtained decree absolute. Please search between [19xx] and [20xx].

[We enclose our cheque in the sum of £[20 for every 10 year period] in respect of your fee./We enclose the application for a fee exemption or remission form.]

The relevant available information is:

1.   Full name of husband (possible petitioner):

2.   Date of marriage:

3.   Date of separation:

4.   Full name of co-respondent (if any):

5.   Date or year the petition was filed:

6.   Registry or court in which the petition was filed:

7.   Date or year in which decree nisi was pronounced:

8.   The court in which decree nisi was pronounced:

9.   Date or year in which the decree nisi was made absolute:

We look forward to hearing from you.

Yours faithfully

Enc. cheque

SECTION 3

ANCILLARY RELIEF

Mark Harper

Ancillary Relief

section 3 ANCILLARY RELIEF

section **3** ANCILLARY RELIEF

AR1   Letter confirming advice given at meeting

Dear [*client*]

YOUR REQUIREMENTS/INSTRUCTIONS

ADVICE GIVEN

I have set out below the advice I gave you at our meeting.

ACTION TO BE TAKEN BY THIS FIRM

ACTION TO BE TAKEN BY YOU

Yours sincerely

AR2   Letter outlining court's approach to ancillary relief claims

Dear [*client*]

With regard to financial arrangements between you and your spouse, the court takes various matters into account when considering what order should be made. The court considers all the circumstances of the case, gives first consideration to the welfare of any children of the family under the age of 18 and, in particular, the court has regard to the following matters:

(a) The income, earning capacity, property and other financial resources which each spouse has or is likely to have in the foreseeable future including, in the case of earning capacity, any increase in that capacity which it would be, in the opinion of the court, reasonable to expect a person to take steps to acquire.

(b) The financial needs, obligations and responsibilities which each spouse has or is likely to have in the foreseeable future.

(c) The standard of living enjoyed by the family before the breakdown of the marriage.

(d) The ages of each spouse and the duration of the marriage.

(e) Any physical or mental disability of each spouse.

(f) The contributions which each spouse has made or is likely to make in the foreseeable future to the welfare of the family, including any contribution by looking after the home or caring for the family.

(g) The conduct of each spouse, if that conduct is such that it would in the opinion of the Court be inequitable to disregard.

(h) The value to each spouse of any benefit which one spouse because of the divorce will lose the chance of acquiring (most usually pension provision).

The aim of the court is to achieve fairness. Following a landmark decision called *White v White* in 2000, the court has to consider an equal division of assets built up during the marriage, unless the marriage was of short duration, or the assets are insufficient to satisfy capital needs in particular rehousing. However, often a key and decisive factor is the reasonable needs (especially housing needs) of yourself and your spouse, which often overrides any possibility of an equal division of assets.

In most cases, the courts no longer have power to make orders for child maintenance except by agreement; an application to the Child Support Agency has to be made for child maintenance to be assessed.

In your case, I advise that the following factors will be particularly relevant:
[   ]

Both you and your spouse have an absolute duty to each other and to the court to disclose fully your financial position (and any significant changes during the case) so that a proper financial arrangement can be made. That is an ongoing duty which continues until an order is approved or made by the court.

Yours sincerely

AR3   Letter to client explaining about pensions

Dear [*client*]

I write to explain what powers the court has regarding pensions.

The first is known as 'off-setting'. This means that the court looks at the transfer value of the pensions and decides that the person without significant pensions should receive an equivalent payment in capital from some other source. This is only possible where there is spare capital available after rehousing you and your spouse.

The second option open to the court is a pension sharing order. This means that an existing pension fund is divided, not necessarily 50–50, and passed over to the other person which, in practice, in most cases, will then have to be invested in a new pension.

The third option, not often used, is pension attachment, formerly known as 'earmarking'. The court has the power to order that a proportion of a pension, once received both as to the annual income and the lump sum, should be paid to the other spouse. The court has the power to order that a proportion of any death in service benefit should be paid to the other spouse as well.

The problem with pension attachment orders is that they are complicated to draft and if the person receiving the attachment order remarries then no continuing annual payment will be made. If someone changes job then that will mean that an order regarding a death in service benefit will be of no effect.

This is a highly complicated area of the law and almost every case is different.

In your case I believe the correct approach is [   ]

Yours sincerely

AR4 Letter explaining court's powers under MCA 1973, section 37

Dear [*client*]

If your [former] spouse has disposed of assets with a view to frustrating your claims for a financial settlement or she/he is about to do so, then it is important that you should know that the court has wide powers to deal with such situations.

Under section 37 of the Matrimonial Causes Act 1973, the court can restrain someone from carrying out a transaction or from transferring assets out of the country or to someone else. In addition, the court can set aside (ie unscramble) certain transactions which have already been carried out where they were completed with the intention of defeating a claim for financial settlement arising from a marriage.

The court can exercise these powers whilst a financial application such as your own is proceeding or, indeed, in some cases after a financial provision order has been made.

However, the court cannot order a transaction to be set aside if someone bought the asset from your [former] spouse in good faith without knowing that the motive behind the sale was to reduce your [former] spouse's assets to frustrate your claim.

If you make such an application to set aside a transaction made by your [former] spouse then, if the transaction took place less than three years before your application, the court will presume that the transaction was completed to frustrate your financial claim unless there is convincing evidence to the contrary.

In addition to these powers, the court also has 'inherent' powers to prevent someone trying to defeat financial claims without the requirement that they have to prove an intention to frustrate their spouse's or former spouse's claim.

If you do consider that your [former] spouse has acted in this way or that there is a risk that she/he will do so, please let me know immediately because I will need to prepare documentation to present to the court to persuade the district judge to exercise the appropriate powers.

I look forward to hearing from you.

Yours sincerely

AR5   Letter explaining to client the difference between not making a claim and having a claim dismissed

Dear [*client*]

It is important that you understand the options available to you before you decide on how to deal with the financial arrangements between you and your former husband/wife.

Spouses and former spouses have rights to make financial claims against each other by applying to the court for orders for any or all of the following:

1.   Maintenance (ie income payments).

2.   Adjustment of property ownership (eg transfer of a house from joint ownership to the sole ownership of one spouse).

3.   Lump sums (ie capital payments).

4.   Pension sharing attachment.

These rights can only be brought to an end in two ways. The first and most usual way is by a court order. Where one or both spouses do not wish to proceed with financial claims then, provided the court agrees that such an order would be appropriate, an order can be made dismissing their financial claims.

The second way is where someone obtains a divorce and then re-marries. In this situation, unless that person has already applied for the orders for a lump sum or transfer of property which they are seeking either in the divorce petition or by way of formal application on Form A before they re-marry, then they are caught in 'the re-marriage trap'. The effect of this trap is that they have lost the right to make those financial claims against their former spouse.

Should the spouses decide not to obtain court orders dealing with financial provision and in the event that the re-marriage trap does not apply, then the claims which each of them have against the other are simply left open. This situation is unsatisfactory in that it creates a degree of uncertainty because it leaves the possibility of one spouse making a claim against the other at any time. On the other hand, where one spouse's financial position is likely to improve substantially it may be in the other's interest to delay a final financial settlement.

Where neither spouse wants to claim against the other it is usually better for an application to be made by consent for the respective claims of each spouse to be dismissed.

Clearly, this is an important matter and please telephone me if you wish to discuss it in further detail.

Yours sincerely

AR6 Letter advising client about mediation

Dear [*client*]

I am a member of Resolution (formerly the Solicitors Family Law Association) and, in accordance with Resolution's code of practice, I always try to deal with clients' cases in a way which will encourage and assist them and their spouse to achieve a constructive resolution of their difficulties.

You may wish to take advantage of a process called mediation which involves an impartial third person assisting those involved in family breakdown to communicate better with one another and to help them to reach their own agreed and informed decisions about some or all of the issues relating to or arising from the separation or divorce including children, finance or property.

One advantage of reaching an agreement through mediation is that it is almost always considerably cheaper because it does not involve going to court.

Another advantage of reaching agreement through mediation is that such agreements usually last and you will therefore be more likely to get on better with your [former] spouse in the future.

There are a number of different organisations which carry out mediation. Please let me know if you would like further details.

Yours sincerely

AR7 Letter explaining council tax

Dear [*client*]

Since you are now living on your own in your property, you must notify your local authority so that you are entitled to a reduction in the amount of council tax you have to pay.

Council tax is based on the assumption that your property is occupied by two adults.

You must therefore write to your local authority and notify them that you are now the only adult in the property and ask for the [25%] reduction.

You should also be aware that if you are on a low income and your savings are less than [£16,000], you may be entitled to council tax benefit by way of help in paying your council tax. I suggest you contact your local authority to whom you pay council tax for further information.

Yours sincerely

AR8 Letter to client who has moved out of the matrimonial home

Dear [*client*]

Since you have moved out of your property, you should notify the local authority in writing so that you cannot be liable to pay council tax on the property. Joint occupiers are jointly liable for the amount payable in full.

Council tax is based on the assumption that each property is occupied by two adults.

Your spouse will be entitled to a [25%] reduction being the only adult in the property.

Yours sincerely

AR9   Letter to client regarding potential earning capacity

Dear [*client*]

In your case, one of the main issues will be to what extent it is reasonable for you to have to work.

I would remind you that one of the specific factors which the court is required to take into account is each person's income and earning capacity 'which both people have or are likely to have in the foreseeable future, including, in the case of earning capacity, any increase in that capacity which it would be, in the opinion of the court, reasonable to expect the person to take steps to acquire'.

Because of the particular facts of your case [and/or the fact that you have children], it may well be that the court would not expect you to work full time.

Please let me have a note of any qualifications you may have, including any examination results, and prepare a list of all the jobs that you have had with the dates that you had those jobs.

Also, please let me know, in your view, what your ability and/or prospects are for obtaining work, whether full time or part time.

Yours sincerely

section 3 ANCILLARY RELIEF

AR10   Letter to client proposing to move out of rented accommodation

Dear [*client*]

I want to ensure that you are fully aware of the implications which arise should you decide to move out of your rented accommodation. If you do move out there is a risk that you may lose your right to live at the property and, in addition, you may prejudice any application to be rehoused by your local council.

By moving out there is a danger that you will lose important rights which protect tenants of council-owned properties and your tenancy could be cancelled. In addition, the council could decide that you have made yourself 'intentionally homeless' which would mean that you would not have an automatic right to be rehoused by a local authority. The law defines someone as being intentionally homeless if they deliberately do or fail to do anything which results in them ceasing to occupy the accommodation which is available and which it is reasonable for them to continue to occupy.

In broad terms, this means that where the council tenancy is in joint names and the court would be likely to transfer it into the sole name of one of the parties to the marriage, then that person is normally expected to apply to the court for the tenancy to be transferred into his/her sole name. This may not apply where that person has been a victim of violence.

This letter can only advise you of the general principles and I must stress that if you are considering moving out or you require further explanation of anything contained in this letter, you should contact [me/my firm's housing department] so that more detailed advice can be given.

Yours sincerely

AR11   Letter to client living in temporary accommodation

Dear [*client*]

I note that you are living in temporary accommodation provided by the local council.

In the light of your circumstances my advice is that you contact one of the housing officers at the housing department of the local council with a view to trying to speed up your application to be permanently rehoused.

Yours sincerely

AR12 Letter cautioning client about discussing financial arrangements with the other person

Dear [*client*]

I always encourage clients to try to speak direct with their spouse/former partner regarding finances, in the hope that this will make it more likely that an agreement can be reached.

However, it is important that you should not specifically say to your spouse/former partner whether any proposals made by him/her are definitely agreed. If proposals are made by him/her which you want to accept, you should normally state that you will discuss those proposals with your solicitor and you should contact me to tell me about the proposals that have been made.

Although it is rare for agreements reached direct between both parties to be upheld by the courts as binding, there is always a danger that this may happen, or that your spouse/former partner will insist that they will not make any other proposals. In any event, negotiations between spouses direct have to be disclosed to the court at the Financial Dispute Resolution Appointment.

Yours sincerely

section 3 ANCILLARY RELIEF

AR13   Letter advising client in respect of joint tenancy and intestacy rules

Dear [*client*]

I suspect that you and your spouse own the property as 'joint tenants'. This means that, if one of you dies, the survivor will be entitled to the whole property, even if divorce proceedings have been started or you are divorced, and irrespective of any provision in a Will or if no Will has been made irrespective of the intestacy rules.

It is possible to prevent this occurring by preparing a simple document known as a notice of severance which you should sign and which must be sent to your spouse for signature. Once you have both signed this it will then be lodged at the Land Registry. After the notice has been sent to your spouse, even if [he/she] does not sign and return it, the property will then be owned by you both as 'tenants in common'. This means that, in the event of you dying before your spouse, your share in the property will pass according to the terms of your Will or under the rules of intestacy if you have no valid Will.

Under the rules of intestacy, in the absence of a valid Will, your spouse will receive a minimum of the first [£125,000] of all your assets ([£200,000] if you have no children). Therefore, in addition, you need to prepare a Will and I can arrange for one of my colleagues to prepare a Will for you. My firm's standard charges are between [£   ] and [£   ] plus VAT depending on the complexity of the individual Wills.

Therefore, in order to ensure that your spouse does not become entitled to your share in the property in the event of your death it will be necessary for you to prepare a Will and a notice of severance. Please let me know if you want me to prepare these documents.

Yours sincerely

AR14   Letter to other joint tenant severing joint tenancy

Dear [other joint tenant]

SPECIAL DELIVERY

We act for [   ] and enclose by way of formal service a notice of severance.

Please acknowledge receipt of this letter and sign and date the enclosed notice of severance where indicated and return it to us as soon as possible.

We recommend that you obtain independent legal advice regarding the contents of this letter. We suggest you contact Resolution (formerly the Solicitors Family Law Association) on 01689 820272 for details of members of Resolution in your area. We recommend that you consult a Resolution member who will normally be a specialist in family law; Resolution members are committed to adopting an amicable approach in all family matters.

Yours sincerely

AR15   Letter to Land Registry enclosing notice of severance signed by both joint tenants

Dear Sirs

[   ] District Land Registry

Title Number: [   ]

Address: [   ]

We act for [   ], one of the registered proprietors of the above property.

We enclose completed Form RX1 with the evidence referred to in section 6.

Yours faithfully

section 3 ANCILLARY RELIEF

AR16   Letter to Land Registry enclosing notice of severance signed by one joint tenant only

Dear Sirs

[   ] District Land Registry

Title Number: [   ]

Address: [   ]

We act for [   ], one of the registered proprietors of the above property.

We enclose a certified copy of a notice of severance sent to the other registered proprietor on [   ], together with a copy of our letter of the same date to that registered proprietor. We have not received a reply to that letter.

We hereby certify that the original notice of severance was served in accordance with section 196(4) of the Law of Property Act 1925. The letter and notice of severance were sent by special delivery and we confirm that the letter has not been returned undelivered by the Royal Mail.

In the circumstances, please register a tenants in common restriction accordingly, for which we understand there is no fee.

Yours faithfully

AR17   Letter advising client in respect of joint bank account

Dear [*client*]

If you have a joint bank account with your spouse, you should ensure that the account is made a joint signatory account requiring two signatures for any money to be withdrawn. Otherwise any money in the account can be withdrawn, or an overdraft run up without your knowledge or permission and you will be jointly liable for any overdraft run up, even if you have not spent the money yourself.

In the same way, you should cancel any joint credit cards or cards for which your spouse is a signatory, otherwise you will be similarly liable for any expenditure incurred by the other holder of the credit card.

Yours sincerely

AR18   Letter advising client regarding financial documents and Hildebrand documents

Dear [*client*]

It is important that you keep all your financial documents, such as bank statements, credit card statements and pay-slips and that you do not destroy them, since you may be required to produce copies of these documents to the court.

Whilst it is usually possible to obtain copies of these documents, institutions such as banks charge as much as [£5] for a copy of each statement. Clearly, you would be well-advised to avoid such expense by keeping the originals of your financial documents from now on.

I would suggest that you keep all financial documents in a safe place, preferably in a ring-binder in date order.

Please note that any original or copy documents belonging to your spouse which have come into your possession have to be returned via me to your spouse's solicitors. This duty exists whenever requested to do so, or by no later than when disclosure is given, usually prior to the first appointment.

Such documents are known as *Hildebrand* documents after a case of that name. You are permitted to locate any documents readily accessible, without breaking open a locked filing cabinet or safe or committing any criminal act.

Any correspondence or emails between your spouse and their lawyer is not covered by this rule. Those documents must never be used by you or me, but you should send them to me for me to return to your spouse's solicitors.

Yours sincerely

section 3 ANCILLARY RELIEF

AR19   Letter enclosing schedule of income and outgoings

Dear [*client*]

With regard to your application for financial provision, it will be necessary for you to give full disclosure of your financial position. This is to show the nature and extent of your income and assets past, present and future.

I would therefore like you to prepare a summary of all your income and outgoings. I attach a Confidential Client Questionnaire for your use. However, I would point out that this Questionnaire is a guide only and will not necessarily cover all aspects.

I would stress that you will be obliged to provide this information in due course. Please ensure that between now and the final hearing or settlement, you remember to keep all documents relating to your financial position, eg bank statements, building society passbooks, insurance policy statements, mortgage statements, pay-slips, P60s and so forth (this list is not exhaustive).

In the event that you do not provide full and frank disclosure, your spouse has the right to request such information and make applications to the court if the information is not provided. You will therefore appreciate that the more complete the information you provide at an early stage, the less costs will be incurred in protracted correspondence and applications to the court.

Yours sincerely

Enc.

AR20   Confidential Client Questionnaire

Please complete this questionnaire and return it to us in advance of our meeting, if possible. Not all questions will necessarily apply to you.

1. YOUR DETAILS

    Your full name: _____

    Your date of birth: _____

    Your age: _____

    Your address (including post code): _____

    _____

    Your correspondence address (if you want us not to write to you at home): _____

    _____

    Your e-mail address: _____

    Your telephone numbers   Home: _____

    Work: _____

    Fax: (do we have to telephone before faxing?) Yes/No: _____

    Mobile: _____

    Your occupation: _____

    Your employer's name (if applicable): _____

2. YOUR SPOUSE'S/PARTNER'S DETAILS

    His/her full name: _____

    His/her date of birth: _____

    His/her age: _____

    His/her address (including post code): _____

    _____

    His/her correspondence address (if you want us not to write to him/ her at home) or name, address and reference of his/her solicitors: _____

    _____

    His/her telephone numbers   Home: _____

    Work: _____

Fax: (do we have to telephone before faxing?) Yes/No: _____

Mobile: _____

His/her occupation: _____

Name and address of his/her employer: _____

_____

3. OTHER PERSON'S DETAILS

Is there another person involved in your case? If so, give that person's name, address and date of birth if known:

_____

_____

4. YOUR MARRIAGE/RELATIONSHIP DETAILS

Date and place of your marriage: _____

Your maiden name (if applicable): _____

When did your relationship begin? _____

When did you start living together? _____

Who has your marriage certificate? _____

If you are now separated, *when* did you separate? _____

Where did you last live together? _____

5. CHILDREN DETAILS

Your children's full names	Date of birth	Age	School	School fees paid (if relevant)	Natural, step or other
1.				£ pa	
2.				£ pa	
3.				£ pa	
4.				£ pa	
5.				£ pa	

Give details if you, your spouse/partner or children have any disabilities or special needs:

_____

_____

6. IS YOUR HOME OWNED?

If so, please complete this page, otherwise move on to 7.

Is the property registered in your name or in joint names? _____

Date of purchase: _____

Number of bedrooms: _____

Number of reception rooms: _____

Purchase price: _____

Original amount of mortgage: _____

Who funded the original purchase price? _____

Who has paid the mortgage? _____

Current value (approx): _____

Outstanding mortgage (approx): _____

Any other loans/charges: _____

Amount of monthly mortgage repayments: _____

Endowment or repayment mortgage: _____

Endowment life policies – details: _____

_____

7. IF YOUR HOME IS RENTED

In whose name is the tenancy? _____

Landlord: _____

London Borough or Local Authority (if not landlord): _____

Date of tenancy: _____

Right to buy Yes/No: _____

Duration of tenancy: _____

Current rent per month: _____

8. YOU AND THE OTHER PERSON'S INCOME AND ASSETS

Your annual *gross* income: _____

Your monthly *net* income: _____

Your assets (including worldwide investments, bank accounts, properties
etc) (Please continue on separate sheet if necessary): _____

_____

section 3 ANCILLARY RELIEF

Your pension transfer values: _____

Your partner's/spouse's annual gross income: _____

Your partner's/spouse's monthly net income: _____

Your partner's/spouse's assets (including as above): _____

_____

Your partner's/spouse's pension transfer values: _____

The other person's annual gross income: _____

The other person's monthly net income: _____

The other person's assets (including as above): _____

The other person's pension transfer values: _____

9. PREVIOUS COURT PROCEEDINGS

Have there been any other/previous court proceedings relating to your marriage, relationship or children? If so, please state court record number and date: _____

_____

10. DO YOU HAVE LEGAL EXPENSES INSURANCE?

Yes/No: _____

11. ARE YOU A BRITISH CITIZEN OR DO YOU HAVE SETTLED STATUS?

Yes/No: _____

(The reason for this question is because your immigration status may be affected by what legal action you may want us to take.) If you are not a British Citizen, are there outstanding immigration issues that may affect the advice you seek from us (give details)?

_____

_____

Your domicile: _____

Your spouse's domicile: _____

Your habitual residence: _____

Your spouse's habitual residence: _____

SIGNED _____

DATED _____

AR21   Letter advising about procedures on settlement

Dear [*client*]

My advice is that you should now instruct me to proceed with your application for the court to make a suitable order dealing with the financial arrangements between you and your spouse.

Even after court proceedings have commenced it is very important that we try to reach agreement with your [former] husband/wife as to the order which should be made. Agreement is generally a more satisfactory way of resolving a dispute than a contentious court hearing because it avoids acrimony, ill-feeling and, importantly, it avoids additional costs being incurred.

Court proceedings can be expensive and, given the possibility that the costs, or at least a proportion of them, may be payable by you (and because the Legal Services Commission's statutory charge may apply), an agreed order may very well save you money.

Having said that, I would stress that we must not aim for an agreed order without ensuring that it is fair. I will only advise you to consent to an agreed order if I consider that the provisions of that order are appropriate.

Should agreement prove possible, it is still necessary to obtain a court order reflecting that agreement. However, there is a simple procedure which avoids either of the spouses or their solicitors having to attend court. This involves preparing a 'statement of information' which is completed with some basic details including ages of the parties to the marriage, the length of the marriage and their respective financial means in terms of income, property and savings. This is then signed by you and your [former] husband/wife. I will also prepare a consent order which embodies the agreement which has been reached and this is signed and sent to the court.

Provided the court is satisfied that the order is appropriate in the light of the information on the statement of information, then the order will be made by the court.

Yours sincerely

section 3 ANCILLARY RELIEF

AR22   Letter to client suspected of not providing full disclosure

Dear [*client*]

I am concerned that your spouse's solicitors are alleging that you have not provided full disclosure of your income and assets and that you have not produced all the information and documents they have asked you for.

I would remind you that in family law cases each spouse is obliged to give full and frank disclosure of all their income and assets. That duty is ongoing and continues until a final order has been agreed or made by the court.

If it becomes clear that you have not made full disclosure of your financial situation, then there is a real possibility that you may be at risk on costs; this means that you could be ordered to pay the costs of your spouse's application to the court generally, which could run to many thousands of pounds.

You must also appreciate that since I am a solicitor, I am an officer of the court. Therefore, I cannot permit you to conduct your case, or prepare any documents on your behalf, in such a way that I know is deliberately misleading to the court.

Therefore, as soon as financial information comes to my attention I am obliged to insist that you disclose that information, otherwise I can no longer represent you.

Yours sincerely

AR23   Letter to court issuing petitioner's ancillary relief proceedings

Dear Sirs

We enclose, for issue, Form A in triplicate.

We also enclose our cheque for [£210] in respect of the issue fee.

Please return two sealed copies of Form A for service upon the mortgagees and notice of first appointment.

Yours sincerely

AR24   Letter to mortgagee serving Form A

Dear Sirs

We act for [   ] regarding divorce and financial settlement.

Pursuant to Family Proceedings Rules 1991, rule 2.59(4), we enclose sealed copy Form A by way of service. Kindly acknowledge receipt.

[Please inform us if you would agree to the transfer of the mortgage into our client's sole name.]

Yours faithfully

AR25PC/PF   Letter to respondent enclosing Form A for private/ publicly funded client

Dear Sirs

We enclose by way of service upon you:

1. Sealed copy Form A.

2. Notice of First Appointment.

[3. Notice of Issue of Public Funding.]

[4. Notice of Acting.]

Please acknowledge receipt.

We look forward to exchanging Forms E on [   ].

Yours faithfully

section 3 ANCILLARY RELIEF

AR26   Case plan letter to client

Dear [*client*]

[As agreed, I have filed Form A at court, a copy of which I enclose.] [Your husband/wife's Solicitors have filed Form A and I enclose a copy.] It would be helpful to you if I provided an overview of what this means.

Form A is a form of application to the court for the court to adjudicate, if no agreement can be reached, on the financial order to be made between you and your [husband/wife]. If your case goes to a final hearing the interval between the filing of Form A and the final hearing may be [10 to 12] months. The reason for this, as will become clear later, is that under the court rules there are stages which cannot be shortened, and cases have to wait their turn to get into the court lists.

Under the court rules there are various stages where the control of the procedure is in the hands of the court. I set out the principal stages in simplified form, which apply to most cases, but which can be altered. Please remember that each stage can be avoided if prior agreement or settlement of claims is reached.

1.   The court has given the date of [   ] for what is known as the first appointment.

2.   At least 35 days before the first appointment ie by [   ], both you and your [husband/wife] have to exchange and file at court full details of your capital and income, assets and liabilities, and details of other matters, in a prescribed sworn form called Form E.

3.   At least 14 days before the first appointment ie not later than [   ] both you and your [husband/wife] have to exchange and file at court:

    3.1 A concise statement of the issues in dispute;

    3.2 A questionnaire setting out what further information and documents should be (in addition to any documents already provided) relevant to the issues stated to be in dispute in the statement of issues;

    3.3 A notice in Form G stating whether each of you will be able to treat the first appointment as an FDR appointment (which I explain below).

4.   This means that at the first appointment at which you and your [husband/wife] and their legal advisers have to attend, the court will be in possession of a substantial amount of information about the financial issues between you and your [husband/wife] and a judge will set out an agenda for your case, which could for example give a time scale within which the questions at 3.2 above must be answered, or that a valuation(s) be made, or other evidence be filed. This agenda will be made in a court order and will invariably include a date for a financial dispute resolution

(FDR) appointment, often 3–4 months later.

5.   The FDR, as with the first appointment, has to be attended by you and your [husband/wife] and your legal advisers. This hearing will be conducted by a judge who will have no part to play if your case proceeds further, and who will have before him/her all offers of settlement which you will have had to make at least seven days beforehand, and all evidence which has come into being before and after the first appointment.

In short, the purpose of the hearing, which may last [an hour] or more, is to see if it is possible to come to an overall financial settlement. Frequently, but not always, this objective is achieved, and the judge can then make an order, which once complied with will mean that your case has been concluded. Only if the FDR is unsuccessful will the judge give further directions (make further orders about the way the case will go forward) and will fix a date for a final hearing, probably several months ahead.

Costs

At every stage of appearance at court we have to provide, as do your [husband's/wife's] solicitors, a schedule of costs to the court, which has to be in prescribed form. The costs incurred by you in the financial court proceedings are incurred in particular in the preparation of your Form E, and before and at each appearance at court.

The vast majority of cases are settled and never go to a final hearing. I cannot promise that this will happen in your case, but my objective is for you to reach an agreement if possible with your [husband/wife] earlier rather than later.

I hope this is helpful as an overview. It is only an interview, and I may well have to advise you along the way of more detailed aspects of each stage.

Yours sincerely

Enc.   Copy Form A

AR27   Letter regarding enclosures to Form E

Dear [*client*]

I am preparing your draft Form E (financial statement) at present, which must be sworn by [   ] at the latest.

The court rules require that you must enclose with the Form E copies of the following documents:

1.   Any written valuation of the matrimonial home which you have obtained in the last six months.

2.   Your most recent mortgage statement, if applicable.

3.   Statements of account for all bank, building society and National Savings accounts, which are in credit, which you hold or have an interest in, including TESSAs or ISAs for the last twelve months.

4.   Any surrender value quotation which you have obtained regarding any life policies.

5.   If you are in business, the last two years' accounts and any other document on which you base your valuation of your interest in the business.

6.   If you have a pension, a valuation of your pension rights if you have been provided with one recently. I attach a copy of section 2.16 of the Form E which I suggest you copy and send to each company with which you have a pension.

7.   If you are an employee, your last three payslips and your P60 for the most recently completed financial year.

8.   If you are self-employed, the accounts for the last two completed accounting years.

I look forward to hearing from you in good time for the deadline stated in the start of this letter.

Yours sincerely

Enc.

AR28   Letter enclosing draft Form E

Dear [*client*]

I enclose a draft Form E (Financial Statement). Please read it very carefully because it is essential that the contents are true. You are under a duty to disclose voluntarily all relevant financial information and, failure to do so, can constitute a 'material non-disclosure' which could result in any final order which is made being set aside (overturned) in the future.

It is worth remembering that if an agreement is not reached and the case proceeds to a contested hearing, then you will almost certainly be cross-examined on the contents of your Form E.

Therefore, please ensure that you understand everything in the Form E and that it accurately reflects your financial position. You should make any amendments or additions by marking the draft and, if I have left out any important details, please let me know as quickly as possible.

Please then return the draft to me.

Yours sincerely

Enc.

AR29   Letter enclosing Form E for swearing

Dear [*client*]

I now enclose your Form E. Please read it carefully to ensure that the details are correct. If you consider that it requires amendment, please telephone me to discuss the amendments.

If you approve Form E in its present form, please contact another firm of solicitors to make an appointment for you to sign and swear it. This is a straightforward procedure which only takes a couple of minutes. The solicitor will charge a fee of [£5 plus £2 per exhibit]. [As you are publicly funded I enclose a cheque for that amount.] Alternatively, you may prefer to go to a county court office to swear the Form E. The court does not charge for this service.

Once you have sworn the Form E, please return it to me [*in the enclosed stamped addressed envelope*]. I will then file the original Form E with the court and send your [former] spouse's solicitor a copy.

Yours sincerely

Enc.

AR30P   Letter to court enclosing Form E for petitioner

Dear Sirs

On behalf of the petitioner, we enclose for filing, Form E sworn on
[   ].

We confirm that we have served a copy on the respondent's solicitors.

Yours faithfully

AR30R   Letter to court enclosing Form E for respondent

Dear Sirs

On behalf of the respondent, we enclose for filing, Form E sworn on
[   ].

We confirm we have served a copy upon the petitioner's solicitors.

Yours faithfully

AR31PC   Letter advising private client of non-receipt of other person's Form E

Dear [*client*]

I have still not received your spouse's Form E. I could therefore apply to the court for an order that [he/she] files [his/her] Form E within 14 days and that there should be a penal notice endorsed on that order.

The effect of that penal notice is that if, once your spouse has had a copy of the order delivered to [him/her] by hand, [he/she] fails to comply with the time-limit set down by the order, [he/she] will be in breach of that order and therefore in contempt of court. It would then be open for you to apply for [him/her] to be committed to prison or punished as the court sees fit. Obviously, that is a drastic step and I hope that it will not be necessary to do so. If it does prove necessary, however, I will first seek your permission.

The hearing of the application is a procedural matter and it is not necessary for you to attend. Please can you telephone me to discuss if you want me to apply for an order for the Form E to be produced. If Form E is not received then the first appointment may have to be postponed.

Yours sincerely

AR31PF   Letter advising publicly funded client of non-receipt of other person's Form E

Dear [*client*]

I have still not received your spouse's Form E. I could therefore apply to the court for an order that [he/she] files [his/her] Form E within 14 days and that there should be a penal notice endorsed on that order.

The effect of that penal notice is that if, once your spouse has had a copy of the order delivered to [him/her] by hand, [he/she] fails to comply with the time-limit set down by the order, [he/she] will be in breach of that order and therefore in contempt of court. It would then be open for you to apply for [him/her] to be committed to prison or punished as the court sees fit. Obviously, that is a drastic step and I hope that it will not be necessary to do so. If it does prove necessary, however, I will first seek your permission and will also need to obtain an amendment to your Public Funding Certificate.

The hearing of the application is a procedural matter and it is not necessary for you to attend. Please can you telephone me to discuss if you want me to apply for an order for the Form E to be produced. If Form E is not received then the first appointment may have to be postponed.

Yours sincerely

AR32   Letter to court enclosing application for issue

Dear Sirs

We now enclose, for issuing, notice of application in duplicate together with our cheque in the sum of [£80].

Please list the application for hearing before a district judge as soon as possible.

We look forward to receiving sealed copy for service upon the petitioner's solicitors.

Yours faithfully

section 3 ANCILLARY RELIEF

AR33   Letter to client confirming hearing date of application

Dear [*client*]

The court has fixed [ ] for the date when the application for the Form E of the other person in your case is to be produced.

As I explained to you before, there is no need for you to attend court.

I will inform you of the outcome of the hearing as soon as it has taken place.

Yours sincerely

AR34   Letter advising client of non-receipt of Form E despite existence of order

Dear [*client*]

Despite the fact that your [former] spouse had a copy of the order dated
[   ] delivered to [him/her], I have still not received [his/her] Form E.

The time-limit specified in the order has now expired and therefore the other person is in contempt of court.

I am sure that you will be reluctant to apply to the court for the other person to be punished but I recommend that we do so, since little or no progress can be made in your case until we do so.

Please confirm that you want me to apply for committal to prison of your [former] spouse. The alternative is for the first appointment to proceed without the Form E or adjourn the first appointment to another date.

Yours sincerely

AR35 Letter to client enclosing draft statement of issues and questionnaire

Dear [*client*]

As explained in my letter dated [   ], I now enclose a draft statement of issues and questionnaire. The statement of issues sets out what I regard to be the main areas of dispute. That document has to be drafted in a neutral and low-key way and is not designed to argue your case but simply to state in outline what your case is on the key areas of dispute.

Please let me know if you have any comments on it.

I also enclose a draft questionnaire which is a request for further information and documents from your spouse. The court rules specifically state that the questionnaire has to refer to the issues in dispute and cannot be a general request for all sorts of information.

I would comment on the statement of issues as follows, using the numbering in the document: [   ].

I would comment on the draft questionnaire as follows, using the numbering in that document: [   ].

The role of the district judge at the first appointment is to decide whether or not the questions in the draft questionnaire are reasonable and the district judge may disallow some which are excessive or irrelevant or unreasonable.

Please let me know if you think we should be asking for any other information or documents from your spouse.

Yours sincerely

Enc.

section 3 ANCILLARY RELIEF

AR36   Letter to client enclosing other person's statement of issues and draft questionnaire

Dear [*client*]

I have now received and enclose your spouse's statement of issues and draft questionnaire. Please read through these carefully.

Using the numbering in the statement of issues I would comment as follows:
[   ].

As regards the draft questionnaire, I advise that the court will order you to answer the questions apart from the following ones, using the numbering in the questionnaire: [   ].

The procedure at the first appointment is relatively straightforward. Unless it is to be used as a financial dispute resolution (FDR) appointment, the district judge will consider the statements of issues and draft questionnaires. The district judge will go through each questionnaire asking for justification of any questions which are disputed by your spouse and then deciding which questions should be answered.

The district judge will then make orders for directions as to how the case should proceed.

The role of the district judge at the first appointment is to decide whether or not the questions in the draft questionnaire are reasonable and the district judge may disallow some which are excessive or irrelevant or unreasonable.

In preparation for the first appointment we now need to consider what directions we should ask the court to make. Directions are orders as to how the future progress of the case should be conducted. I recommend that we seek the following directions:

1.   That the valuation of [   ] be agreed and if no agreement can be reached then a jointly nominated valuer should be appointed, with the costs to be borne equally.

2.   Both you and your spouse should answer the questionnaires as approved/ amended by the district judge within 21 days of the date of the first appointment.

3.   That the matter should be listed for an FDR appointment.

Please can you let me have your comments on the documents enclosed with this letter.

Yours sincerely

Enc.

AR37 Letter advising client regarding completion of Form G

Dear [*client*]

In preparation for the first appointment I have to prepare Form G and send it to the court and the other solicitors 14 days before that hearing.

Form G has to state whether you will be in a position at the first appointment to treat that hearing as if it were a financial dispute resolution (FDR) appointment.

The advantage of using the first appointment as if it were an FDR appointment is that a great deal of time and legal expense will be saved. However, only if the value of all relevant assets are known and sufficient financial information has been provided will it be possible to treat the first appointment as an FDR appointment.

Therefore I advise that it [will/will not] be possible to treat the first appointment as an FDR appointment. Please can you telephone me as soon as possible to discuss this.

Yours sincerely

AR38 Letter to client reporting on outcome of first appointment

Dear [*client*]

I write to confirm the outcome of the first appointment. I enclose a copy of the order for directions made and my comments on them are as follows:
[   ].

Please note that the financial dispute resolution (FDR) appointment has been fixed for [ ]. It will take place in the same court building as before. It is essential that you attend. [I propose instructing a barrister to represent you at the FDR which I will discuss with you].

If there are any significant changes in your financial or personal situation between now and the FDR, please can you let me know well in advance of the FDR since those changes may alter the case.

Yours sincerely

AR39PC Letter advising private client about application for answers to the questionnaire

Dear [*client*]

You will recall that your spouse was ordered to produce further information and documents. As I have not received [all/any] of the information requested, I could apply to the court for an order that the information be provided within 14 days and that there be a penal notice endorsed on that order.

The effect of that penal notice is that if, once your spouse has had a copy of the order delivered to [him/her] by hand, [he/she] fails to comply with the time-limit set down by the order, [he/she] will be in breach of that order and therefore in contempt of court. It would then be open for you to apply for [him/her] to be committed to prison or punished as the court sees fit. Obviously, that is a drastic step and I hope that it will not be necessary to do so. If it does prove necessary, however, I will first seek your permission.

The hearing of the application is a procedural matter and it is not necessary for you to attend. Please can you telephone me to discuss if you want me to apply for an order for the information and documents to be produced. If they are not produced there is a risk that the financial dispute resolution appointment will have to be postponed.

Yours sincerely

AR39PF Letter advising publicly funded client about application for answers to the questionnaire

Dear [*client*]

You will recall that your spouse was ordered to produce further information and documents. As I have not received [all/any] of the information requested, I could apply to the court for an order that the information be provided within 14 days and that there be a penal notice endorsed on that order.

The effect of that penal notice is that if, once your spouse has had a copy of the order delivered to [him/her] by hand, [he/she] fails to comply with the time-limit set down by the order, [he/she] will be in breach of that order and therefore in contempt of court. It would then be open for you to apply for [him/her] to be committed to prison or punished as the court sees fit. Obviously, that is a drastic step and I hope that it will not be necessary to do so. If it does prove necessary, however, I will first seek your permission and will also need to obtain an amendment to your Public Funding Certificate.

The hearing of the application is a procedural matter and it is not necessary for you to attend. Please can you telephone me to discuss if you want me to apply for an order for the information and documents to be produced. If they are not produced there is a risk that the financial dispute resolution appointment will have to be postponed.

Yours sincerely

section 3 ANCILLARY RELIEF

AR40 Letter advising client of hearing date

Dear [*client*]

The court has fixed [   ] to be the date when the application will be made for an order that your spouse must produce the outstanding information and documents.

As I explained to you before, there is no need for you to attend court.

I will inform you of the outcome of the hearing as soon as it has taken place.

Yours sincerely

AR41   Letter to client concerning appointment of surveyor to value property

Dear [*client*]

It is now necessary to make suitable arrangements for the valuation of
[   ]. My advice is for you to instruct a qualified chartered surveyor
rather than an unqualified estate agent because, if the valuation is not agreed
by your [former] spouse, then it will be necessary to call the valuer to
give evidence. In my view, the district judge will usually consider that the
evidence of a qualified chartered surveyor carries more weight than that of an
unqualified estate agent.

Please let me know which firm of chartered surveyors you wish me to instruct.
If you do not have a specific individual or firm in mind, I could suggest names
of suitable firms, but I must point out that I may not have personal experience
of their work.

Yours sincerely

AR42   Letter to client concerning appointment of surveyor to value property, as per order for directions

Dear [*client*]

In accordance with the order for directions, it is now necessary to make
suitable arrangements for a valuation of [   ]. My advice is for you to
instruct a qualified chartered surveyor rather than an unqualified estate agent
because, if the valuation is not agreed by your [former] spouse, then it will
be necessary to call the valuer to give evidence. In my view the district judge
will usually consider that the evidence of a qualified chartered surveyor carries
more weight than that of an unqualified estate agent. Please let me know which
firm of chartered surveyors you wish me to instruct. If you do not have a
specific individual or firm in mind, I could suggest names of suitable firms, but
I must point out that I may not have personal experience of their work.

Since this is to be a joint valuation, normally you will be bound by it for the
purposes of the financial dispute resolution appointment only; after then, you
may be able to obtain your own valuation.

Yours sincerely

AR43PC Letter instructing surveyors to value property for private client

For the attention of [   ]

Messrs

Surveyors and valuers

Dear Sirs

Proceedings between [   ] as petitioner

And [   ] respondent

Case no [   ] in the [Principal Registry of the Family Division]

We act for [   ] in connection with his/her [divorce/relationship breakdown]. [   ] act for [   ].

At a directions appointment on [   ], the court directed that the [former matrimonial] home at [   ], ('   '), which is owned by Mr/s [and] Mr/s [   ] [jointly], should be valued independently by a jointly appointed expert. The parties have agreed that your firm should conduct the independent valuation.

As the valuation will be required for court proceedings, it will be governed by Part 35 of the Civil Procedure Rules ('CPR'). Consequently, your overriding duty in preparing the report will be to the court. Although you may already be familiar with the Practice Direction, which supplements CPR Part 35, we enclose, for ease of reference, a copy of paragraphs 1 and 2 of the Practice Direction, together with an example declaration which you may wish to use in your report. Office Copy Entries from the Land Registry are also enclosed with this letter.

In the preparation of your report, we should be grateful if you would bear in mind the following:

1. The valuation of [   ] is to be carried out on the basis of 'market value' as defined by The Royal Institute of Chartered Surveyors as follows: 'the estimated amount for which an asset should exchange on the date of valuation between a willing buyer and a willing seller in an arms length transaction after proper marketing wherein the parties had each acted knowledgably, prudently and without compulsion'.

2. Please set out the factors which you have taken into account in formulating your valuation.

3. [Please include your opinion of the current market rent attributable to the property].

section 3 ANCILLARY RELIEF

4. Please have regard to recent sales [and current rental values] of comparable properties, setting out in your report details of such comparable properties, to include (where appropriate) asking and completed sale prices.

5. Please provide your opinion on: [here set out any other matters, such as sale by lot, or application for planning permission, or income possibilities, or any other relevant matter and also specifically state if a structural survey is required, as this is not required for a formal valuation unless specifically requested].

6. Kindly ensure that your report is addressed to the court and not to the parties or their solicitors.

7. [   ] currently resides at the property. Please do not liaise with either Mr/s or Mr/s [   ] directly in relation to the valuation. Neither Mr/s or Mr/s [   ] should be present when you attend at the property for inspection/both Mr/s and Mr/s [   ]/and [   ] will be present during the inspection of the property. Kindly refrain from discussing the valuation directly with them. Please liaise with [   ] telephone number [   ] to make arrangements for access to and inspection of the property.

8. Kindly direct any enquiries you may have in respect of the property or in respect of any other information or documentation which you require in order to carry out your valuation report in writing to [solicitors] [   ] and copy to [   ]. Similarly, please copy to [   ] any correspondence which you receive in response to such enquiries to include a schedule of any documents received. Following the preparation of your valuation report, please forward one copy to both firms of solicitors quoting the above reference.

9. A court appointment has been listed in this matter on [   ]. Given the court timetable, it is important that the valuation be produced as soon as possible, and any event, no later than [   ]. However, it would assist the parties if you were able to prepare your report in advance of that date. Kindly confirm whether or not this will be possible.

10. It has been agreed between the parties that Mr/s and Mr/s [   ] will be settling your firm's fees (equally). Please send separate invoices requesting one half of the valuation fee to [   ] and to [   ].

Before proceeding with this matter, kindly provide us with an estimate of your likely charges for producing the above report, for approval. Please also confirm that you have had no prior dealings with either party which could cause conflict of interest.

We look forward to hearing from you.

Yours faithfully   Yours faithfully

_____   _____

[   ]   [   ]

Encls:

1.   Copy title register;
2.   Extract from Practice Direction to CPR Part 35;
3.   Example expert's declaration

AR43PF   Letter instructing surveyors to value property for publicly funded client

For the attention of [   ]

Messrs

Surveyors and valuers

Dear Sirs

Proceedings between [   ] as petitioner

And [   ] respondent

Case no [   ] in the [Principal Registry of the Family Division]

We act for [   ] in connection with his/her [divorce/relationship breakdown]. [   ] act for [   ].

At a directions appointment on [   ], the court directed that the [former matrimonial] home at [   ], ('   '), which is owned by Mr/s [and] Mr/s [   ] [jointly], should be valued independently by a jointly appointed expert. The parties have agreed that your firm should conduct the independent valuation.

As the valuation will be required for court proceedings, it will be governed by Part 35 of the Civil Procedure Rules ('CPR'). Consequently, your overriding duty in preparing the report will be to the court. Although you may already be familiar with the Practice Direction, which supplements CPR Part 35, we enclose, for ease of reference, a copy of paragraphs 1 and 2 of the Practice Direction, together with an example declaration which you may wish to use in your report. Office Copy Entries from the Land Registry are also enclosed with this letter.

In the preparation of your report, we should be grateful if you would bear in mind the following:

1. The valuation of [   ] is to be carried out on the basis of 'market value' as defined by The Royal Institute of Chartered Surveyors as follows: 'the estimated amount for which an asset should exchange on the date of valuation between a willing buyer and a willing seller in an arms length transaction after proper marketing wherein the parties had each acted knowledgably, prudently and without compulsion'.

2. Please set out the factors which you have taken into account in formulating your valuation.

3. [Please include your opinion of the current market rent attributable to the property].

4. Please have regard to recent sales [and current rental values] of comparable properties, setting out in your report details of such comparable properties, to include (where appropriate) asking and completed sale prices.

5. Please provide your opinion on: [here set out any other matters, such as sale by lot, or application for planning permission, or income possibilities, or any other relevant matter and also specifically state if a structural survey is required, as this is not required for a formal valuation unless specifically requested].

6. Kindly ensure that your report is addressed to the court and not to the parties or their solicitors.

7. [   ] currently resides at the property. Please do not liaise with either Mr/s or Mr/s [   ] directly in relation to the valuation. Neither Mr/s or Mr/s [   ] should be present when you attend at the property for inspection/both Mr/s and Mr/s [   ]/and [   ] will be present during the inspection of the property. Kindly refrain from discussing the valuation directly with them. Please liaise with [   ] telephone number [   ] to make arrangements for access to and inspection of the property.

8. Kindly direct any enquiries you may have in respect of the property or in respect of any other information or documentation which you require in order to carry out your valuation report in writing to [solicitors] [   ] and copy to [   ]. Similarly, please copy to [   ] any correspondence which you receive in response to such enquiries to include a schedule of any documents received. Following the preparation of your valuation report, please forward one copy to both firms of solicitors quoting the above reference.

9. A court appointment has been listed in this matter on [   ]. Given the court timetable, it is important that the valuation be produced as soon as possible, and any event, no later than [   ]. However, it would assist the parties if you were able to prepare your report in advance of that date. Kindly confirm whether or not this will be possible.

10. Mr/s [   ] and Mr/s [   ] accept that a fee will be payable for your advice and the firms jointly confirm that they will be responsible for your reasonable charges subject to the level of your charges having been agreed in advance. However, since Mr/s [   ] has the benefit of public funding, there may be some delay in the payment of your fee, pending receipt of the funds from the Legal Services Commission.

Before proceeding with this matter, kindly provide us with an estimate of your likely charges for producing the above report, for approval. Please also confirm that you have had no prior dealings with either party which could cause conflict of interest.

section 3 ANCILLARY RELIEF

We look forward to hearing from you.

Yours faithfully　　　　　　　　　　　Yours faithfully

_____　　　　　_____

[　　　　]　　　　　　　　　　　　[　　　　]

Encls:

1.　Copy title register;
2.　Extract from Practice Direction to CPR Part 35;
3.　Example expert's declaration

AR44 Letter advising client to consider making settlement proposals

Dear [*client*]

Now that the financial court proceedings have been commenced you are under a duty to make proposals in settlement, to try to reach an agreement with your spouse.

Since the financial court proceedings were not started by you, you are technically the 'respondent'.

The Court of Appeal has made it clear that respondents to financial applications are under a duty to make proposals in settlement and that any proposal should be 'a serious offer worthy of consideration'. You are also under a duty to try to reach an agreement. You are not expected to make proposals until there has been adequate disclosure of the other person's income and assets.

At the forthcoming financial dispute resolution hearing, if you have not made proposals you are likely to be criticised by the district judge.

[In my view there has been adequate disclosure and I therefore recommend that you consider making proposals.]

[In my view there has not been adequate disclosure, but nonetheless you should be considering what proposals you are prepared to make.]

Yours sincerely

AR45   Letter making proposals to other party's solicitor

Dear Sirs

We have now had an opportunity to consider this matter carefully with counsel and our client. In an effort to compromise this matter and thereby avoid the necessity of a [full] day hearing at court, we are instructed to put forward the following proposals for settlement:

1.   That the former matrimonial home, [   ], be placed on the market for sale at the best possible price.

2.   That the net proceeds of sale (ie gross proceeds less estate agent's fees, mortgage redemption monies and legal costs) be divided as to [   ].

3.   [   ]

4.   [   ]

5.   [   ]

6.   That the above settlement shall be in full and final satisfaction of all or any claims that either party may have against the other under the Matrimonial Causes Act 1973, the Married Women's Property Act 1882 or any other relevant legislation.

7.   That neither party shall be entitled to apply against the estate of the other under the Inheritance (Provision for Family and Dependants) Act 1975.

8.   That there be no order for costs [save public funding assessment of [   ] costs].

If the above is agreed, we would suggest that it should be incorporated into a consent order to be approved by the court.

We intend referring this letter to the attention of the court as to costs if this offer is not accepted.

Yours faithfully

AR46 Letter advising client about and enclosing a letter making proposals

Dear [*client*]

I enclose a copy of a letter dated [   ] from which you will see that the following proposals are being made by your [former] spouse to try to reach an agreement or 'settle' the case as follows:

1.

2.

3.

The Court of Appeal has made it clear that once an offer is made, and providing full financial disclosure has been made, the person receiving the offer is under a duty to respond to the offer, giving reasons for rejecting the offer, if that is the case, and to respond to the offer within a reasonable period.

[In my view, these proposals are a reasonable offer and you should give serious thought as to whether you want to accept them.]

[Since you have the benefit of public funding, I may have to consider notifying the Legal Services Commission that you have not accepted this offer, which may result in your public funding being discharged (ie cancelled). Under public funding rules, I am required to notify the Legal Services Commission if someone refuses to accept reasonable proposals to compromise a case.]

[Because I believe these proposals are a reasonable offer there is a danger that if you do not accept these proposals, then at the final hearing you could be ordered to pay all or part of your spouse's costs.]

[If you are considering accepting these proposals, then please let me know if there are any other matters which need to be sorted out. Please also let me know if there are any other joint assets such as life policies which need to be transferred into sole names; it is important that all aspects have been included.]

Yours sincerely

AR47   Letter advising client about proposals and costs rules

Dear [   ]

I write to explain the costs rules in financial cases introduced in April 2006, which apply to your case.

The general rule is now that the court will not make an order requiring one spouse to pay the costs of the other spouse. However the court may make such an order at any stage of the case where it considers it appropriate to do so because of the way in which one spouse has conducted their case, which includes before the case was started.

Therefore costs incurred by both spouses will be a liability, which will normally have to be financed out of existing assets during the case, in so far as this is possible.

In deciding what order if any the court should make regarding costs, contrary to the general rule that there should be no order made regarding costs, the court must have regard to:

(a)   any failure by a spouse to comply with court rules and guidance;
(b)   any open offer to reach agreement made in the case – this excludes any letters written on a 'without prejudice' or 'without prejudice save as to costs' basis;
(c)   whether it was reasonable for either spouse to raise, pursue or contest a particular allegation or issue;
(d)   the manner in which a spouse has pursued or responded to the financial claims made, or any particular allegation or issue;
(e)   any other aspect of a spouse's conduct/behaviour only in respect of the case itself, which the court considers relevant; and
(f)   the financial effect on either spouse of any costs order.

It is not possible to rely on any offer made, regarding costs, which is 'without prejudice'. It is no longer possible to make proposals to reach an agreement on a 'without prejudice save as to costs' basis, under what was known as the Calderbank rule.

I will write to you in due course if it is appropriate to seek an order for costs in your case.

Yours sincerely

AR48   Letter to client explaining about procedure at the financial dispute resolution (FDR) appointment

Dear [*client*]

I write to explain about the procedure at the forthcoming FDR Appointment which has been listed for hearing on [   ].

[I will be representing you at the hearing] [your barrister will be representing you at the hearing and/my assistant [   ] will be attending the hearing with you]. It is essential that you attend.

It is often necessary to arrive at court a good hour before so that negotiations can begin before the court hearing. Depending on what progress is made with the negotiations we will then go before the district judge and explain the sets of proposals which have been made.

[I] [your barrister] will argue your case as will your spouse's barrister. In most cases the district judge will give an indication as to what order is likely to be made at a final hearing. The district judge will encourage both of you to try to reach an agreement and compromise wherever appropriate and possible.

The negotiations before and after the FDR appointment may go on for several hours and therefore you should make arrangements to be free for most of the day.

Sometimes at the FDR appointment it is possible to reach an overall agreement, in which case a financial consent order will be prepared, signed by all concerned and then approved by the district judge.

Please let me know if you have any questions as to the procedure at the FDR appointment.

Yours sincerely

section 3 ANCILLARY RELIEF

AR49   Letter to client enclosing draft consent order

Dear [*client*]

I enclose a statement of information and a draft financial consent order for your approval.

The statement of information simply sets out the basic facts of your case. Please read through this document carefully, making any amendments as necessary in neat writing, and then sign and return the document to me. Please do not date the document.

The financial consent order is a more complicated document and you should study it carefully to ensure that you fully understand it. It is very important that you understand it properly and that the document records all the terms of agreement reached since this will be the main document which will be referred to at any time in the future.

The consent order is divided into two main parts. The first is a series of recitals and undertakings, and the second is the formal part of the court order itself.

A recital is a clause setting out the fact of an agreement on a particular point.

An undertaking is a legally binding promise to the court and if that undertaking is broken, then the person who is to benefit from the undertaking can apply to the court for the other person, who is in breach of the undertaking, to be punished by the court and even to be committed to prison. In most cases it is possible to enforce undertakings of a financial nature in this way.

The formal part of the court order contains the orders which are to be made by the court.

I have set out below an explanation of the various clauses in the consent order.

[   ]

Please let me know if you approve the terms of the consent order and, if so, please sign and return the consent order to me but do not date the document.

Yours sincerely

Enc.

AR50 Letter to court enclosing consent order

Dear Sirs

We enclose, by way of application for consent order:

1. Petitioner's Form A.

2. Respondent's Form A.

3. Petitioner's Form M1.

4. Respondent's Form M1.

5. Consent order plus duplicate clean copy.

[6. Notice of acting.]

7. Cheque for £[40] by way of fee.

Please place this letter before a district judge.

We look forward to receiving the consent order as soon as possible.

Yours faithfully

AR51 Letter to private client prior to application for a final hearing

Dear [*client*]

You now have to consider whether or not to try to make further proposals to reach an agreement, or whether you now want to proceed with your case to a final hearing.

You should appreciate that substantial extra costs will be incurred in the last month before any final hearing, and the costs of the final hearing itself, when you will be represented by a barrister, will also be substantial. You may end up spending substantial further costs and this must be borne in mind.

You should also appreciate that some clients find going to court distressing, particularly if clients have not seen their spouses or former spouses for some time.

I look forward to hearing from you as soon as possible.

Yours sincerely

AR52   Letter to private client after agreement not reached at financial dispute resolution (FDR) resolution

Dear [*client*]

As you know, the date for a final hearing has been fixed on [   ] at
[   ] at [   ] with a time estimate of [   ] days. Please put
this in your diary now as you will have to attend. Your barrister is [   ]
whom I have booked to represent you. I and/or [*assistant*] will be present
with you throughout the hearing. Should it be necessary, I have arranged a
pre-hearing conference with [*Barrister*] on [   ] at [   ] which I
would ask you also to put in your diary.

As I have already advised you, the majority of cases never go to a final hearing
because agreement is reached beforehand, but if this is not achievable in your
case, it would be helpful for you to have an overview of what has to be done,
the criteria that the court is obliged to consider and the question of costs.

What has to be done between now and (final hearing date)

The court has to have before it completely up-to-date information about the
finances and other relevant matters of both you and your [husband/wife].
Please tell me if your finances or your personal situation change in any way.
As a minimum your bank statements, credit card statements and any changes
to your capital and income situation must be provided. Particulars of properties
which you consider suitable for your [husband/wife] and which are currently
available have to be provided. If it is necessary for you, by affidavit, to update
your financial situation I shall advise you.

Where it is necessary we shall with [*Barrister*] have to agree whether any
witnesses are needed, and if so whom, and what evidence they will file on your
behalf.

Both you and your [husband/wife] will have to make and file at court not
less than 14 and 7 days before [   ] open letters with proposals for
settlement. Your proposals will first be agreed with [*Barrister*].

We shall prepare for you to be made available when the hearing starts a
schedule of your costs of the case, to include an estimate of the costs of the
hearing. This will cover my firm's costs, all disbursements such as fees of
[*Barrister*] and VAT.

Costs

Where a case goes to a final hearing, there are many steps which have to be
taken in order that your case is prepared as well as possible and [*Barrister*] has
all the documents to be able to represent you and present your case as strongly
as possible. These steps, some of which I have referred to above, mean that
there will be a substantial increase in the level of your costs in the run up to the

final hearing. This illustrates why it is desirable to settle your case as early as possible.

As I advised you on my first administrative letter dated [   ], were your case to go to a major hearing, I would have to ask you in good time to put me in funds to cover the estimated costs of it and to include the fees of any barrister instructed on your behalf. It is too early for me to give you a precise estimate, which I shall do not less than six weeks before the final hearing, but the best provisional estimate that I can now make is that the cost would be about £[   ] inclusive of VAT and disbursements. I need to let you know this provisional advice so that you can begin to make arrangements to have funds available when I give you the detailed estimate referred to above.

Whatever the outcome of the final hearing, you are liable for my firm's costs.

About two to four weeks before [*hearing date*] I shall have to deliver a brief (detailed instructions and every document that is relevant to your case properly indexed and paginated) to [*Barrister*]. When the brief has been delivered [his/her] fees become payable irrespective of whether the final hearing takes place. If your case does not litigate it may be possible, dependent on how far in advance of [*final hearing date*] agreement is reached to agree a reduced brief fee, but this is by concession and cannot be guaranteed.

I mentioned above that this is an overview to give you some framework of what is involved in the preparation for the final hearing. It is not possible, without going into enormous detail, to go further and in any event experience has shown that, for example, as information is provided, or valuations are produced, or affidavits filed, the precise needs and manner of preparing a case for hearing will change.

Please contact me about any aspect of this letter, or if you have any queries.

Yours sincerely

AR53   Letter advising client of need to make substantial payment on account prior to final hearing

Dear [*client*]

As you know the final hearing of your case is listed for [   ], some six weeks away. I write to you regarding the question of payment of money on account of costs prior to the final hearing.

You will recall that my firm's Terms of Business (provided to you on [   ]) stated that before a final hearing we required clients to pay funds up front on account of legal fees to be held in our client account in your name against any future bills at the end of the hearing.

I can only, at this stage, give a very broadbrush estimate for costs to the conclusion of the hearing if an agreement is not reached before the final hearing, but I hope that even a broad estimate will help you. I cannot obviously predict with 100% accuracy how many hours it will take me fully to prepare the case but I have tried to do my best below.

I would estimate that your barrister's brief fee would be between £[   ] and £[   ] including VAT to the conclusion of the hearing.

Giving you an accurate estimate of my firm's costs from now on is not easy since it very much depends on what work is necessary. I set out below a list of the work which I expect will be necessary together with my estimate of the time to be spent on each item. These are very rough and ready figures and could change significantly depending on developments in the case. The details are:

Type of work	(Name of solicitor)	(Name of Assistant/Trainee)
1. Preparation for further Conference	[ ] hours	
2. Attending Conference		
3. Updating disclosure		
4. Open proposals		
5. Preparing Court bundles		
6. Negotiations		
7. Meetings		
8. Miscellaneous and other correspondence		
9. Preparation of brief for final hearing		
10. Final hearing		
Totals:		

Therefore the total cost to you could be:

1. Estimated future work by [   ] xx hours × £[   ] plus VAT =
    £[   ] including VAT.

2. Estimated future work by [   ] xx hours × £[   ] plus VAT =
    £[   ] including VAT.

3. Your Barrister's fees up to £[   ].

Therefore the total estimated fees are £[   ].

If I am able to delegate routine work to a more junior member of staff I will do so and the costs may be reduced.

Therefore, unfortunately, I have to ask you to send me £[   ] by close of business on [   ] which I will place on deposit here until conclusion of the final hearing. [If I do not receive this payment by that date then I may have no option but to apply to be removed from the court record and regrettably you would have to represent yourself at the final hearing.]

I am also required to let you know that your barrister's fees mentioned above will become due and payable on [   ]. After that date, even if an agreement is later reached you will be obliged to pay those fees although I may be able to negotiate a reduction depending on how close it is to the final hearing when an agreement is reached and depending on what work your barrister has had to do. Therefore, of course, if an agreement is to be reached it would be preferable if it was reached before [   ].

I am sorry to have to write to you in these terms but it is important that you are aware of the costs implications of the final hearing. Please telephone me if you have any questions about this letter.

Yours sincerely

AR54   Letter to client requesting further information for final hearing

Dear [*client*]

It is now only six weeks before the final hearing of your case and I am making preparations for that hearing.

There is a great deal of work to be done and considerable costs will be incurred from now on. Therefore, please inform me if there has been any change in your financial circumstances since we last met.

Also, if you have not already done so, please let me have up-to-date copies of all relevant financial documents such as payslips, P60s, credit card statements, bank statements and so on.

Please also let me know if you think there has been a change in the value of any properties involved in your case.

Finally, also let me know if you believe that there has been any recent change in the financial circumstances of your spouse.

Yours sincerely

AR55 Letter advising client of procedure at final hearing

Dear [*client*]

I write to advise you as to the procedure at the final hearing itself.

The final hearing has been fixed for [   ] days. Normally, the court will only hear the case from [10.30 am to 1 pm] and from [2 pm to 4.30 pm], without a break, apart for lunch.

The main issues still in dispute are:

[   ]

Your barrister will represent you at the hearing and your case will be conducted by him/her. You will have to give evidence and that will involve both answering questions put to you by your barrister and also being cross-examined by the other side's barrister.

You are liable to be cross-examined on any statements made in your Form E and any affidavits which have been sworn by you and you may be asked to explain any documents which have been produced. In addition, you could be asked any question to do with finances which is considered relevant to your case.

Yours sincerely

AR56   Letter to client concerning choice of counsel

Dear [*client*]

I am writing to ask if you have any preference as to which barrister you want me to instruct to represent you in your case.

I would strongly recommend [   ] who is a specialist Family Law Barrister of [ ] years' experience from a leading family law chambers of barristers.

I will assume unless I hear from you to the contrary within seven days that you have no objection to me instructing this barrister and that you do not have any other particular barrister you would prefer me to instruct.

I should say that if you do want me to instruct a different barrister I would be extremely reluctant to instruct a barrister of whom I have no experience, but we will discuss this if it applies to your case.

Yours sincerely

AR57   Letter to client ordered to pay maintenance

Dear [*client*]

I write to report on the outcome of your case.

ANY FURTHER ACTION YOU ARE REQUIRED TO TAKE

ANY FURTHER ACTION WE WILL TAKE

ACCOUNTING FOR OUTSTANDING MONEY

ORIGINAL DOCUMENTS

I am returning to you a bundle of original documents which are no longer needed by me.

[As agreed, I will keep some other original documents, namely [   ].]

RETRIEVAL OF PAPERS

Once my firm's costs have been paid [by the Legal Services Commission], your file of papers will be placed in storage and will normally be kept for a period of [15 years]. If, however, you wish to keep your file of papers, we will gladly send them to you but we may need to make copies of the papers.

If you ever need access to your file of papers, you should contact this firm. [It may take a week or so for the papers to be retrieved since we normally store them in a different building.] [My firm may have to make a small charge for retrieval of the papers.]

FUTURE REVIEW

The final order provides that you are to pay maintenance to your former spouse. If, for any reason, there is a significant change in your circumstances or her/his circumstances, you can always apply to the court for the maintenance to be reduced and, similarly, she/he can apply to the court for the maintenance to be increased, if only to keep in line with inflation.

If your former spouse remarries, her/his claims for maintenance automatically terminate. If your former spouse starts to cohabit then, unless there is a reference in the order to the maintenance ending when she/he cohabits, the maintenance in theory remains payable and you should contact me.

You should not simply stop paying maintenance in any circumstances but rather contact me so that a formal application to the court can be made for the maintenance to be varied so as to be reduced. If you simply stop paying the maintenance, your former spouse could enforce the arrears of maintenance without giving you any notice that she/he intends to do so.

Yours sincerely

AR58   Letter to client awarded maintenance

Dear [*client*]

I write to report on the outcome of your case.

ANY FURTHER ACTION YOU ARE REQUIRED TO TAKE

ANY FURTHER ACTION WE WILL TAKE

ACCOUNTING FOR OUTSTANDING MONEY

ORIGINAL DOCUMENTS

I am returning to you a Bundle of original documents which are no longer needed by me.

[As agreed, I will keep some other original documents, namely [   ].]

RETRIEVAL OF PAPERS

Once my firm's costs have been paid [by the Legal Services Commission], your file of papers will be placed in storage and will normally be kept for a period of [15 years]. If you wish to keep your file of papers, we will gladly send them to you but we may need to take copies of the papers.

If you ever need access to your file of papers, you should contact this firm. [It may take a week or so for the papers to be retrieved since we normally store them in a different building.] [My firm may make a small charge for retrieval of the papers.]

FUTURE REVIEW

Since the final order in your favour provides that maintenance should be paid to you, you should always consider whether you should apply to the court at some point in the future for the maintenance to be increased.

The order for maintenance is not index linked, and therefore the value of the maintenance order will gradually erode in time with inflation.

In addition, you could always apply for an increase in the maintenance if you are working and you lose your job, or if you become ill for some reason, or there is some other major change in your circumstances or a significant improvement in the circumstances of your former spouse.

Yours sincerely

AR59 Letter advising client about the Inheritance (Provision for Family and Dependants) Act 1975

Dear [*client*]

Where someone who was domiciled in England or Wales dies, then any person who falls into one of the five categories specified in the Inheritance (Provision for Family and Dependants) Act 1975 can apply to the court for money from the deceased's estate on the grounds that the effect of the Will, or any intestacy in the absence of any Will, is such that that person has not been provided with reasonable financial provision from the deceased.

The four relevant categories for your case are:

(a)   former spouse or civil partner;
(b)   a child; and
(c)   'any person who immediately before the death of the deceased was being maintained, either wholly or partly, by the deceased';
(d)   any person who was cohabiting as husband and wife with the deceased for two years prior to the death of the deceased.

The definition of reasonable financial provision is: 'such financial provision as it would be reasonable in all the circumstances of the case for the applicant to receive for his maintenance'.

Although the Act refers to maintenance, the court has power to order not only payment of maintenance out of the estate but also payment of a lump sum or a transfer of property order.

The Act provides that a person shall be treated as being maintained by the deceased 'either wholly or partly … if the deceased, otherwise than for full valuable consideration, was making a substantial contribution in money or money's worth towards the reasonable needs of that person'.

In considering what order should be made, the court is required to have regard to the following matters, namely:

(a)   the financial resources and financial needs which the applicant has or is likely to have in the foreseeable future;
(b)   the financial resources and financial needs which any other applicant for an order under the Act has or is likely to have in the foreseeable future;
(c)   the financial resources and financial needs which any beneficiary of the estate of the deceased has or is likely to have in the foreseeable future;
(d)   any obligations and responsibilities which the deceased had towards any applicant or towards any beneficiary of the estate;
(e)   the size and nature of the net estate of the deceased;
(f)   any physical or mental disability of any applicant for an order;
(g)   any other matter, including the conduct of the applicant or any other person, which in the circumstances of the case the court may consider relevant.

When considering what money should be paid out of the estate to a spouse or former spouse of the deceased, the court must have regard to:

(a) the age of the applicant and the duration of the marriage;

(b) the contribution made by the applicant to the welfare of the family of the deceased, including any contribution made by looking after the home or caring for the family.

The court is also required to take into account an applicant's earning capacity, financial obligations and responsibilities.

The purpose of the Act is to ensure that someone who was previously dependent on the deceased does not suffer hardship on the death of the deceased by no longer receiving financial support.

The Act is not about what other people may believe to be morally right or just.

To start the court proceedings, you would have to swear an affidavit setting out the facts of your case, based on a statement which I will be preparing. Then the others involved in the case will have to prepare affidavits in reply.

The court considers what orders are necessary for the future conduct of the case and all necessary documents have to be listed and disclosed to the others involved in the case. It is therefore important that you keep all relevant documents including any financial documents.

After all relevant documents have been exchanged, it will then be necessary to instruct a barrister to advise as to whether or not the case is ready. It will also be necessary to obtain a valuation of any properties. Only then will it be possible to obtain a final hearing date.

Because of severe delays at court, it could be at least [one year] from the date that court proceedings are started until the final hearing.

Even if it is necessary to start court proceedings, that does not mean that the case must go all the way to a final hearing. Most cases are resolved by agreement long before a final hearing.

Yours sincerely

section 3 ANCILLARY RELIEF

AR60   Letter advising client about methods of enforcement of a maintenance order

Dear [*client*]

You should appreciate that in the event that the order for maintenance is not complied with there are a number of steps you could take to enforce arrears of maintenance.

First of all you should be aware that there is a strict rule that if any arrears of maintenance are more than one year old, then you need leave (permission) from the court to enforce those arrears. Normally, the court will not give permission to enforce arrears which are more than one year old.

This is because once the court has made an order for maintenance in your favour, the court expects you to return to the court to enforce that order if it is not complied with.

I have listed below the various methods of enforcing orders for maintenance:

CHARGING ORDER

If your former spouse has any property then you could apply for a charging order on that property, somewhat like a mortgage. Whether claimed or not, interest accruing on the original order and the costs of enforcing the security are included in the sum charged by the charging order; and recovery of such sums is not subject to any limitation period. It would then be necessary to obtain a separate order to force a sale of the property.

GARNISHEE ORDER

If you know that your former spouse has money in a bank or building society account, or is owed money by a third person, then we could apply to the court for what is known as a garnishee order. This is an order which requires the bank, building society or other creditor to pay the money directly to you, rather than to your former spouse.

ATTACHMENT OF EARNINGS

If your former spouse is employed, then we can apply to the court for an order that your maintenance is paid direct to you out of your former spouse's salary. This can be extremely effective provided that your former spouse does not change job or is not on a low wage.

The advantage of an attachment of earnings application is that continuing future maintenance can be included, as well as existing arrears.

JUDGMENT SUMMONS

It is possible to apply for a judgment summons where your former spouse is threatened with being sent to prison for not paying the arrears of maintenance. This can be complex and you need to prove beyond reasonable doubt that your former spouse has the money to pay the arrears. [Unfortunately, public funding is not available for this in most cases.]

In any event, it is rare for a judge to make an order sending someone to prison for not paying maintenance.

You should also appreciate that as soon as any steps are taken by you to enforce arrears of maintenance, then if your former spouse's financial circumstances have changed since the original order was made, it is highly likely that your former spouse will apply to the court for that earlier order to be varied so as to be reduced and for any arrears to be remitted (ie cancelled).

If your former spouse is successful in that application to the court then that will prevent you from recovering all or some of the arrears, and only once the application for variation has been heard by the court, can you recover any maintenance.

Yours sincerely

SECTION 4

CHILDREN

Lisa Fabian Lustigman

Children

section **4** CHILDREN

C1 General letter of frequent issues relating to separated parenting

Dear [*client*]

As promised, I am writing to set out the various issues relating to your children. Much of what I say may seem like commonsense, but one aspect of any separation and divorce in which minor children are involved that in my experience needs to be tackled as a priority, is the question of the parents' continuing relationship with and involvement in the lives of their children.

When considering the [financial division], first consideration is given to the needs of children. Equally, if the court has to deal with any matter relating to any child, then the welfare of that child is regarded as paramount. In essence, English law is very much child-centred in its approach to [marital] breakdown.

I will deal with the principal issues by reference to main headings, as follows:

1. The role of the parents in the family

It is important that you and your [spouse/partner] communicate with one another at all times in respect of issues regarding your [children]. Whilst it will need to be understood by all that there is no prospect of reconciliation between the two of you as [husband and wife], you should seek to maintain a united front in your role as parents in the best interests of the children. That requires consultation, honesty and openness in dealings regarding the children.

2. Residence

I understand that it is agreed that [you]/[your] [spouse/partner] will continue to have primary care of the children at the former [matrimonial] home. Plainly, when you [he/she] get your own home, it is important that the children regard both properties as home, and are encouraged to do so.

3. Contact

The law says that it is the right of the children to see the parents, and not the other way round.

You and your [spouse/partner] need to speak regularly to discuss the child[ren]'s upbringing and [his/her] their daily/weekly/monthly programmes, so that contact can work as well as is possible.

I understand that the intention is that there will be a [two-weekly] cycle, with your [spouse/partner] having the children one weekend, you having the children the next weekend. That seems perfectly satisfactory. Punctuality on both sides is important.

At present, you are seeing the children at the [former matrimonial home], and [you also see them overnight on [   ] night]. [I suspect that there may well be a gradual phasing out of the [   ] night arrangement, but if it works well for all concerned, then no changes are necessary.]

It is fairly important that you and your [spouse/partner] keep each other generally informed as to where the children and each of you may be contacted. This is particularly important so that if either [child/son/daughter] suffers any illness, then the other parent can be informed promptly.

4. School requirements

There does need to be flexibility in arrangements so that school requirements are adhered to – homework must be done, and both children will want to be able to participate fully in school events. A proper balance needs to be kept as regards the children's right to see each parent and their school requirements.

5. Holiday requirements

You and your [spouse/partner] need to organise and arrange holiday contact with each other, sufficiently in advance. For example, you should not make bookings or arrangements without first having consulted with one another and agreed dates.

6. Wishes of the children

This is an important consideration, but should be kept in proportion with the age and understanding of each child. Plainly, the wishes of your older [son/daughter] will carry greater weight than those of your younger [child/ren], because of [his/her/their] age(s) and maturity. Having said that, it is important to establish the children's wishes and listen carefully to them. This does not mean that the children get to dictate the holiday.

7. School events

Where there are one-off school events (such as, for example, sports day) then you might consider it sensible for you to attend together, but where there are events taking place over more than one evening (for example, a school play) you might consider attending separately. This is up to the two of you, but does need to be discussed. This is an area that is all the more delicate if either of you has another partner that you may wish to bring along to a school event. If there are one-off occasions that both of you wish to attend, and one of you objects to the partner of the other attending, then it is probably inappropriate for the third party to be present.

8. Birthdays etc

You and your [spouse/partner] do need to address who is to hold the birthday party for each child, and whether it is right that there should be two separate birthday parties, whether for friends or family. Your child[ren] will no doubt want to be involved in the decision-making in respect of parties, and those parties will need to be planned well in advance. You need to consider, also, whether the other parent should be invited. Similar considerations apply in respect of Christmas and other festivals. Often, parents will alternate festivals so that, for example, one parent has the whole of Christmas Day with the children one year, and the other the next and so on.

9. New partners

It is absolutely vital that any new partner is introduced, intentionally, to the children only after careful consultation with the other parent. It is the introduction of third parties into the equation that, in my experience, is the most frequent area of tension between parents over children, and this is something that you need to avoid.

I hope that this letter is instructive in giving you some pointers as to matters that need to be addressed. A key point to take on board is that if you and your [spouse] tackle a potential issue early on, then the opportunities for misunderstandings and disagreements are so much lessened. If you and your [spouse/partner] find difficulty over any issue, then I would recommend that you talk things through with a trained mediator, rather than resorting to the courts, if at all possible. However, if reasonable discussion is not possible, the court does have to be involved. I can let you have details of trained mediators that I would recommend.

Yours sincerely

C2 Letter advising client about the Children Act 1989

Dear [*client*]

The advent of the Children Act 1989 changed the arrangements relating to custody, care and control, and access, as they used to be called.

The Act introduced three new arrangements in connection with children, namely, *residence, contact,* and *parental responsibility.* Although the Act is over 15 years old, people still tend to muddle the terminology although, broadly speaking, they mean the same thing. I will refer to the 'new' 1989 terminology as the courts do not use 'custody, access or care and control'.

I hope the first two are self-explanatory. In brief, a residence order will determine where the child[ren] will live although in practice no orders are made as to residence unless it is necessary to make such an order. A contact order sets out the type of contact and the frequency of it. Parental responsibility is shared jointly between all married parents, even after a divorce, so long as the child is under 18. Unmarried fathers can acquire parental responsibility either by agreement with the mother of the child/ren or by order of the court, and now, if the father's name is on the birth certificate of the child/ren

The court also has power to make two other types of order, namely prohibited steps and specific issue orders.

A prohibited steps order limits when certain parental rights and duties can be exercised.

A specific issue order contains directions to resolve a particular issue in dispute in connection with the child.

A prohibited steps or specific issue order could be obtained where there is a dispute as to the child's education, determining whether the child can be taken abroad, or preventing a parent from seeing the child.

The court will give the following three principles the highest priority:

1. The children's welfare is of the paramount importance;
2. The court shall have regard to the general principle that any delay is likely to prejudice the welfare of the children; and
3. The court shall not make an order unless it considers that doing so would be better for the children than making no order at all.

In deciding whether an order should be made, the court will have regard to:

(a) the ascertainable wishes and feeling of the child concerned (considered in the light of the child's age and understanding);
(b) the child's physical, emotional and educational needs;
(c) the likely effect on the child of any change in his/her circumstances;
(d) the child's age, sex, background, and any other characteristic which the

court considers relevant;

(e) any harm which the child has suffered or is at risk of suffering;

(f) how capable each of the child's parents, and any other person in relation to whom the court considers the question to be relevant, is of meeting the child's needs;

(g) the range of powers available to the court under the Children Act in the proceedings in question.

Under the Children Act, the court will only make a formal residence order, or any other order, if there is a dispute – otherwise no order will be made. There is also a presumption that the court should not intervene unless it is in the best interests of the child. When making any decision, the court's paramount consideration is the welfare of the child. The court recognises that delay is likely to be harmful to the child's welfare, which is entirely separate to the delay when listing a matter for hearing if the court calendar is exceptionally heavy or busy. If the matter is urgent, then it is possible to request an early date due to the nature of the application.

Yours sincerely

C3 Letter advising client about availability of prohibited steps and specific issues orders

Dear [*client*]

You have outlined to me your concerns about the behaviour of [other parent]. [Following our discussion/your letter to me] I write to let you know that the court has power to make two types of order under the Children Act 1989 which may be helpful, namely prohibited steps and specific issue orders.

A prohibited steps order limits when certain parental rights and duties can be exercised.

A specific issue order contains directions to resolve a particular issue in dispute in connection with the child.

A prohibited steps or specific issue order could be obtained when there is a dispute as to the child's education, determining whether the child can be taken abroad, or preventing a parent from seeing that child.

The court does not grant either of these orders lightly. They are never granted in order to put unwarranted obstacles to contact or other issues by one parent against the other.

Please let me know if you would like to discuss these applications further in order to help you make an informed decision.

Yours sincerely

C4 Letter advising father client about parental responsibility

Dear [*client*]

Since you are not married to the child[ren]'s mother, it is essential that you apply for what is known as 'parental responsibility' in respect of your child[ren].

Although this may seem unfair to you, because you were not married to the child[ren]'s mother at the date of your child[ren]'s birth and have not since married the child[ren]'s mother, OR, if the birth was not jointly registered after 1 December 2003, in theory you have no right or duties in connection with the child[ren] until given them by agreement or court order.

Parental responsibility encompasses all the rights and duties which a parent has regarding a child, including the right to decide where the child should go to school, what form of religious upbringing the child should have, and what medical treatment the child should receive.

In practice, it can often mean that schools, doctors, hospitals, social services and other organisations may not deal directly with an unmarried father who is separated from the mother unless the father has parental responsibility.

Also, without parental responsibility, the child[ren]'s mother does not have to consult you on important decisions about the child[ren] and could take the child[ren] out of the country for holidays for a specific period without having to obtain your permission. If she wanted to take the child[ren] abroad for any longer period of time having parental responsibility would strengthen your position.

It is possible to obtain parental responsibility either by agreement with the child[ren]'s mother or by court order, if your name is not on the birth certificate.

In order to obtain parental responsibility by agreement, it is possible to complete a simple form which has to be signed by you and the child[ren]'s mother in the presence of independent witnesses, and that form then has to be lodged at court.

Please let me know if you think the child[ren]'s mother would agree to you having parental responsibility and then I will send the requisite form for her to sign.

If no agreement can be reached, then it will be necessary for you to make an application to the court. Initially, the application is relatively straightforward since standard forms have to be completed.

When considering whether a parental responsibility order should be made, the court will take into account:

section 4 CHILDREN

1.   the commitment shown by you towards the child[ren];
2.   the strength of the attachment between you and the child[ren];
3.   why you are applying for a parental responsibility order.

Broadly speaking, if you have not had contact with the child[ren] for a considerable period of time, it may be extremely difficult to obtain a parental responsibility order.

For you to be successful in obtaining a parental responsibility order, you will have to show that it is in the child[ren]'s best interests for you to have parental responsibility. Fortunately, the current climate is towards both parents having an equal say about parental responsibility issues.

Yours sincerely

C5   Framework of letter confirming advice given to client

Dear [*client*]

YOUR REQUIREMENTS/INSTRUCTIONS

ADVICE GIVEN

I have set out below the advice I gave you at our meeting.

1.   Divorce

2.   Finances

3.   Children

4.   Other

ACTION TO BE TAKEN BY THIS FIRM:

ACTION TO BE TAKEN BY YOU:

ACTION TO BE TAKEN BY THIRD PARTIES:

Yours sincerely

C6   Letter to client enclosing case plan for application for residence and/or contact

Dear [*client*]

I enclose a case plan in respect of your application for residence/contact. You will see that I have set out the most important events in the case with an estimated date of the final hearing, assuming that an agreement cannot be reached.

I will let you know if this case plan is changed in any significant way, or if there is to be any significant delay.

There can often be delays in the progress of a case because of delays at court, or because of delays by the other parent in providing information and documents or taking part in the court's proceedings.

If an agreement cannot be reached quickly, we will have to start court proceedings, which will involve us in preparing the application forms on your behalf.

Once the forms have been sent to the court, the court will then list for hearing what is known as a conciliation [mediation and directions] appointment at which the court will try to see if an agreement can be reached. If no agreement can be reached, the court will give directions as to how the case should progress.

You will then have to prepare a statement setting out the facts of the case.

That statement will be sent to the court and a copy sent to the other parent who will then have to prepare a statement in reply. Sometimes the court insists on statements being prepared simultaneously, although the district judge could order that the statements be served consecutively, so that we [the other side] can see the case we/they have to answer.

You may be given an opportunity to reply to the other parent's statement, by filing a further statement.

If we do not receive that statement, we may have to apply to the court for an Order that the other parent's statement is provided.

We will then have to consider what evidence, information and documents we need to obtain in support of your case and it may be that there are points in the other person's statement which we will try to disprove with documentary evidence.

At the directions hearing, the court will normally order that a CAFCASS (Children and Family Court Advisory and Support Service) officer must prepare a report on your case. The CAFCASS officer or reporter is an independent person who will investigate the case and will normally make a recommendation as to what order should be made.

It is important that you co-operate fully with the CAFCASS officer, since he or she is an important person whose recommendations will have a strong impact on the outcome of your case.

At the directions hearing, the court will sometimes fix a date for the final hearing, or alternatively the court will require a further short directions hearing to take place once the CAFCASS officer's report is received. It may be that only then will the final hearing date be fixed. There are currently delays of [three months] or more in obtaining hearing dates.

Therefore, it could be [nine months] or more since the start of your case before the final hearing takes place.

I fully appreciate that from the date of the application to the date of the final hearing, a considerable amount of time will have elapsed. There may be a number of intervening events of significance. Please therefore keep me abreast of information at all times, as I will update the events in the case plan.

Yours sincerely

C7   Letter to client about the availability of mediation

Dear [*client*]

You should consider whether or not you want to try through mediation to reach agreement with the other parent before starting court proceedings.

Since I am a member of Resolution (formerly the Solicitors Family Law Association) and, in accordance with Resolution's code of practice, I will always endeavour to advise, negotiate and conduct court cases in a manner calculated to encourage and assist both people to achieve a constructive resolution of their difficulties as quickly as possible.

Mediation is a process in which an impartial third person assists those involved in family breakdown to communicate better with one another and to reach their own agreed and informed decisions about some or all of the issues relating to or arising from the separation, divorce, children, finance or property.

One advantage of reaching an agreement through mediation is that mediation does not involve going to court and it is therefore almost always considerably cheaper.

Another advantage of reaching agreement through mediation is that such agreements usually last and you will therefore be more likely to have a better relationship with your ex-spouse [co-habitant] in the future. In cases where children are concerned, you will always have a connection to your ex [-spouse] [co-habitant] through your child[/ren]. It is extremely important for the sake of your child[/ren] that both parents can parent effectively and without rancour.

There are a number of different organisations and individuals who carry out mediation and conciliation. Please let me know if you want further details of these organisations. I am also able to recommend certain mediators to you.

Yours sincerely

C8 Letter to client confirming conciliation [mediation and directions] appointment

Dear [*client*]

The court has now fixed a Conciliation Appointment [Mediation and Directions Appointment] for [   ] [am/pm]] on [   ] 200[   ], at the [Principal Registry of the Family Division, 42–49 High Holborn, London WC1V 6NP].

Please make a note in your diary as you are required to attend. I would suggest that I meet you there approximately 15 minutes before the time fixed so that we may have an opportunity to review the case. Please confirm, preferably in writing, that you will attend the Conciliation [Mediation and Directions] Appointment. [You/[your husband/wife] should bring your child[ren] with you as [he/she/they] is/are over 9 years old.] [You/[your wife/your husband] should also bring the younger children too.]

Please let me know if there are any significant developments or changes in the arrangements for contact between now and the Conciliation [Mediation and Directions] Appointment.

A Conciliation [Mediation and Directions] Appointment is the first appointment following your/[your wife/your husband]'s application for residence/contact/specific issue orders. The purpose of the appointment is to see whether it is possible to reach an agreement which can be incorporated in a consent order and there by avoid a contested final hearing.

It is an informal hearing before a district judge at which an officer from CAFCASS (Children and Family Court Advisory and Support Service) is also present. Both the district judge and the CAFCASS officer will try to establish whether there is any possibility of reaching agreement by identifying the problems between you both and seeing whether those problems can be resolved by discussion and the assistance of themselves as independent 'arbitrators'. An order can only be made on that appointment by consent.

If no agreement is reached, the district judge simply gives directions for the future progress of the case as to preparing statements, the preparation of a CAFCASS report, when the final hearing date is to be fixed and any other necessary directions. The report can take up to 12 weeks to be produced, and depending on how busy the service is, it can even take longer.

If no order by consent is made, you will not see that particular district judge or CAFCASS officer again, thus ensuring that the discussions are kept confidential and are not brought up in the context of the contested hearing.

Yours sincerely

C9   Letter to applicant client explaining court procedure relating to s 8 Applications – scenarios for courts in and outside London

Dear [*client*]

I enclose a draft application relating to residence [contact/specific issue] for your comments. I also think it helpful to refresh you about the procedure.

Once issued, I will serve a copy on [other parent]. S/he must complete a form acknowledging that s/he has received the papers and then return it to the court.

Conciliation [Mediation and Directions] Appointment

Your application will be listed for a short hearing, known as a Conciliation [Mediation and Directions] Appointment. You must attend the appointment with me. It will last for approximately half an hour. [Other parent] is required to attend as well.

[I will let you have a 'Guide for the Parties' issued by the Principal Registry of the Family Division (the particular court that will deal with the case) which gives some background information.] I draw your attention to a number of other points. I will consider with you as to whether we issue your application in the High Court or the [Principal Registry].

The Children and Family Reporter

Children under the age of 9 are not expected to attend the hearing. Arrangements for [named child/ren] to be cared for while you and [other parent] are at the hearing will need to be put in place.

The purpose of the appointment is for the district judge to see if an agreement can be brokered between you and [other parent]. Agreement at this stage would save time and money and avoid the stress and strains of litigation.

A Children and Family Court Reporter [mediator] will be present at court. [He or she will sit next to the district judge and may ask you and [other parent] questions directly at the hearing]. [Child/ren] will not be in the courtroom at any time. [In some courts, the mediator meets with the parents for anything up to an hour before the parties see the judge. The mediator canvasses views and opinions, but does not pass any views or opinions him/herself. When the parties are before the district judge, he/she will simply give directions for the future conduct of the case, which may or may not include a direction for a CAFCASS report].

[The nature of the application and matters in dispute will be outlined to the district judge and the Children and Family Court reporter. If the dispute continues, you both may be given the opportunity of retiring to a private room, together with the Children and Family Court reporter, to attempt to reach settlement. This time set aside for negotiations would enable us better to identify [other parent]'s specific objections. These particular negotiations would be 'without prejudice'; they could not be referred to in open court and should enable you and [other parent] to explore possible solutions without a district judge hearing about the path of the negotiations. The Children and Family Court reporter may also speak independently and privately to any child 9 years of age or over.]

If you cannot reach agreement with [other parent] the district judge will make such directions, if any, as may be appropriate to see the matter to an end. These may include setting a general timetable for the conduct of the case. The district judge is also likely to direct the Children and Family Court reporter to investigate the case, to prepare a report and attend the final hearing to give oral evidence. In preparing the report, the Children and Family Court reporter is likely to interview you, [other parent], [child/ren] and any others as thought appropriate (for example his teacher). The court will list the matter for a final hearing.

As you can see, a Directions Hearing [Mediation and Directions] is purely procedural. Neither of you will be required to give formal evidence at court. I will try to agree the directions with [other parent] before the hearing.

At the Conciliation Appointment [Mediation and Directions Appointment] the district judge is likely to require both of you to file a statement setting out your respective cases by a specified time. It is usual for both statements to be filed at the same time, although they can be ordered to be filed consecutively. We will discuss the contents of your statement at some length, but to reiterate, it will be important to set out clearly your proposals for [child/ren]'s future to include schooling, health care, contact with his/her mother/father and so forth.

In most litigation it is usual for an order to be made that costs will be 'in the application'. This means that the person who ultimately pays the costs of the application will pay for the costs of that hearing. However, in applications relating to children, the court resists making any orders for costs unless there are exceptional circumstances. It is likely, therefore, that, whatever the outcome, you will be responsible for all of this firm's costs in relation to the application.

Final hearing

The report made by the Children and Family Court Reporter will not be disclosed to you or [other parent] until two or three weeks before the final hearing. The report is highly persuasive at the final hearing as district judges are often reluctant to ignore a specialist's opinion. [In large and complex cases there may be a pre-trial review after all evidence has been filed.]

If you have not been able to reach an agreement by the time of the final hearing, then the final hearing will take place. I will instruct a barrister to appear on your behalf at that hearing. It is usual to have a conference, ie a

section 4 CHILDREN

meeting with your barrister, at about the time that your statement is being prepared so that the barrister who is instructed can advise on your case at a key stage and represent you at the hearing.

If your case does reach a final hearing, the usual procedure would be for your barrister to take the district judge through your application forms, any statements, and then put your case. You will then be required to give evidence on which you will be cross examined by [other parent]'s barrister if s/he has one. You may be re-examined or asked further questions by your barrister in respect of any matters arising out of the cross-examination process. I will explain the process more fully if we reach that stage.

[Other parent] will then be required to give evidence. S/he will be cross-examined by your barrister. S/he may subsequently be re-examined by his/her own barrister. If appropriate [other parent]'s barrister (or [other parent]) will then put his/her case. Your barrister will then conclude. The district judge will then make his or her decision, usually giving in full the reasons for the judgment. Sometimes he or she will reserve judgment. This means that the district judge does not give a decision on the day, but lists the matter for a further short hearing a week or so later and will then give judgment.

The court's approach

You and [other parent] have what is known as parental responsibility which is shared jointly between all married parents, even after a divorce, so long as the child is under 18. It represents a bundle of rights, responsibilities and duties which those with parental responsibility have towards the child.

It is important to bear in mind that the court will give the following three principles the utmost priority:

1.   The children's welfare is of the paramount importance;

2.   The court shall have regard to the general principle that any delay is likely to prejudice the welfare of the children; and

3.   The court shall not make an order unless it considers that doing so would be better for the children than making no order at all.

In deciding whether an order should be made, the court will have regard to the following factors:

(a)   the ascertainable wishes and feelings of the children concerned (considered in the light of the child's age and understanding);
(b)   their physical, emotional and educational needs;
(c)   the likely effect on the children of any change in their circumstances;
(d)   their age, sex, background, and any characteristic of theirs which the court considers relevant;
(e)   any harm which they have suffered or are at risk of suffering;
(f)   how capable each of their parents, and any other person in relation to

whom the court considers the question to be relevant, is of meeting their needs;

(g) the range of powers available to the court under the Children Act in the proceedings in question.

You will see on page [   ] of the application that we are seeking the following orders: [   ].

I know that there is a lot of detail in my letter but I thought it sensible to set the procedure out now together with the way the court will approach your case. If you have any questions, please contact me.

Yours sincerely

C10   Letter advising client of appointment of CAFCASS officer

Dear [*client*]

The court has made an Order that a Children and Family Court reporter should investigate your case and prepare a report. You will shortly be contacted direct by a member of the Children and Family Court Advisory and Support Service, generally known by its initials, CAFCASS.

The person from CAFCASS is known as a CAFCASS officer or reporter. He or she will interview both parents, and speak to the child[ren] both with the parents and on their own. The CAFCASS officer will *not* ask the child[ren] directly what the child[ren] would want the court to order since the CAFCASS officer will not want to pressurise the child[ren] into feeling responsible for making the decisions. However, the CAFCASS officer will try to explore the child[ren]'s perspective by talking to them and may also contact the school or any other relevant person or organisation.

Although the judge who makes the final decision in your case does not have to follow the recommendations of the CAFCASS officer, it is unusual for the judge not to follow those recommendations.

Therefore, it is important that you co-operate fully with the CAFCASS officer and that you are as helpful as possible to the CAFCASS officer. Although it is tempting to discuss with the child[ren] what they should say to the CAFCASS officer, he or she will probably notice if the child[ren] have in any way been 'coached' about what to say.

If you are dissatisfied with your meeting with the CAFCASS officer, or if you have not been contacted by him or her within the next four weeks, please let me know.

Yours sincerely

C11 Letter to CAFCASS Officer

Dear [*CAFCASS officer*]

We act for [   ] and we note that you have been appointed to prepare the CAFCASS report.

Please note that the order for directions requires you to attend court at the final hearing, which will take place on [   ]. Therefore, please confirm that you will be available to attend court on that date.

Yours faithfully

C12 Letter to client enclosing the CAFCASS report

Dear [*client*]

I have now received, and enclose, a copy of the CAFCASS report. Please read through this carefully and, if possible, let me have your written comments on the report. If this is not possible for any reason, please telephone me.

Please note that the contents of the report are confidential and you should not disclose a copy of the report, or refer to the contents of the report, to anyone else other than the other parent, the court, me, or the CAFCASS officer. If you do not keep the report confidential, then ultimately you could be punished by the court.

In summary, the CAFCASS report contains the following recommendations [   ].

The judge making the final decision in your case does not have to follow the recommendations of the CAFCASS officer, but it is unusual for his or her recommendations to be ignored unless there are very good reasons to do so.

The CAFCASS officer does not usually attend court unless one of the parents requests their attendance [or there is a direction of the court ordering attendance]. I would advise that [   ].

Yours sincerely

section 4 CHILDREN

C13   Letter of joint instruction to a medical expert

[Medical Expert]

Dear [   ]

In the Matter of [   ] – dob [   ] (Male/Female)

In this case [   ] of [   ], Tel: [   ] ; Fax:
[   ],represents Mr/s [   ], ['s] father/mother, who has
applied for a [residence] Order in respect of [   ].

[   ] of [   ], Tel: [   ], Fax: [   ], represents Mr/
s [   ] , ['s] mother/father, who is resisting Mr/s ['s]
application.

Pursuant to the order of [   ] dated [   ], you are being
instructed jointly by the above solicitors on behalf of each of the parties
named, but on the basis that you will provide an independent expert opinion.
While, of course, it is expected that you may speak to the parents it is essential,
nevertheless, both to your role as independent expert and to the parties'
perception of your independent status that there are no informal, unrecorded
discussions or correspondence with any of the professionals involved in the
case. If you need any further information, please contact the parties' solicitors
in writing and they will liaise and provide the necessary information to you.
Where possible, communication should be by email, fax or by letter.

(The court has given you permission to see [   ].)

The following contact details may be helpful:

Mr/s [   ]
(address)
Tel: (Work) [   ]   Mobile: [   ]

Mr/s [   ]
(address)
Tel: [   ]   Mobile: [   ]
Fax: [   ]

We enclose copies of the applications and orders in this matter, as follows:

Applications

1.
2.

Orders

1.
2.

Statements

1.
2.

In brief, the background to the current application and to your instruction in this matter is as follows:

You are kindly requested to report on the [residence, contact, and leave to remove] aspects of this case, together with the effect on [   ] of the ongoing proceedings.

[As your report is required for court proceedings, it will be governed by Part 35 of the Civil Procedure Rules 1998 ('CPR'). As such and as you will be aware, your overriding duty is to the court and your expert evidence in this matter will be presented to the court. Although you may already be familiar with the Practice Direction which supplements CPR Part 35, for ease of reference we enclose a copy of paragraphs 1 and 2 of the Practice Direction to CPR Part 35 and a copy of the President's Ancillary Relief Advisory Group Best Practice Guide for Instructing a Single Joint Expert.

Your report must be verified by a statement of truth the form of which is as follows:

> 'I believe that the facts I have stated in this report are true and that the opinions I have expressed are correct'.]

Your report should be filed with the court and served on or before 4pm on [   ] 20[   ]. This means that by that time and date copies of your report must reach the following address:

The Court Manager
The Court Office
[Principal Registry of the Family Division
First Avenue House
42-49 High Holborn
London WC1V 6NP]

Please address your report to the Court Manager and quote the case number which is: [   ]. Your report should also be served on each of our firms at the addresses given above. The final hearing is listed for [   ] days commencing [   ]. Your attendance at the hearing may be required.

(In the first instance, would you please send your account to Mr/s [   ] at [   ]).

Yours faithfully

[   ]   [   ]

[Encls: extract from Practice Direction to CPR Part 35; Best Practice Guide for Single Joint Expert]

C14   Letter advising client of need to ascertain child[ren]'s wishes

Dear [*client*]

At this stage it is necessary for me to consider what the child[ren]'s views are in your case. This does not mean that it is necessary or appropriate for me to speak to the child[ren].

Therefore, if I have not already obtained the relevant names and addresses from you, please let me know the names and addresses of the child[ren]'s teachers, health visitors, childminders, or any of your relatives, if appropriate, for me to contact. Please also confirm that you agree to me contacting these people.

If any of these people can confirm that the child[ren] support your views, that would help your case. However, you should not specifically discuss the case with the child[ren] [so far as possible]. All too frequently judges hear about children being 'caught in the middle' of their parents' views/disagreements, which is extremely upsetting for the child[ren]. It is therefore important that we conduct our enquiries in such a way so as to ensure that child[ren] do not feel torn between their parents, or that their 'loyalties' are being divided.

Yours sincerely

C15 Letter advising client of availability of interim residence and/or contact order

Dear [*client*]

Under the Children Act 1989, it is possible to obtain an interim order for residence and/or contact.

An interim Order is an Order which is temporary, pending a final decision by the court at the main hearing.

Please let me know if you want me to discuss whether it is appropriate in your case to apply for an interim order. However, you should be aware that some judges are reluctant to make an interim order, particularly for residence/contact where there has been little or no contact recently, without first having a CAFCASS report prepared.

[In some cases it may not be appropriate for interim contact to take place.]

The other problem is that because of delays at court, it can take several weeks, if not months, to obtain a hearing date with a sufficiently long time allowed for the hearing of an interim application for residence/contact. Please let me know if the matter is one of urgency, in which case I will make enquiries at the court office to see if the matter can be listed as an urgent appointment.

Yours sincerely

C16 Letter advising client about variation or discharge of residence or contact order

Dear [*client*]

As you know, the other parent has obtained an interim order for residence/contact. You should be aware that if either your own circumstances, or those of the child[ren], have changed since the order was made, it may be possible for you to apply for the interim order to be varied or discharged. If an interim contact order is varied, that could increase or decrease the amount of contact.

If interim order was discharged (ie terminated), then it would have no effect.

Please let me know, in the light of any changes that may have occurred, if you want me to apply for the interim order to be varied or discharged. Please remember that 'change' does imply any change of significance. If you are not certain as to whether a change could be deemed to be significant, please let me know and we can discuss the matter further.

Yours sincerely

section 4 CHILDREN

C17 Letter advising client about other parent's parental responsibility

Dear [*client*]

Although the child[ren] is/are currently living with you, all experts involved in children's work strongly emphasize the importance of involving the other parent in the upbringing of the child[ren].

It is therefore important that, through practical arrangements (such as shared involvement in school events) and by consultation on important questions, the other parent is involved in the upbringing of the child[ren]. This does not mean that you are required to consult on the day-to-day matters which affect your household, ie your daily activities.

You should also be aware that the other parent shares parental responsibility with you for the child[ren] and, if you take major decisions without consulting with the other parent, then that parent could apply to the court to prevent you from taking or implementing such decisions.

In practical terms, you should ensure that the other parent receives copies of the child[ren]'s school reports and is involved in the important decisions affecting the child[ren]. These decisions include medical issues and religious education/training and upbringing.

Yours sincerely

C18 Letter advising non-resident parent client about parental responsibility

Dear [*client*]

Although [the child[ren]] is/are not currently living with you, nonetheless you share parental responsibility for the child[ren] with the other parent.

This means that you should be consulted about the major decisions concerning the child[ren] and, if that does not occur, then ultimately you could apply to the court for an order preventing the other parent from making major decisions concerning the child[ren], without your involvement. Parental responsibility does not mean that you are entitled to a say in the daily running of the other parent's household unless you feel that as a result of the way the household is managed, detriment could be caused to your child[ren].

Major decisions include (amongst others) those concerning education, religious education and upbringing and medical issues.

You are also entitled to receive copies of the child[ren]'s school reports and to be involved in school events. You should contact the school direct to ensure that this happens.

Yours sincerely

C19 Letter explaining how step-parents can acquire parental responsibility

Dear [*client*]

As you are now remarried, I am writing to let you know that it is possible for your new spouse to acquire parental responsibility for your child[ren] by your former husband/wife.

The Adoption of Children Act 2002, s 112, inserts a new section 4A into the Children Act 1989, in order to make this possible for step-parents. It can be achieved either by agreement between the step-parent and the parents who have parental responsibility for the child/ren, or by order of the court.

Please let me know if you would like to discuss this further.

Yours sincerely

section 4 CHILDREN

C20 General letter explaining child abduction pitfalls (married parents and fathers with parental responsibility)

Dear [*client*]

I am writing to set out the procedure which must be followed if you wish to take your child/ren out of the jurisdiction on a holiday, without falling foul of the Child Abduction Act 1984.

If you have a residence order made by the court in respect of your children, this will contain a provision preventing the other parent from removing the child or children from the UK without your consent, or by order of the court. Removal from the jurisdiction means outside of England and Wales and it therefore follows that a visit to Scotland for the purposes of the Family Law Act 1986 is a visit out of the jurisdiction. Permission will therefore be required if your former spouse/partner wishes to go abroad or even to Scotland.

It is easy to be caught by the Child Abduction Act 1984 and it is important to know that if you have a residence order for your children in your favour, you will commit no offence if you take or send the child/children out of the UK for a period of less than one month, or a series of periods of less than one month. Equally, if you have the consent of the other parent, no offence will be committed if you take or send the child/children out the UK for more than one month.

If however you do not have a residence order in your favour and the child/children merely live with you, you must obtain the consent of your former spouse/partner if he or she has parental responsibility for the child/children.

Generally speaking, following a divorce, when no residence order has been made, each of you have parental responsibility, however neither of you can take the child/children out of the UK for any time whatsoever without committing a criminal offence under the Child Abduction Act 1984 without first obtaining the necessary consents of your former spouse.

Commonsense, courtesy and good manners must prevail here. The watchword is, that each of you should obtain the consent of the other for a holiday abroad and when doing so, you should each provide to the other, full details to include information about flights, hotels, dates, and a contact number at all times.

Yours sincerely

C21 Letter to client advising on leave to remove children permanently from the jurisdiction

Dear [*client*]

[At our meeting,] we discussed that the court has power to grant an order giving a parent permission (known as 'leave') to remove their children from the jurisdiction of England and Wales. Because you want to take your children abroad to live permanently in a foreign country and you do not have the agreement of your [ex] husband/wife, it is necessary for you to apply for leave. [This may not apply if you are not married to the child's father.]

Generally speaking, it is usually (but not always) the case that the parent seeking leave is the parent with whom the children mainly live. The situation is far more complicated where there is a shared care agreement in place.

The case law surrounding leave to remove applications makes clear the principle that the welfare of the children is the paramount consideration, but that leave should not be withheld unless the interests of the children and those of the primary carer are clearly shown to be incompatible. Although there is much current debate about whether judges too readily grant leave to remove to the parent with care, the trend has been that the courts are slow to interfere with the way of life chosen by the parent who has the principal care of the children (in this case yourself) particularly since any interference by the court may cause that person unhappiness or distress or even bitterness and this will reflect adversely upon that parent's care for the children and therefore upon the children's welfare.

This does not mean that the court will automatically give permission to the parent with whom the child[ren] live[s]. There is a two-part test that the courts apply. In the first instance, the judge will need to be satisfied that there is a genuine motivation for the move and that it is not the intention of the parent applying to exclude the other parent from the children's life and thereby bringing contact between the children and the other parent to a rather abrupt end. Secondly, the applicant parent's proposals will be given very careful scrutiny to decide if they are reasonable, and founded on well-researched and soundly investigated practical proposals with particular emphasis on:

1. contact with the parent with whom the children do not live;
2. contact with the extended family;
3. accommodation;
4. education;
5. location.

If the court is satisfied that the primary carer's plans are reasonable, and that the person's motivation is genuine, they will then consider the other parent's position, including whether their concerns are motivated by genuine concern for the children's welfare or driven by some ulterior motive. A judge will have foremost in his mind the likely impact of the proposed move on the other

section 4 CHILDREN

parent's relationship with the child, and particularly with their ability to have contact with the children.

When giving judgment, the judge will balance his decision against a review of the children's welfare as the paramount consideration, as set out under the statutory checklist:

(a) the ascertainable wishes and feelings of the child concerned (considered in the light of the child's age and understanding);
(b) his physical, emotional and educational needs;
(c) the likely effect on him of any change in his circumstances;
(d) his age, sex, background and any characteristic of his which the court considers relevant;
(e) any harm which he has suffered or is at risk of suffering;
(f) how capable each of his parents, and any other person in relation to whom the court consider the question to be relevant, is of meeting his needs; and
(g) the range of powers available to the court under the Children Act in the proceedings in question.

In these cases, great weight is given to the emotional and psychological well-being of the primary carer. If the children are of a sufficient age for their wishes and feelings to be taken into account, the court will consider these. In all cases, a child and family reporter will be appointed to prepare a report after meeting with both parents and the children. The judge does not have to follow the recommendations (if there are any) contained in the report, and the judge will no doubt want to hear evidence from the children and family reporter if the matter proceeds to a final hearing.

In granting permission, the court may set certain conditions by way of safeguards to protect the children's ongoing relationship with the other parent. A common condition is the court requiring that the parent seeking leave to remove from this jurisdiction to obtain an order in the country they are moving to in the same terms as the English order (**'a mirror order'**) to protect the arrangements for contact in the new country. This would make it easier for the other parent to enforce than the English order.

Procedurally, the application for leave to remove is made on Form [C1/C2]. The court will fix a conciliation appointment. All parties have to attend, including any children over the age of nine years. The district judge will sit with the Children and Family reporter. The proposals will be explored, questions will be asked and if resolution cannot be achieved at that appointment, the district judge will give directions for the future conduct of the case. This will most likely include filing statements by certain dates, replying to those statements and a date for the Children and Family reporter to make his or her report to the court and the parties. A date will be fixed for the final hearing.

Please let me know if you want to make an application for leave to remove.

Yours sincerely

C22 Letter to a non-resident father without parental responsibility whom the resident mother thinks may be going abroad with a child without consent

Dear Sir

We act for [name of client]. [Client] has instructed us that you may be considering taking [name of child/children] out of the jurisdiction of England and Wales, where he/she/they are habitually resident, to [name of country]. Please note that you do not have parental responsibility for the children. [Name of client] does not consent to your taking the children out of the jurisdiction, and if you do so without her permission, this will be construed as an abduction. It is a criminal offence under the Child Abduction Act 1984 for a parent or guardian of the child to take or send the child out of the United Kingdom without the consent of any other person who is a parent or guardian of the child, and in this case, (name of client).

If you are in any doubt as to the contents of this letter, we urge you to take independent legal advice. You can obtain the name of a specialist family solicitor in your area by telephoning Resolution (formerly the Solicitors Family Law Association) on: 01689 820272.

Yours faithfully

C23 General letter advising on child abduction

Dear [client]

I am writing following our [meeting/telephone discussion] to set out what would constitute an abduction of your child[ren] by your spouse/partner in the family law arena.

In family law, abduction is defined as the removal or retention of a child by parents, guardians, or close family members, without the consent of the parent, guardian or person who has the right in law to care for that child or children, ie, you.

An abduction would typically take place following the breakdown of the relationship between two parents. It can involve one parent who has gone abroad, and following the breakdown of the relationship with the spouse or partner, has returned the children to his or her family and/or country of origin.

Child abductions within the jurisdiction are hard enough to deal with, but when the child is taken out of the jurisdiction to another country, the problems can become severe. Countries who are signatories to the Convention mentioned below should, in theory and in practice, co-operate in accordance with the Schedules to the Child Abduction and Custody Act. Clearly, abductions of children to countries who are not signatories to the Hague Convention cause serious difficulties. I emphasise that if you have any concerns about abduction of your child[ren], please contact me immediately.

Schedule 1 of the Child Abduction and Custody Act 1985 covers the Convention on the Civil Aspects of International Child Abduction ('The Hague Convention'). The advent of Brussels II (Regulation 1347/1000 (EC)) in March 2005 signalled changes to the intra EU Child Abduction Provisions. As a result, the Hague Convention remains in force, but judges within the EC (except for Denmark) will apply the new provisions of Brussels II as an adjunct to the Hague Convention provisions, as well as in priority to them. This may sound complicated, but effectively, it means that the parent from whom a child has been abducted has the right to ask the 'home' court to retain jurisdiction over the matter before jurisdiction shifts to the new country court. There are provisions setting out when jurisdiction changes.

Section 1 of Child Abduction Act 1984 makes it a criminal offence for a person connected with a child under the age of 16, to take or send the child out of the UK without the appropriate consent. Section 2 makes it a criminal offence if a person, without authority or reasonable excuse, takes or detains a child under the age of 16 so as to remove that child from the lawful control of any person having such lawful control.

Reunite (the International Child Abduction Centre) has produced an extremely helpful and important information pack which you can obtain by contacting Reunite on: 020 7375 3440 (the advice line), or 020 7375 3441 (the administration line).

Please contact me as a matter of urgency if you think your spouse or partner is intending to abduct your child[ren].

Yours sincerely

C24   Letter outlining Court's approach to claims pursuant to Schedule 1 to the Children Act 1989 to Respondent

Dear [client]

The courts have the jurisdiction to make orders in relation to capital and property for the benefit of children. Your partner [   ] can bring a claim against you seeking the transfer and/or settlement of a property and/or a lump sum.

The factors which the court must take into account are all the circumstances, including:

(a)   the income, earning capacity, property and other financial resources which each of you has or is likely to have in the foreseeable future;
(b)   the financial needs, obligations and responsibilities which each of you has or is likely to have in the foreseeable future;
(c)   the financial needs of the child(ren);
(d)   the income, earning capacity (if any), property and other financial resources of the child(ren);
(e)   any physical or mental disability of the child(ren); and
(f)   the manner in which the child(ren) was being, or was expected to be, educated or trained.

If the resources are available, a lump sum order will be made, which would be used to finance the purchase of a new property, to be put in trust, for your partner [   ] to live in, until the children are 18 or 21.

If a lump sum is ordered to help your partner [   ], to pay off debts or to reimburse specific costs, eg baby equipment, it would not be repayable.

If there was an order that a property was put in trust for your children, it would only be for their minority, ie until they reached the age of 17 or finish in full-time secondary (or tertiary) education whichever was the later. There would be a trust deed setting out the precise terms of occupation. It is normal for the carer of the children (usually the mother) to have the right to live in that property free of rent during that period. When the children reach the age of 17 or finish in full-time education the property would then be sold and the entire proceeds on sale (or proportion of the property that you had invested expressed as a percentage of that property) would be paid to you.

In most cases, the courts no longer have power to make orders for child maintenance; an application to the Child Support Agency has to be made for child maintenance to be assessed.

In your case, I advise that the following factors will be particularly relevant:

[   ]

Both of you have a duty to give full and proper disclosure of your financial position so that a proper financial arrangement can be made.

Yours sincerely

C25 Letter to client explaining new rules on child support payments

Dear [client]

I am writing to let you know about the new rules on child support payments which came into effect in April 2003. In effect, these rules have become the benchmark for calculation of all future child support payments. They apply to people earning more than £2,000 net per week. Please note that investment income is not included in the calculation of net income.

The Government has opted for a relatively simply formula, which is readily understandable, but because of its rough and ready nature, there are some injustices in it.

The formula looks at your [gross salary including bonuses] [taxable profit as per Inland Revenue returns or gross receipts] but excluding benefits in kind, investment and dividend incomes and then to calculate your net income you deduct income tax, Class 1 National Insurance contributions and full pension contributions made by you (unless you have a pensions mortgage in which case there is a cap of 75% of such contributions). For the purposes of calculating net income, there is a cap, or upper limit of £104,000 net a year, meaning that any net income above that figure is ignored by the CSA.

Since you have [1/2/more than 2] children, under the Formula you will have to pay [15/20/25%] of your net income in child support payments, subject to possible reductions.

The reductions to child support payments are:

1. By one-seventh if [/the children] stay with you for between 52 and 103 nights a year and two-sevenths if [stays/they stay] with you between 104 and 155 nights a year. If the children stay with you more than 155 nights per year, greater reductions apply.

2. By 15% if you live in a household with one other child or stepchild, by 20% for 2 and 25% for more than 2.

It is possible also to ask the Child Support Agency (CSA) to vary the amount payable in certain circumstances. Variations can be sought to take account of the following:

1. whether the net income declared is inconsistent with your lifestyle, or you have assets apart from your home and business in excess of £65,000;
2. your travel costs for having contact with [the children];
3. the costs of illness or disability of any of your children;
4. the repayment of debts incurred (other than, for example, gambling debts or fines);
5. the boarding school element of private school fees (to be ascertained by calculating the difference between the day school and boarding rate);

6.   costs incurred by you in supporting loans and other expenses for the main home of [/your children].

Notwithstanding the CSA changes, the court will continue to be able to make agreed orders regarding child support. It will also be able to make certain other orders, for example school fees orders and where the CSA confirms that the income cap of £104,000 net a year applies, orders topping up the total amount payable.

If the first child maintenance order is made after the new rules came into effect, it is not possible for either parent to opt out of the new CSA system even by agreement. Once the order has been in existence for 12 months notice can be given to opt into the CSA regime. The notice period is a further 2 months; after then the CSA can assess themselves the level of child maintenance. This means that a post-April 2003 court order could be brought to an end after 14 months.

But, if the first child support order was made before April 2003, the court will ordinarily retain sole jurisdiction over the regulation of the amount of child support payable from time to time, the only exception being if [your wife] goes on to state benefits after which the new rules will, however, automatically apply.

Yours sincerely

C26   Letter to unmarried parent explaining relevance of CSA application in Schedule 1 Children Act 1989 proceedings

Dear [   ]

Child Support Agency ('CSA') application

As I have previously explained to you, as [   ][,] [and] [   ] [currently live with you] [are within your day-to-day care], you are able to make an application to the CSA for maintenance in respect of [him][her][them].

Different rates of maintenance will apply depending on your child[ren]'s father's net weekly income, which is calculated by deducting income tax, National Insurance contributions and pension scheme contributions from his gross yearly earned income and dividing the figure by 52.

As you have [   ] child[ren], your child['s][ren's] father will be required to pay [15][20][25]% of his net weekly income by way of maintenance, subject to any deductions that may be made by the CSA, for example, to acknowledge any overnight contact your child[ren] [has][have] with [his][her][their] father in excess of 51 nights a year.

I should point out that an income ceiling is imposed by the CSA, so that any income exceeding £2,000 net per week, or £104,000 net per annum, earned by your child[ren]'s father will be ignored, by the CSA but not necessarily the court.

Despite the ceiling, there are substantial advantages to your making a CSA maintenance application to assess the father's means. If, for example, it is found that his income exceeds the ceiling, the court will then be able to make what is known as 'top-up orders', pursuant to a further application by you under Schedule 1 to the Children Act 1989, which has the effect of 'topping-up' the level of maintenance your children receive. Such maintenance can include any expenses for the child[ren], to include (for example), the costs of hiring a carer for [your] [the] child[ren] or a carer's allowance for you in lieu of maintenance for yourself, although it should be noted that a separate application will need to be made if you wish to obtain payments from your child[ren]'s father in respect of school fees or additional payments in respect of any disabilities your child[ren] may have.

I appreciate that this may seem rather complicated, and I will be pleased to answer any questions you may have in relation to CSA and Schedule 1 Children Act applications.

Yours sincerely

C27 Letter to respondent re application brought by other partner

Dear [*respondent*]

As [I have not heard from you/we do not appear to be making any progress], my client has instructed me to make an application to the Child Support Agency for a maintenance assessment in relation to your children [   ] and [   ].

She has also instructed me to make an application under Schedule 1 Children Act 1989 for an order for a lump sum and/or settlement of property to enable her and the children to rehouse themselves. This will be served upon you shortly.

Yours sincerely

C28   Letter to applicant re procedure of Schedule 1 Children Act 1989 application (case plan)

Dear [*client*]

I write to confirm that, as agreed, I will issue an application for a lump sum and/or settlement of property order at the [   ] County Court.

In order to proceed with your application, you must complete, sign and return to me the following forms:

1.   Application for an order, Form C1.

[2.   Form C1A.]

2.   Application for a financial order, Form C10.

3.   Supplementary application for a financial order, Form C10A.

Please check these forms. If they are correct, sign them in ink where I have indicated in pencil and return them to me.

I shall then send them to the court with the court fee of £[   ] and your application will be issued.

I will then serve your application by sending the forms to your former partner by first class post. Your former partner, [   ], must complete a form acknowledging that he has received the papers, together with Form C1A if you have ticked 'yes' to box 7 of Form C1, and return this form to the [   ] Court. He must also complete the financial form C10A which the Court will have sent him. Copies of these documents will be sent to you by the Court.

I will then list your application for a short directions hearing which you should attend. It will only last for half-an-hour or so. Your former partner, [   ], will be required to attend as well. I will try and agree the directions with your [former partner/former partner's solicitor].

At that hearing a judge will look at your application and the documents filed at court and make an order for directions. He or she may require both of you to file a statement setting out your respective cases. It is usual for your statement to be filed first as you are the applicant. Your former partner, [   ], will then have the opportunity to respond in his statement to your arguments. Sometimes, you will be given the opportunity to reply to your former partner [   ]'s statement. If there are any queries over the value of any properties which you may own or any other significant assets the court may direct that valuations are carried out. Often it is simpler to deal with any queries dealing with your former partner [   ]'s financial position by putting a list of questions to him. If this is done the court may, with your agreement, order that those questions be answered but the court cannot order this of its own volition in these types of cases.

Finally, the court will list the matter for a final hearing. It is usual for an order to be made that costs will be in the application. This means that the person who ultimately pays the costs of your application will pay for the costs of that hearing. As you can see, a directions hearing is purely procedural. Neither of you will be required to give evidence at court.

By a specified time after the directions hearing you will then need to prepare your statement within a certain time frame, usually 28 days, and your former partner, [   ], will need to do the same subsequently. Any queries in relation to each other's financial disclosure will need to be dealt with and valuations carried out, all within the timetable imposed by the court.

If you have not been able to reach an agreement by the time of the final hearing, then the final hearing will take place. I will instruct a barrister to appear on your behalf at that hearing. It is usual to have a conference ie a meeting with the barrister at about the time that your statement is being prepared so that the barrister who is instructed can advise on your case at a key stage.

If your case does proceed to court, the usual procedure would be for your barrister to take the judge through your application forms, any statements, and all documents and then to put your case. You will then be required to give evidence on which you will be cross-examined by your former partner [   ]'s barrister. You may be re-examined or asked further questions by your barrister in respect of any matters arising out of the cross-examination process. I will take you through this procedure nearer the time.

Your former partner, [   ], will then be required to give evidence too. He will be cross-examined by your barrister. He may be subsequently re-examined by his own barrister. Your former partner [   ]'s barrister will then put his case. Your barrister will then conclude. The judge will then make his or her decision, usually giving a full and reasoned judgment. Sometimes he or she will reserve judgment. This means that the judge does not give his decision on the day, but lists the matter for a further short hearing a week or so later, and then give judgment.

After the judge has made his or her decision he or she will make a decision on the question of legal costs, in respect of which I have written to you separately.

Yours sincerely

C29   Letter to court enclosing application for orders under Schedule 1 Children Act 1989

Dear Sirs

We act for the applicant in this matter. We enclose, for issue please, the following documents (with copies for service and the court where appropriate):

1.   Application for an order in Form C1 [and Form C1A].

2.   Financial Form C10.

3.   Supplemental Financial Form C10A.

4.   Cheque for £[   ].

Please return these documents to us so that we can serve them upon the respondent.

Thank you for your assistance.

Yours faithfully

Enc.

C30   Letter to respondent serving application for orders under Schedule 1 Children Act 1989

Dear [*respondent*]

Further to my recent letter, I enclose by way of service:

1.   My client's application for various orders under Schedule 1 to the Children Act 1989 in Forms C1 [and C1A].

2.   My client's financial application Form C10.

3.   My client's supplemental application Form C10A.

4.   Notice of proceedings form issued by the court together with a blank acknowledgement of service form which you will need to complete and send to the [   ] court at [   ] within 14 days.

5.   Statement of Means C10A which you will also need to complete and file at court within 21 days.

I recommend that you obtain independent legal advice regarding the contents of this letter. I suggest that you contact Resolution, (formerly the Solicitors Family Law Association) on 01689 820272 for details of specialist family solicitors.

Yours sincerely

Enc.

C31   Letter to client enclosing draft consent order

Dear [*client*]

I enclose a copy of the draft consent order which has been prepared setting out the terms of agreement that have been reached.

Please read through the consent order carefully to ensure that you fully understand it and also to make sure that all the necessary points are included in the consent order.

I will now explain the main terms of the consent order.

[   ].

If you agree with the terms of the consent order, please sign and return the consent order to me as soon as possible. If you have any questions or queries, please contact me so that we can go through the items in issue.

Yours sincerely

C32 Letter advising client about consequences of failure to reach agreement

Dear [*client*]

You now have to consider whether or not to try to make further proposals to reach an agreement, or whether you now want to proceed with your case to a final hearing. In brief, the proposals on each side thus far are:

1.

2.

3.

It is important to understand that significant extra costs will be incurred in the last month before any final hearing. Also, the costs of the final hearing itself, when you will be represented by a barrister, will also be substantial. You may end up spending another [several thousand] pounds and this must be borne in mind.

Also, some clients find going to court distressing, particularly if clients have not seen their spouses or former spouses for some time. We can talk about ways to minimise this type of anxiety, if you think this would be helpful.

I would like to stress that until your [spouse] closes the door on negotiations, that door remains open for settlement. We have spoken about your barrister's brief fees, which will become due on [a fixed] [date], even if we subsequently settle before the final hearing. This does not mean that you should still press on and go forward with a final hearing regardless.

Please let me know if you would like to go through the various proposals and options. It is important that we make any new proposals in a timely manner.

Yours sincerely

C33 Letter to court with statement

Dear Sirs

We act for the [applicant/respondent] in this matter. We enclose our client's statement for filing. Please note that a copy of this has been served upon the [applicant/respondent].

Yours faithfully

Enc.

C34 Letter serving statement on respondent's solicitors

Dear Sirs

We enclose by way of service a copy of our client's statement dated
[   ]. You will recall that district judge [   ] ordered your client
to file a statement within [   ] days of the same. Please confirm that we
can expect to receive it on [   ], so as to avoid any unnecessary delay.

Yours faithfully

Enc.

C35 Letter to other party's solicitors proposing directions

Dear Sirs

We refer to the directions hearing which has been fixed for [   ] and
write to propose the following directions:

1. That our client file a statement setting out her case within 28 days.

2. That your client file the same in reply within 28 days.

3. That our client file a statement in reply if so advised within 21 days
   thereafter.

4. The value of the property/ies known as [   ] be agreed, if possible,
   and in default of agreement as to a jointly nominated valuer, the said
   property be valued by a valuer appointed by the President of the Royal
   Institution of Chartered Surveyors, the costs of such valuation to be paid
   by the parties jointly.

5. That discovery be effected by way of voluntary questionnaires, if so
   advised, to be served within 21 days of the conclusion of filing of any
   evidence, such replies to be provided within 28 days thereafter. In this
   way discovery will be streamlined as it is pursuant to rule 2.63 of the
   Family Proceedings Rules 1991.

6. [That the matter be listed for a Directions Appointment to last for one
   hour], to be treated as a quasi FDR type appointment.]

7. The matter be listed for a hearing with a time estimate of [   ]
   day(s) as soon as possible after the filing of all evidence and any replies
   being served [and the further directions appointment/quasi FDR type
   appointment.

Kindly confirm that you agree to these directions so that an order can be made
by consent [without attendance].

Yours faithfully

C36 Letter instructing surveyors to value property for private client

For the attention of [   ]

Messrs

Surveyors and valuers

Dear Sirs

Proceedings between [   ] as petitioner

And [   ] respondent

Case no [   ] in the [Principal Registry of the Family Division]

We act for [   ] in connection with his/her [matrimonial/Children Act] affairs. [   ] act for [   ].

At a directions appointment on [   ], the court directed that the [former matrimonial] home at [   ], ('   '), which is owned by Mr/s [and] Mr/s [   ] [jointly], should be valued independently by a jointly appointed expert. The parties have agreed that your firm should conduct the independent valuation.

As the valuation will be required for court proceedings, it will be governed by Part 35 of the Civil Procedure Rules ('CPR'). Consequently, your overriding duty in preparing the report will be to the court. Although you may already be familiar with the practice direction, which supplements CPR Part 35, we enclose, for ease of reference, a copy of paragraphs 1 and 2 of the Practice Direction, together with an example declaration which you may wish to use in your report. Office Copy Entries from the Land Registry are also enclosed with this letter.

In the preparation of your report, we should be grateful if you would bear in mind the following:

1. The valuation of [   ] is to be carried out on the basis of 'market value' as defined by The Royal Institute of Chartered Surveyors as follows: 'the estimated amount for which an asset should exchange on the date of valuation between a willing buyer and a willing seller in an arms length transaction after proper marketing wherein the parties had each acted knowledgably, prudently and without compulsion'.

2. Please set out the factors which you have taken into account in formulating your valuation.

3. [Please include your opinion of the current market rent attributable to the property].

4. Please have regard to recent sales [and current rental values] of comparable properties, setting out in your report details of such comparable properties, to include (where appropriate) asking and completed sale prices.

5. Please provide your opinion on: [here set out any other matters, such as sale by lot, or application for planning permission, or income possibilities, or any other relevant matter and also specifically state if a structural survey is required, as this is not required for a formal valuation unless specifically requested].

6. Kindly ensure that your report is addressed to the court and not to the parties or their solicitors.

7. [   ] currently resides at the property. Please do not liaise with either Mr/s or Mr/s [   ] directly in relation to the valuation. Neither Mr/s or Mr/s [   ] should be present when you attend at the property for inspection/both Mr/s and Mr/s [   ]/and [   ] will be present during the inspection of the property. Kindly refrain from discussing the valuation directly with them. Please liaise with [   ] telephone number [   ] to make arrangements for access to and inspection of the property.

8. Kindly direct any enquiries you may have in respect of the property or in respect of any other information or documentation which you require in order to carry out your valuation report in writing to [solicitors] [   ] and copy to [   ]. Similarly, please copy to [   ] any correspondence which you receive in response to such enquiries to include a schedule of any documents received. Following the preparation of your valuation report, please forward one copy to both firms of solicitors quoting the above reference.

9. A court appointment has been listed in this matter on [   ]. Given the court timetable, it is important that the valuation be produced as soon as possible, and any event, no later than [   ]. However, it would assist the parties if you were able to prepare your report in advance of that date. Kindly confirm whether or not this will be possible.

10. It has been agreed between the parties that Mr/s and Mr/s [   ] will be settling your firm's fees (equally). Please send separate invoices requesting one half of the valuation fee to [   ] and to [   ].

Before proceeding with this matter, kindly provide us with an estimate of your likely charges for producing the above report, for approval. Please also confirm that you have had no prior dealings with either party which could cause conflict of interest.

We look forward to hearing from you.

section 4 CHILDREN

Yours faithfully   Yours faithfully

....

[   ]   [   ]

Encls:

1. Copy title register;
2. Extract from Practice Direction to CPR Part 35;
3. Example expert's declaration.

C37   Letter to client concerning instruction of counsel

Dear [*client*]

I am writing to ask if you have any preference as to which barrister you want me to instruct to represent you in your case.

I would strongly recommend [   ] who is a specialist family law barrister of [   ] years' experience from a leading Family Law Chambers of Barristers.

I will assume unless I hear from you to the contrary within seven days that you have no objection to me instructing this barrister and that you do not have any other particular barrister you would prefer me to instruct.

I should say that if you do want me to instruct a different barrister I would be extremely reluctant to instruct a barrister of whom I have no experience, but we will discuss this if it applies to your case. In any event, it is important that we instruct the counsel of your choice as soon as possible, as the Bar tends to be booked months in advance.

Yours sincerely

C38   Letter to client prior to final hearing

Dear [*client*]

It is now only a few weeks before the final hearing of your case and I am making preparations for that hearing.

There is a great deal of work to be done and considerable costs will be incurred from now on. Therefore, please inform me if there has been any change in your circumstances since we last met, or if anything has happened that could be relevant to your case. For example, please let me know if there has been any [sudden] increase or decrease to the current contact regime, or if there are any difficulties with those arrangements. If there have been any issues about schooling or holidays, it is important that I have the most up to date position in order to properly instruct your barrister. Please also send me copies of all written communications between you and [other parent].

I enclose a checklist of things we need to complete/discuss/consider:

[   ]

[If there has been any change in your financial circumstances, please let me have up-to-date copies of all relevant financial documents such as payslips, P60s, credit card statements, bank statements and so on.]

[Please also let me know if you think there has been a change in the value of any properties involved in your case. It may be that we will have to request an update on the previous valuation.]

[Finally, also let me know if you believe there has been any recent change in the financial circumstances of [the other parent].]

Yours sincerely

C39   Letter advising client about procedure at final hearing

Dear [*client*]

I write to advise you as to the procedure at the final hearing itself.

The final hearing has been fixed for [   ] days. Normally, the court will only sit from [10.30 am to 1 pm] and from [2 pm to 4.00/30 pm], without a break, apart for lunch.

The main issues still in dispute are:

[   ].

Your barrister [   ], will represent you at the hearing and your case will be conducted by your him/her. However, you will have to give evidence and that will involve both giving evidence to your barrister and also being cross-examined by the other barrister.

You are liable to be cross-examined on anything referred to in any statements which have been prepared by you and you may be asked to explain any documents which have been produced. [You could also be asked any question to do with finances, which is considered relevant to your case.] Would you please telephone me to discuss this further, as there are a number of 'tips' I can give you to help you give your evidence effectively. Unless you are familiar with the process, giving evidence can be stressful. Whilst I cannot 'rehearse' your evidence with you, I would like to dispel any fears you may have, in order to minimise the stress of this experience.

Yours sincerely

section **4** CHILDREN

C40   Letter advising client of outcome of case

Dear [*client*]

I write to report on the outcome of your case.

ANY FURTHER ACTION YOU ARE REQUIRED TO TAKE

ANY FURTHER ACTION WE WILL TAKE

ACCOUNTING FOR OUTSTANDING MONEY

ORIGINAL DOCUMENTS

COPY OF THE ORDER/TRANSCRIPT

I am returning to you a bundle of original documents which are no longer needed by me.

[As agreed, I will keep some other original documents, namely [   ]].

RETRIEVAL OF PAPERS

Once [the balance of] my firm's costs have been paid [by the Legal Services Commission], your file of papers will be placed in storage and will normally be kept for a period of [15 years]. If, however, you wish to keep your file of papers, we will gladly send them to you but we may retain a complete copy of the file in accordance with practice approved by The Law Society.

If you ever need access to your file of papers, you should contact this firm. [It may take a few days/a week or so for the papers to be retrieved, since we normally store them in a different building.] [My firm may make a small charge for retrieval of the papers.]

Yours sincerely

SECTION 5

INJUNCTIONS

Lisa Fabian Lustigman

Injunctions

section 5 INJUNCTIONS

IN1 Letter to client applying for injunctions about application with notice

Dear [*client*]

I write further to our meeting on [   ].

You have instructed me to apply to the court for an injunction against [   ]. I have now drafted your application and supporting statement which is enclosed.

Please ensure that your sworn statement is factually correct because you may be questioned in court very closely on its contents. If any amendments are required, please let me know. Please take the statement to another firm of solicitors for it to be sworn. There will be a statutory swear fee of £5 plus £2 for each exhibit. Alternatively, you may take it to your local county court at [   ]. There is no fee.

I have advised you that you have sufficient grounds on which to make an application for an injunction. I have explained the two ways in which you can apply for an injunction – with or without notice. A without notice application is one which is made without your husband/partner, [   ], knowing about it. Such applications can only be made where there is a real and immediate danger of serious injury or irreparable harm. As there does not appear to be such a threat in your case, I have advised you that it is inappropriate to apply without notice. I have advised you that it would be better to apply on notice.

If your application is granted, the injunction will forbid your husband/partner, [   ], from:

(a)   using or threatening violence against you [and the children].
(b)   intimidating, harassing or pestering you [and the children].

This type of order is known as a non-molestation order.

The application is also for an order requiring your husband/partner, [   ], to vacate your property. This is known as an occupation order.

When deciding whether to make an order requiring your husband/partner, [   ], to vacate your property, the court will consider various factors:

[*If right to occupy*]

The court will have regard to all the circumstances including:

1.   the housing needs and housing resources of each of you and of any children;
2.   your respective financial resources;
3.   the likely effect of any order, or of any decision by the court not to exercise its powers, on the health, safety or wellbeing of each of you and of any children; and

4.   the conduct of each of you in relation to each other and otherwise.

The court will also apply what is known as 'the balance of harm' test. If it appears to the court that you or any children are likely to suffer significant harm attributable to the conduct of your husband/partner, [   ], the court must make an occupation order unless it appears to the court that you or your children are likely to suffer even greater harm if such an order is made.

If such an order were made in your favour it could be for a specified period, until the occurrence of a specified event or until another order is made by the court. If it is for a specified period, then it is often for six months.

[If applicant is a former spouse and has no existing right to occupy]

The court will have regard to all the circumstances including:

1.   the housing needs and housing resources of each of you and of any children;
2.   your respective financial resources;
3.   the likely effect of any order, or of any decision by the court not to exercise its powers, on the health, safety or wellbeing of each of you and of any children; and
4.   the conduct of each of you in relation to each other and otherwise.

The court will also apply 'the balance of harm' test. If it appears to the court that you or any children are likely to suffer significant harm attributable to the conduct of your former husband/partner, [   ], the court must make an occupation order unless it appears to the court that you or any children are likely to suffer even greater harm if such an order is made.

There are three additional factors that the court must consider:

1.   the length of time which has elapsed since you last lived together;
2.   the length of time which has elapsed since the marriage was dissolved or annulled (if relevant); and
3.   the existence of any current legal proceedings between you for a financial order pursuant to the divorce, or for an order under Schedule 1 Children Act 1989 for financial relief or relating to the legal or beneficial ownership of the property. *[Delete as appropriate]*.

If such an order were made in your favour, it would be for a period of six months only but may be extended repeatedly for further six-month periods.

[If applicant is a cohabitant/former cohabitant and has no existing right to occupy]

The court will have regard to all the circumstances including:

1.   the housing needs and housing resources of each of you and of any children;
2.   your respective financial resources;
3.   the likely effect of any order, or of any decision by the court not to

exercise its powers, on the health, safety or wellbeing of each of you and of any children; and
4.   the conduct of each of you in relation to each other and otherwise.

In addition, the court will consider:

1.   whether you have any children, or whether there are children involved for whom either of you have or have had parental responsibility;
2.   the length of time during which you have lived together as husband and wife;
3.   the length of time which has elapsed since you stopped living together; and
4.   the existence of any current legal proceedings between you for an order under Schedule 1 Children Act 1989 for financial relief or relating to the legal or beneficial ownership of the property.

The court must also consider whether you or any children are likely to suffer significant harm attributable to the conduct of your former partner, [   ]; the court may make an order unless it appears to the court that either you or the children are likely to suffer even greater harm if such an order is made.

If such an order were made in your favour, it would be for a period of six months and can be renewed for a further period of six months, ie in total twelve months.

[*Where neither applicant nor respondent have right to occupy*]

The court will have regard to all the circumstances including:

1.   the housing needs and housing resources of each of you and of any children;
2.   your respective financial resources;
3.   the likely effect of any order, or of any decision by the court not to exercise its powers, on the health, safety or wellbeing of each of you and of any children; and
4.   the conduct of each of you in relation to each other and otherwise.

The court will also apply 'the balance of harm' test. If it appears to the court that you or any children are likely to suffer significant harm attributable to the conduct of your husband/partner, [   ], the court must make an occupation order if you are or were married and may make an order if you are or were cohabiting, unless it appears to the court that you or the children are likely to suffer even greater harm if such an order is made.

If such an order were made in your favour, it would be for a period of six months on a renewable basis, if you are or have been married, but only for six months and one further six month period if you are or have been cohabiting.

As your application is on notice, if it appears to the court that your husband/partner, [   ], has used or threatened violence against you or your children, then the court must attach a power of arrest to the injunction.

This means that if your husband/partner, [   ], were to breach the injunction in any way, you could immediately telephone the police who could arrest him straightaway. The police would have to bring him before the judge within 24 hours, excluding Sundays, Christmas Day and Good Friday.

If no power of arrest is attached and your husband/partner, [   ], does breach an order made, you may wish to consider applying to the court for his committal to prison for contempt of court. [Should this be necessary, I would need to obtain an amendment to your Certificate of Public Funding to apply for his committal to prison.]

I am making arrangements for your application to be issued at the court. The court will advise me of the hearing date. It will then be necessary for me to arrange for the application and sworn statement to be personally delivered. Your husband/partner, [   ], must have two clear days' notice of your application.

To assist in identifying him, please let me have a recent photograph of him, as previously requested, and details of his routine and general whereabouts. It would also be helpful to let me know what car (if any) he drives, so that the people who are personally delivering the court papers can find and then identify him easily.

I will let you know when you are required to attend court and the name of the barrister who will represent you.

Please return your sworn statement to me as soon as possible. Also, please inform me immediately of any incidents which may occur between now and the hearing.

Yours sincerely

Enc.

IN2　Letter to client applying for injunctions about application without notice

Dear [*client*]

I write further to our meeting on [   ].

You have instructed me to apply to the court for an injunction against your husband/partner, [   ]. I have now drafted your application and supporting Statement which is enclosed.

Please ensure that your Statement is factually correct because you may be questioned in court very closely on its contents. If any amendments are required, please let me know. Please take the Statement to another firm of solicitors for it to be sworn. There will be a statutory swear fee of £5 plus £2 for each exhibit. Alternatively, you may take it to a local county court at [   ]. There is no fee.

I have advised you that you have sufficient grounds on which to make an application for an injunction. I explained the two ways in which you can apply for an injunction – with or without notice. A without notice application is one which is made without your husband/partner, [   ], knowing about it. Such orders will only be made in an emergency where there is a real and immediate danger of serious injury or irreparable harm. The court will have regard to all the circumstances of the case, including any risk of significant harm to you or the children if an order were not made immediately. The court will also consider whether you would be deterred or not make an application at all if an immediate order were not made. The judge will also consider whether there is any reason to believe your husband/partner, [   ], is deliberately evading service and you or the children will be seriously prejudiced by any delay involved in trying to locate him.

As there does appear to be such a threat in your case, I have advised you that it is appropriate to apply without notice.

If your application is granted by a judge, the injunction will forbid your husband/partner, [   ], from:

(a)　using or threatening violence against you [and the children];

(b)　intimidating, harassing or pestering you [and the children].

This type of order is known as a non-molestation order.

The application is also for an order requiring your husband/partner, [   ], to vacate your property. This is known as an occupation order. It is not usually made in cases such as yours where your husband/partner, [   ], knows nothing about your application, as it is an order with far-reaching and serious consequences. Your husband/partner, [   ], would normally be given the opportunity to make representations. In your case it would appear that your situation is sufficiently serious to warrant applying for such an order. The court will look at all of the circumstances of the case including the risk of significant harm to you and the children, whether you would delay or put off bringing this application if an order were not made immediately, and whether or not your husband/partner, [　　　　], is likely to deliberately evade service.

When deciding whether to make an order requiring your husband/partner, [　　　　], to vacate your property, the court will consider various factors:

[If right to occupy]

The court will have regard to all the circumstances including:

1. the housing needs and housing resources of each of you and of any children;
2. your respective financial resources;
3. the likely effect of any order, or of any decision by the court not to exercise its powers, on the health, safety or wellbeing of each of you and of any children; and
4. the conduct of each of you in relation to each other and otherwise.

The court will also apply what is known as 'the balance of harm' test. If it appears to the court that you or any children are likely to suffer significant harm attributable to the conduct of your husband/partner, [　　　　], the court must make an occupation order unless it appears to the court that you or your children are likely to suffer even greater harm if such an order is made.

If such an order were made in your favour it could be for a specified period, until the occurrence of a specified event or until another order is made by the court. If it is for a specified period, then it is often for six months.

[If applicant is a former spouse and has no existing right to occupy]

The court will have regard to all the circumstances including:

1. the housing needs and housing resources of each of you and of any children;
2. your respective financial resources;
3. the likely effect of any order, or of any decision by the court not to exercise its powers, on the health, safety or wellbeing of each of you and of any children; and
4. the conduct of each of you in relation to each other and otherwise.

The court will also apply 'the balance of harm' test. If it appears to the court that you or any children are likely to suffer significant harm attributable to the conduct of your former husband/partner, [　　　　], the court must make an occupation order unless it appears to the court that you or any children are likely to suffer even greater harm if such an order is made.

There are three additional factors that the court must consider:

1. the length of time which has elapsed since you last lived together;
2. the length of time which has elapsed since the marriage was dissolved or annulled (if relevant); and
3. the existence of any current legal proceedings between you for a financial order pursuant to the divorce, or for an order under Schedule 1 to the Children Act 1989 for financial relief or relating to the legal or beneficial ownership of the property. [*Delete as appropriate.*]

If such an order were made in your favour, it would be for a period of six months only but may be extended repeatedly for further six-month periods.

[*If applicant is a cohabitant/former cohabitant and has no existing right to occupy*]

The court will have regard to all the circumstances including:

1. the housing needs and housing resources of each of you and of any children;
2. your respective financial resources;
3. the likely effect of any order, or of any decision by the court not to exercise its powers, on the health, safety or wellbeing of each of you and of any children; and
4. the conduct of each of you in relation to each other and otherwise.

In addition, the court will consider:

1. whether you have any children or whether there are children involved for whom either of you have or have had parental responsibility;
2. the length of time during which you have lived together as husband and wife;
3. the length of time which has elapsed since you stopped living together; and
4. the existence of any current legal proceedings between you for an order under Schedule 1 Children Act 1989 for financial relief or relating to the legal or beneficial ownership of the property.

The court must also consider whether you or any children are likely to suffer significant harm attributable to the conduct of your former partner, [   ]; the court may make an order unless it appears to the court that either you or the children are likely to suffer even greater harm if such an order is made.

If such an order were made in your favour, it would be for a period of six months and can be renewed for a further period of six months, ie in total twelve months.

[*Where neither applicant nor respondent have right to occupy*]

The court will have regard to all the circumstances including:

1. the housing needs and housing resources of each of you and of any

children;
2.   your respective financial resources;
3.   the likely effect of any order, or of any decision by the court not to exercise its powers, on the health, safety or wellbeing of each of you and of any children; and
4.   the conduct of each of you in relation to each other and otherwise.

The court will also apply 'the balance of harm' test. If it appears to the court that you or any children are likely to suffer significant harm attributable to the conduct of your husband/partner, [   ], the court must make an occupation order if you are or were married and may make an order if you are or were cohabiting, unless it appears to the court that you or the children are likely to suffer even greater harm if such an order is made.

If you are or have been cohabiting, the court will also take into account the fact that you have not given each other the commitment involved in marriage. In practice, that tends not to be a significant factor.

If such an order were made in your favour, it would be for a period of six months on a renewable basis, if you are or have been married; but only for six months and one further six-month period if you are or have been cohabitants.

If it appears to the court that your husband/partner, [   ], has used or threatened violence against you and there is a risk of significant harm to you [and/or the children] attributable to your husband/partner [   ]'s conduct, then the court may attach a power of arrest to the injunction.

This means that if your husband/partner, [   ], were to breach an injunction in any way, you could immediately telephone the police who could arrest him. The police would have to bring him before the judge within 24 hours, excluding Sundays, Christmas Day and Good Friday.

As soon as you have sworn your statement, you must attend [   ] court at [   ] on [   ], when a representative from this firm will attend together with [   ], an experienced barrister.

If successful, this order may well last only until the matter comes back before the court within a week or so. At the second hearing your husband/partner, [   ], will be given an opportunity to make representations in relation to your applications.

It will be necessary to personally deliver a sealed copy of any order made and the other court documents, including your sworn statement, to your husband/partner, [   ]. As soon as the order and other documents have been delivered to him, whether or not your husband/partner, [   ], is willing to accept them, the order is binding on him. If he breaches the order, he is liable to be arrested and brought before a judge.

To assist in identifying him, please let me have a recent photograph of him, as previously requested, and details of his routine and general whereabouts.

It would also be helpful to let me know what car (if any) he drives, so that the people who are personally delivering the court papers can find and then identify him easily.

Please return your sworn statement to me as soon as possible.

Yours sincerely

Enc.

IN3   Letter to court on behalf of petitioner/applicant

Dear Sirs

We act for the petitioner.

We enclose, for issue please, the following documents (with copies for service and the court where appropriate):

1. petition for a divorce;
2. statement for arrangements for children form;
3. marriage certificate;
4. certificate as to a reconciliation;
5. the court filing fee or application for a fee exemption or remission form;
6. notice of application for a non-molestation and/or occupation order;
7. sworn statement in support;
[8. notice of issue of emergency Certificate of Public Funding;]
9. draft order.

Please issue the relevant divorce papers which we will serve at the same time as our client's application for a non-molestation and/or occupation order, which we would be grateful if you could list for a hearing as soon as possible, bearing in mind that we must give two clear days' notice to the respondent.

Thank you for your assistance.

Yours faithfully

Enc.

IN4   Letter to court on behalf of applicant

Dear Sirs

We act for the applicant. We enclose, for issue please, the following documents (with copies for service and the court where appropriate).

1.   application for a non-molestation and/or occupation order;
2.   sworn statement in support;
[3.   notice of issue of emergency Certificate of Public Funding;]
4.   the court filing fee or exemption of fees form;
5.   draft order.

Please can you issue our client's application and list the matter for hearing as soon as possible, bearing in mind that we must give two clear days' notice to the respondent.

Thank you for your assistance.

Yours faithfully

Enc.

IN5 Letter to process server requesting service of order with return date

Dear Sirs

Further to our telephone conversation today, we enclose the following documents (and copies for your affidavit) for personal service on [   ] of [   ]:

1. letter addressed to [   ] dated [   ];

2. a sealed copy of the order of [   ] dated [   ] with/without penal notice endorsed. You will see that the return date is [   ]. For service to be effective, you will recall that there must be two clear working days' notice. [   ] must therefore be served by 4pm on [   ];

3. a copy of our client's notice of application;

4. A copy of our client's sworn statement dated [   ];

5. notice of issue of ertificate of Public Funding dated [   ];

6. [add *divorce papers if relevant*].

If possible, please draw to the attention of [   ] the hearing date as listed on the order, which is on [   ], and the penal notice [and power of arrest] attached to the order.

I enclose a photograph of [   ].   His description is as follows:

(a) Height   :
(b) Build   :
(c) Hair   :
(d) Eyes   :
(e) Spectacles   :
(f) Other distinguishing features   :
(g) Car   :
(h) Ethnic Origin   :
(i) Age   :

His likely whereabouts are [   ].

You may find it useful to liaise directly with our client to obtain details of [   ]'s likely whereabouts and normal routine. Her telephone number is [   ].

[*We also enclose a letter to the police and a copy of the order. Please deliver to the police station.*]

Once service has been effected, please let us know immediately. Please then let us have your sworn affidavit of service, containing the appropriate endorsement in the top right-hand corner and exhibiting the copies of those documents you have served, in time for the return date so that we can hand it to the judge. In addition, please enclose your invoice.

Thank you for your assistance.

Yours faithfully

Enc.

IN6   Letter serving respondent with order

Dear [*respondent*]

We act for [   ].

We have been instructed by our client that there have been various incidences of a [*violent/threatening*] nature recently which has led our client to instruct us to apply for an injunction. We have now done so. Such an order was made by [   ] at the [   ] court today.

We therefore enclose, by way of service upon you, the following documents:

1.   a sealed copy of the order made by [   ] of [   ] court, dated [   ];

2.   sealed notice of application dated [   ];

3.   a copy of our client's sworn statement in support of her application, dated [   ];

[4.   notice of issue of Certificate of Public Funding dated [   ];]

You must attend [   ] county court [   ] at [   ] on [   ].

This order forbids you from using or threatening violence against our client or intimidating, harassing or pestering our client or encouraging anyone else to do so.

In addition, please note that there is a penal notice endorsed on the order. This means that if you breach the order, our client will consider making an immediate application to the court for your committal to prison.

We strongly recommend that you obtain independent legal advice regarding the contents of this letter. We suggest you contact Resolution (formerly the Solicitors Family Law Association) on 01689 820272 for details of members of Resolution in your area. We recommend that you consult a Resolution member who will normally be a specialist in family law. Resolution members are committed to adopting an amicable approach in all family matters.

Yours faithfully

Enc.

IN7   Letter serving respondent with order containing undertaking

Dear [*respondent*]

We enclose, by way of formal service upon you, the order dated [   ] containing the undertaking(s) which you gave to the court when you personally attended before [   ] on [   ].

As the judge explained to you, an undertaking is a legally binding promise made to the court. If that undertaking is broken then our client can apply to the court for you to be punished. You could even be committed to prison.

The undertaking(s) forbid(s) you from using or threatening violence against our client [and the children] or intimidating, harassing or pestering our client in any way – to include communicating with our client [and the children] except through us.

There is a penal notice endorsed on the undertaking(s). If you breach the undertaking(s), our client will consider making an immediate application to the court for your committal to prison.

We recommend that you obtain independent legal advice regarding the contents of this letter.

We suggest you contact Resolution (formerly the Solicitors Family Law Association) on 01689 820272 for details of members of Resolution in your area. We recommend that you consult a Resolution member who will normally be a specialist in family law. Resolution members are committed to adopting an amicable approach in all family matters.

Yours faithfully

Enc.

IN8   Letter to police enclosing order

Dear Sirs

We act for [   ] of [   ].

We enclose a sealed copy of an order which was made by [   ] in the [   ] court on [   ]. You will see that a power of arrest is attached to that order. Please can you alert the Domestic Violence Unit and ensure that the control room has a copy of this order, so that the police are aware of it in the event that our client should need to contact you directly.

Thank you for your assistance.

Yours faithfully

Enc.

IN9 Letter to client enclosing 'without notice' non-molestation order – no power of arrest

Dear [*client*]

I write further to the hearing which took place before [   ] at the [   ] court today. I enclose a copy of the order which was made by the court for you to keep safely.

The order forbids your husband/partner, [   ], from using or threatening violence against you [and the children] or intimidating, harassing or pestering you [and the children], or communicating with you [and the children] except through me. [*Check what order says.*]

I am making arrangements for a sealed copy of the order to be personally delivered to your husband/partner, [   ]. Until the order is personally delivered to him, it does not take effect.

Although the police do not have to arrest your husband/partner, [   ], if he is in breach of the order unless a criminal offence is committed, you should telephone the police immediately if there are any further incidents and ask for their help.

Please notify me immediately if your husband/partner, [   ], breaches the order, because you may want to apply to the court for his committal to prison [for contempt of court.] [I will need to obtain an amendment to your Certificate of Public Funding to apply for this.] [Breach of a non-molestation order is now a criminal offence under the Domestic Violence Crime and Victims Act 2004.*]

In the usual course of things, your case will be heard again by the judge on [   ]. You must attend that hearing which will be at [   ] county court [   ] at [   ] on [   ]. Please be there by [   ]. You will be represented by [   ], an experienced barrister.

Please keep in regular touch with me between now and the next hearing and let me know about any further incidents so that, if necessary, I can prepare a further sworn statement on your behalf.

Yours sincerely

Enc.

NB [*not yet in force, although it received the Royal Assent in November 2004. Breach of a non-molestation order will be punishable by up to 5 years imprisonment.]

IN10   Letter to client enclosing a 'with notice' non-molestation and occupation order (including to vacate property) – no power of arrest

Dear [*client*]

I write further to the hearing which took place before [   ] at the
[   ] court today. I enclose a copy of the order which was made by the
court for you to keep safely.

The order forbids your husband/partner, [   ], from using or threatening
violence against you [and the children] or intimidating, harassing or pestering
you [and the children] or communicating with you [and the children] except
through me. [*Check what order says.*]

The order also requires your husband/partner, [   ], to vacate your
property by [   ] on [   ].

I am making arrangements for a sealed copy of the order to be personally
delivered to him. Until the order is personally delivered to your husband/
partner, [   ], it does not take effect.

Although the police do not have to arrest him if he is in breach of the order
unless a criminal offence is committed, you should telephone the police
immediately if there are any further incidents and ask for their help. [Please
note that it is now a criminal offence to breach a non-molestation order under
the Domestic Violence Crime and Victims Act 2004*.]

Please notify me immediately if your husband/partner, [   ], breaches
the order because you may want to apply to the court for his committal to
prison [for contempt of court.] [I will need to obtain an amendment to your
Certificate of Public Funding to apply for this.]

Yours sincerely

Enc.

NB [*not yet in force, although it received the Royal Assent in November
2004. Breach will no longer be enforceable as contempt of court.]

IN11 Letter to client enclosing a 'without notice' non-molestation order – containing power of arrest

Dear [*client*]

I write further to the hearing which took place before [   ] at the
[   ] court today. I enclose a copy of the order which was made by the
court. Please keep it safely.

The order forbids your husband/partner, [   ], from using or threatening
violence against you [and the children] or intimidating, harassing or pestering
you [and the children] or communicating with you [and the children] except
through me. [*Check what the order says.*]

I am making arrangements for a sealed copy of the order to be personally
delivered to him. Until the order is personally delivered to your husband/
partner, [   ], it does not take effect.

A power of arrest is attached to the order. If your husband/partner, [   ],
breaches the order in any way, you should immediately telephone the police.
The police will arrest him without first obtaining a warrant if they have
reasonable cause to believe that he has breached the order. They will bring him
before a judge within 24 hours, excluding Sundays, Christmas Day and Good
Friday.

If your husband/partner, [   ], breaches the order, [breach is no longer
enforceable as contempt of court under the Domestic Violence Crime and
Victims Act 2004. Under the DVCVA, breach of a non-molestation order will
be punishable by up to 5 years imprisonment*] you may also wish to consider
applying to the court for his committal to prison for contempt of court. [I will
need to obtain an amendment to your Certificate of Public Funding to apply for
this.]

In the usual course of things, your case will be heard again on [   ].
You must attend that hearing which will be at [   ] county court at
[   ] on [   ]. Please be there by [   ]. You will be
represented by [   ].

Please keep in regular touch with me between now and the next hearing and
let me know about any further incidents so that, if necessary, I can prepare a
further sworn statement on your behalf.

Yours sincerely

Enc.

NB [*not yet in force, although it received the Royal Assent in November
2004. Breach will no longer be enforceable as contempt of court.]

IN12 Letter to client enclosing a 'with notice' non-molestation and occupation order (including to vacate property) – containing power of arrest

Dear [*client*]

I write further to the hearing which took place before [   ] at the [   ] court today. I enclose a copy of the order which was made by the court. Please keep it safely.

The order forbids your husband/partner, [   ], from using or threatening violence against you [and the children] or intimidating, harassing or pestering you [and the children] or communicating with you [and the children] except through me. [*Check what the order says.*]

The order also requires your husband/partner, [   ], to vacate your property by [   ] on [   ].

I am making arrangements for a sealed copy of the order to be personally delivered on him. Until the order is personally delivered to your husband/partner, [   ], it does not take effect.

A power of arrest is attached to the order. If your husband/partner, [   ], breaches the order in any way, you should immediately telephone the police. The police will arrest him without first obtaining a warrant if they have reasonable cause to believe he has breached the order. They must bring him before the judge within 24 hours, excluding Sundays, Christmas Day and Good Friday.

If your husband/partner, [   ], breaches the order, [breach is no longer enforceable as contempt of court under the Domestic Violence Crime and Victims Act 2004. Under the DVCVA breach of a non-molestation order will be punishable by up to 5 years imprisonment*] you may also wish to consider applying to the court for his committal to prison for contempt of court.] [I will need to obtain an amendment to your Certificate of Public Funding to apply for this.]

Yours sincerely

Enc.

NB [*not yet in force, although it received the Royal Assent in November 2004. Breach will no longer be enforceable as contempt of court.]

IN13 Letter to client – undertaking given

Dear [*client*]

I write to report on the outcome of your case. At court, on [   ],
your husband/partner, [   ], gave an undertaking, which is a legally
binding promise, to the court not to use or threaten violence against you [or
the children] and not to intimidate, harass or pester you [or the children]. [He
was also required by the terms of this undertaking to vacate your property by
[   ] on [   ] and not to return there [save for the purposes of
contact and only then as previously agreed in writing].]

If your husband/partner, [   ], breaches the terms of his undertaking,
then you can apply to the court for him to be punished and even to be
committed to prison [for contempt of court.]

It is unusual for a person to be sent to prison for a first breach of an
undertaking, although in serious cases a person can be sent to prison in such
circumstances. If he breaches the terms of this undertaking repeatedly, you
may wish to consider applying to the court for his committal to prison. [I will
need to obtain an amendment to your Certificate of Public Funding to apply for
this.]

Please therefore contact me immediately if your husband/partner, [   ],
breaks the terms of his undertaking.

I am making arrangements for a sealed copy of the undertaking to be
personally delivered to him. You may be unable to enforce this undertaking by
way of applying for his committal to prison until the papers are served on him.
I shall let you know as soon as the undertaking has been served.

Your husband/partner [   ]'s undertaking expires on [   ]. It may
be necessary to seek an extension of his undertaking shortly before this date.
Alternatively, nearer the time, if you think you will need stronger protection,
you can reapply to the court for a non-molestation [and occupation] order to be
made against him.

Yours sincerely

IN14 Letter to client wanting to discontinue application

Dear [*client*]

I refer to our telephone conversation on [   ] when you instructed me not to continue with your application for an injunction.

[I have not as yet arranged for a sealed copy of your application and supporting sworn statement to be personally delivered to your husband/partner, [   ].]

or

[I have personally delivered sealed copies of your application for an injunction and supporting sworn statement on your husband/partner, [   ]. It will therefore be necessary for me to write to him accordingly informing him of your instructions not to proceed.]

It will not be difficult to cancel the hearing listed for [   ]. However, because the hearing is not due to take place until [   ] it will be possible for you to keep the hearing date open for, say, one week to see if any further problems develop. If you then decide that you do want to continue with your application, you will be able to do so. Please let me know. I do, however, advise you to continue with your application to avoid any further possible incidents; at least then you will have the protection of a court order.

If I do not hear from you by [   ], I will cancel the hearing [and write to the Legal Services Commission asking them to discharge your Certificate of Public Funding].

Yours sincerely

IN15 Letter to court vacating hearing

Dear Sirs

[   ] Case No [   ]

[Names of Parties]

We refer to our letter dated [   ] and our client's application for a non-molestation and occupation order due to be heard on [   ] at [am/pm].

Our client has now informed us that s/he does not wish to proceed with his/her application. Therefore, we would be grateful if you could vacate the hearing.

[We confirm that we have not served our client's wife/husband/partner, [   ], with the sealed copy of the application.]

or

[We have notified our client's husband/partner, [   ], that our client is not proceeding with her application.]

Yours faithfully

IN16 Warning letter to respondent

Dear [*respondent*]

We have been consulted by [   ], as a result of recent problems which have arisen between you [in your marriage].

Our client instructs us that for the last [   ] months you have been violent to her on a number of occasions, the last being on [   ], and you have often threatened her with violence, using abusive and aggressive language to her [   ], sometimes in the presence of the children [   ].

We have advised our client that she is in a position to obtain a court order to protect herself [   ] and the children [   ] from you using or threatening to use violence against [her/them] or intimidating or harassing [her/them].

However, our client would prefer at this stage to try to resolve matters between you without the need for a court order. This is provided that you stop your aggressive behaviour towards her immediately and take immediate steps to find somewhere else to live.

We must warn you that if as a result of this letter you attempt to threaten or intimidate our client in any way, or you are violent towards her, we shall have no hesitation in applying to the court for an order to protect her.

Our client is prepared to allow you until [   ] on [   ] to vacate the house. If you have not left by that time, we have instructions to apply to the court for an order to protect our client by ordering you to leave. If it becomes necessary to apply for such an order we would ask the court to order you to pay for her legal costs.

We recommend that you obtain independent legal advice regarding the contents of this letter. We suggest you contact Resolution on 01689 820272 for details of members of family law specialists in your area. We recommend that you consult a Resolution member who will normally be a specialist in family law. Resolution members are committed to adopting an amicable approach in all family matters.

If you consult solicitors you should take this letter with you. If you do not intend to consult solicitors please contact the writer of this letter, who is [   ], by telephone or in writing.

Yours sincerely

IN17 Authority to release client's medical records

Dear Sir or Madam

Please accept this letter as my authority and request for you to release copies of my medical records and other information to my solicitors [*name and address, reference*].

Thank you for your assistance.

Yours faithfully

Signed:

Date:

IN18 Letter advising respondent client of effect of order made against him

Dear [*client*]

I write further to our meeting on [   ].

You gave me a copy of an order made against you, dated [   ].

The order forbids you from using or threatening to use violence against
[   ] [and the children] or intimidating, harassing or pestering
[   ] [and the children] or communicating with your wife/partner
[   ] [and the children]; except through her solicitors. The order will
remain in effect until [   ] on [   ]. The order also requires you
to vacate the property at [   ] by [   ] on [   ].

A power of arrest was attached to the order. This means that if you breach the
order in any way, your wife/partner, [   ], could immediately telephone
the police. The police must arrest you immediately if they have reasonable
cause to believe that you have breached the order. They must bring you before
the judge within 24 hours, excluding Sundays, Christmas Day and Good
Friday. If you breach the order, your wife/partner, [   ], may wish to
apply to the court for your committal to prison [for contempt of court.]

[I confirm that you have been granted an emergency Certificate of Public
Funding to defend these proceedings.]

I have now drafted your statement in reply which is enclosed.

Please ensure that your statement is factually correct, because you are liable
to be cross-examined on its contents. If any amendments are required, please
let me know. If not, please take the statement to another firm of solicitors for it
to be sworn. There will be a statutory swear fee of £5 plus £2 for each exhibit.
Alternatively, you may take it to the local county court at [   ]. There is
no fee.

[I have advised you that you have sufficient grounds to defend the
proceedings.]

When deciding to make an order requiring you to vacate the property, the court
will consider all the circumstances of the case, including the housing needs
and resources of each of you, your financial resources, the effect of any order
on the health, safety and wellbeing of both of you [and the children] and your
conduct. If it appears to the court that your wife/partner, [   ], [or the
children] [is/are] likely to suffer significant harm at your hands it [must make
an order if you are or were married/may make an order if you are or were
cohabitants].

[*If former spouse and no right to occupy*]

The court will also consider how long it is since you lived together, how long it is since the marriage was dissolved/annulled and the existence of any current legal proceedings.

[*If cohabitant/former cohabitant with no right to occupy*]

The court will also consider whether you have children in respect of whom you have parental responsibility, how long you have lived together, how long it is since you stopped living together and the existence of any legal proceedings.

The case will next be heard by the court on [   ]. You must attend the hearing which will be at [   ]. Please be there by [   ]. You will be represented by [   ], an experienced barrister. A representative from this firm will also be in attendance.

Please keep in regular touch with me between now and [   ] and inform me of any further incidents so that I can prepare a further sworn statement on your behalf, if necessary.

Yours sincerely

Enc.

IN19 Letter to client advising on the key changes to Part IV of the Family Law Act 1996 as a result of the introduction of the Domestic Violence, Crime and Victims Act 2004, section 42A

Dear [*client*]

We have discussed applying/We have applied on your behalf for a non-molestation order/occupation order against your husband/wife/partner.

[I am writing to let you know that the Domestic Violence Crime and Victims Act 2004 (DVCVA) will/has insert(ed) a new section into the Family Law Act 1996, making the breach of a non-molestation order a criminal offence, punishable by up to five years imprisonment. Essentially, your husband/wife/partner will be guilty of an offence if s/he does anything that s/he is forbidden from doing by a non-molestation order, *and* they were aware of the existence of the order at the time of the offence. Where a person is so convicted, the conduct or breach will no longer be punishable as contempt of court. However, your husband/wife/partner cannot be convicted of an offence for any conduct which has been punished as a contempt of court.]

[A non-molestation order can be made against a person who is 'associated' with the applicant. The DVCVA has widened the definition of 'associated persons' by inserting a new paragraph defining an associated person as having or having had an intimate personal relationship with another, which is or was of significant duration. I do not imagine this will apply to all boyfriend/girlfriend relationships but it could apply to couples who each have their own home, who have never cohabited, but have had a sexual relationship over several years.] [At this stage, it is not known whether a relationship of several months will be sufficient to amount to 'significant duration'. If it does not, we can consider whether you will be able to apply under the Protection from Harassment Act 1997 instead, if this level of relationship is not applicable.] [Also of note is that the definition of cohabitant will now extend to same-sex couples.]

[Please let me know as a matter of urgency if your husband/wife/partner has breached the order.]

[Insofar as occupation orders are concerned, the effects of the amendment to the definition of cohabitants is to make available occupation orders under the Family Law Act 1996 to same sex cohabitants, whether or not they own the home in which they cohabit (subject to the satisfaction of certain sections of the Act) and to allow same sex couples to apply for the transfer of certain tenancies.]

[We do not know when the new section will actually come into law, but it is expected to during 2006.]

Yours sincerely

SECTION 6

COSTS

Andrea Woelke

Costs

CO1PC Letter confirming first appointment to client paying privately

Dear [*client*]

I refer to our telephone conversation and confirm your appointment to see me at [   ] on [   ].

To help me assess what advice you need, I enclose a confidential questionnaire for you to complete and return to me, preferably before our meeting. Please complete it as best you can.

[From the information you gave me, you are not entitled to advice under the Legal Help scheme but you may be entitled to *Family Legal Help and Legal Representation*. Therefore, before legal aid pays for your costs, you will have to pay for any work I do for you yourself.]

My current hourly charging rate is £[   ] plus VAT and expenses. [Therefore please bring a minimum of £[500] on account of costs to the first meeting. If you decide that you want me to take action on your behalf or advise you further, I may have to ask you to pay more money on account of costs, depending on the work involved. If the charges for the work I do for you are less than what you have paid me on account of costs, I will of course send any balance back to you.]

For money laundering regulations I will have to verify your ID. Could you please bring:

1.   one photo ID, such as your passport or a photo driving licence; and
2.   one address ID, such as a recent utility bill or a bank statement.

[*I also enclose this firm's terms of business. I will ask you to sign one copy when we meet.*]

Also, please remember to bring with you to the first meeting all relevant papers. If you are not sure which papers are relevant, bring anything you think will be helpful. This will make it much quicker and easier to find out what your problem is and how we can help you with it.

I look forward to meeting you.

Yours sincerely

Enc. client questionnaire
       terms of business letter

CO1LH   Letter confirming first appointment to client eligible for Legal Help

Dear [*client*]

I refer to our telephone conversation and confirm your appointment to see me at [   ] on [   ].

To help me assess what advice you need, I enclose a confidential questionnaire for you to complete and return to me, preferably before our meeting. Please complete it as best you can.

From the information you gave me on the telephone, you are entitled to advice under the Legal Help scheme. If you are on Income Support or Income-based Job Seeker's Allowance, please bring your benefits book or the letter confirming your benefits to our meeting.

If you are working, please bring:

1.   a copy of your last three payslips,
2.   details of your income from any other sources,
3.   confirmation of the value of any savings or other money or assets you own (such as a savings account passbook or recent bank statement) and
4.   confirmation of the amount of your mortgage or rent payments.

For money laundering regulations I will have to verify your ID. Could you please bring:

1.   one photo ID, such as your passport or a photo driving licence; and
2.   one address ID, such as a recent utility bill or a bank statement.

[*I also enclose this firm's terms of business. I will ask you to sign one copy when we meet.*]

Also, please remember to bring with you to the first meeting all relevant papers. If you are not sure which papers are relevant, bring anything you think will be helpful. This will make it much quicker and easier to find out what your problem is and how we can help you with it.

I look forward to meeting you.

Yours sincerely

Enc. client questionnaire
        terms of business letter

section **6** COSTS

CO2LH   Letter to overly zealous client on Legal Help

Dear [*client*]

I am slightly concerned by the frequency and, indeed, length of your telephone calls to me.

Although I am always willing to take your instructions by telephone, if I spend a lot of time on the telephone to you, the time-limit that is imposed on Legal Help will soon be exhausted and I may not be able to do all the necessary work for you.

[*In addition all the time I spend forms part of any future statutory charge and later on you will have to pay a corresponding amount to the Legal Services Commission from any money or property you recover or preserve in court proceedings that are related to your current issues. The more time I spend, the more you may later have to pay.*]

Therefore, please bear in mind that it is far better for you to give me your instructions in writing, unless of course you need to call me urgently.

Yours sincerely

CO3NOSC   Letter to overly zealous client on CLS funding – no contributions nor statutory charge

Dear [*client*]

I am slightly concerned by the frequency and, indeed, length of your telephone calls to me.

The Legal Services Commission will only pay for work that the court later thinks was reasonably necessary for the case and some of what you are asking me to do may later fall outside this. The partners in this firm do not allow me to work for free and therefore I will not be able to reply to every question you have immediately; I may also need to ask you to cut your telephone calls short. That way, I can advise you fully.

Therefore, please bear in mind that it is far better for you to give me your instructions in writing, unless of course you need to call me urgently.

Yours sincerely

CO3SC   Letter to overly zealous client on CLS funding – contributions or statutory charge

Dear [*client*]

I am slightly concerned by the frequency and, indeed, length of your telephone calls to me.

The Legal Services Commission will only pay for work that the court later thinks was reasonably necessary for the case and some of what you are asking me to do may later fall outside this. The partners in this firm do not allow me to work for free and therefore I will not be able to reply to every question you have immediately; I may also need to ask you to cut your telephone calls short. That way, I can advise you fully.

In addition all the time I spend forms part of any future statutory charge and later on you will have to pay a corresponding amount to the Legal Services Commission from any money or property you recover or preserve in court proceedings that are related to your current case. The more time I spend, the more you may later have to pay.

Therefore, please bear in mind that it is far better for you to give me your instructions in writing, unless of course you need to call me urgently.

Yours sincerely

CO4   Letter to overly zealous privately-paying client

Dear [*client*]

[I enclose an up-to-date note of my firm's charges. Please let me have payment as soon as possible.]

I am slightly concerned by the frequency and, indeed, length of your telephone calls to me.

Although I am always willing to take your instructions by telephone, your costs will increase significantly if you want me to spend the amount of time on the telephone with you that I have done recently. It will also increase your overall costs and I will have to revise the costs estimates that I have given you upwards.

If you are able to obtain an order that the other person in your case will have to pay some or all of your costs, it is likely that when my firm's costs are assessed by the court, the time spent on some of the telephone attendances will be disallowed. If this happens, you will still have to pay for these yourself.

Therefore, please bear in mind that it is far better for you to give me your instructions in writing, unless of course you need to call me urgently.

Yours sincerely

CO5   Letter filing Emergency Certificate of Public Funding

Dear Sir or Madam

We enclose our client's Emergency Certificate of Public Funding for the court file.

Yours faithfully

CO6   Letter filing Certificate of Public Funding

Dear Sir or Madam

We enclose our client's Certificate of Public Funding for the court file.

Yours faithfully

CO7   Letter filing amended Certificate of Public Funding

Dear Sir or Madam

We enclose our client's amended Certificate of Public Funding for the court file.

Yours faithfully

CO8   Letter filing discharged Certificate of Public Funding

Dear Sir or Madam

We enclose our client's discharged Certificate of Public Funding for the court file.

Please ensure that our name is accordingly removed from the court record.

Yours faithfully

CO9 Letter to publicly funded client explaining application for costs in publicly funded cases – abolition of indemnity rule

Dear [*client*]

I must consider, as part of my obligation to the Community Legal Services Fund, whether it is appropriate to ask for your legal costs to be paid by the other person in your case if you are successful in your application. If the court makes an order for all or part of your costs to be paid by the other person in your case, these will have to be paid at the ordinary private rates and not at the rates at which the Community Legal Service Fund pays solicitors.

There is a difference between the rates. For example, for preparation and attendance on a client whose case is not publicly funded I would usually expect the court to allow me approximately £[   ] per hour plus VAT. In the case of a client whose case is publicly funded, I would normally only be able to charge £[   ], which is the current prescribed rate [together with an increase as a result of my accreditation].

There are no circumstances in which you will have to pay the higher hourly rates for work covered by your Certificate of Public Funding. You will only have to pay the lower rates where the statutory charge applies. The higher rates will only apply if the court orders someone else to pay your costs and they actually pay.

My firm can only work for you on the basis of public funding on the strict understanding that you agree to my firm seeking an order for costs where appropriate. I will notify you either when an agreement is being negotiated or before a final hearing, if it is appropriate to seek an order for costs on your behalf.

[*In many types of cases the court does not usually order one party to pay the other party's costs, even if they are successful in their application. This includes disputes about children and finances on divorce. The court will only consider an application for costs in exceptional cases, for example if one party has deliberately been lying to the court.*]

If the other person in your case has to pay your costs as part of an agreement or a court order, this firm can enforce the costs order even if you later decide that you do not want it to be enforced.

Yours sincerely

CO10 Letter to publicly funded client immediately before application for costs – abolition of indemnity rule

Dear [*client*]

I write to notify you that I propose seeking an order for costs on your behalf against the other person in your case in the negotiations for an agreement and/ or at the final hearing. There is more information about costs in court cases in the terms-of-business letter I sent you dated [   ].

If the court orders the other person in your case to pay your costs, my firm and your barrister will be paid at a higher rate, closer to the rates you would have to pay if you were paying privately for your case.

[*If you did not seek an order for costs, all your legal costs would result in a high statutory charge on any property or money you preserve or recover. If, however, the other person in your case is ordered to pay your costs, this is likely to cover the bulk of your costs and the statutory charge will be very low. From experience I estimate that the other person in your case would be ordered to pay about 80% of your costs.*]

If an order for costs is made, and those costs are actually paid, I estimate that my firm's total costs will be £[   ] plus VAT and disbursements of £[   ], making a total of £[   ], whereas if an order for costs is not made, then the totals will be £[   ], £[   ] and £[   ] respectively.

The law permits my firm, once an order is made, to enforce the costs against the other person in your case at the higher rate, independent of your views.

Yours sincerely

CO11PC   Initial letter to expert witness for private client

Dear [   ]

Please telephone me to advise me what your likely fee will be for preparing a report and possibly attending court and how this is broken down, for example by hourly rates. Before I can confirm that I will be responsible for your reasonable fee, I need to obtain my client's authority.

[*I enclose a letter of authority addressed to you, authorising you to discuss my client's medical issues with me.*]

Although I hope that the contents of your report will be agreed by the other party, it may be necessary to call you to give evidence in court if this is not possible.

Please let me have a copy of your CV including your qualifications and whether or not you have experience of giving evidence in court.

Yours faithfully

[*Enc. letter of authority*]

CO11CLS Initial letter to expert witness for client on CLS funding

Dear [   ]

Please telephone me to advise me what your likely fee will be for preparing a report and possibly attending court and how this is broken down, for example by hourly rates. Before I can confirm that I will be responsible for your reasonable fee, I need to obtain my client's authority.

[*I enclose a letter of authority addressed to you, authorising you to discuss my client's medical issues with me.*]

Although I hope that the contents of your report will be agreed by the other party, it may be necessary to call you to give evidence in court if this is not possible.

Please let me have a copy of your CV including your qualifications and whether or not you have experience of giving evidence in court.

Please note that since my client has the benefit of public funding, there may be some delay in payment of your fee pending receipt of money from the Legal Services Commission. This firm is not able to pay you until we receive the money from the Commission, which can take six weeks or more.

In addition, since this is a publicly funded case, your fee, as with this firm's costs, has to be assessed by the court as to whether or not it is reasonable. Although I will be able to pay your fee in full as soon as I receive payment from the Legal Services Commission, your instructions are on the basis that in the event that your fee is reduced by the court on detailed assessment, you will refund the difference immediately.

Yours faithfully

[*Enc. letter of authority*]

CO12 Letter to expert witness pending payment of fees by Legal Services Commission

Dear [Sir/Madam]

Thank you for your letter dated [   ].

We have requested payment on account of your fee from the Legal Services Commission and as soon as we receive payment from them we will be able to pay your account.

Yours faithfully

CO13 Letter to expert witness enclosing fee

Dear [Sir/Madam]

We have now received payment of your fee from the Legal Services Commission and accordingly enclose our cheque for £[   ], together with your invoice dated [   ] for receipting and return please.

Yours faithfully

Enc. cheque
     invoice

CO14   Periodic letter to client paying a contribution to CLS funding – no Statutory Charge

Dear [*client*]

This is a standard letter which I am required to write, as part of the terms of my firm's Community Legal Service Franchise.

I am now required to inform you regularly of the amount of costs incurred in your case. Please note that as you are paying a contribution, the contribution will not be repaid to you unless the total of your publicly funded costs is less than the amount of your contribution. In almost all cases, the costs exceed the contribution.

However, apart from the contribution, you will not be required to pay any more towards these costs as the Statutory Charge will not apply in your case. I am only sending you this information to comply with the requirements under the Community Legal Service Franchise.

Your costs incurred to date are as follows:

	VAT	£
Legal Help costs		
My firm's costs		
Expenses		
Barrister's fees		
Sub-totals	————	————
Total		————

I now estimate that, if your case proceeds to a final hearing, your total costs are likely to be £[   ] including VAT and expenses. Needless to say, I hope it will be possible to resolve your case before the final hearing takes place.

Most cases do not go to a final court hearing.

[*I enclose a revised costs schedule for the future estimated costs in your case.*]

[*The estimate I have given is higher than I anticipated because [   ].*]

Please note that this is only a rough estimate based on approximate times, and not a detailed breakdown of all costs incurred and likely to be incurred in your case.

At the conclusion of your case, your costs will be assessed, normally by the court, and the court will only allow my firm those costs that it regards as reasonable. You will have an opportunity to express your views to the court if you wish, and, if necessary, have a formal court hearing about my firm's costs.

Neither my firm nor the Legal Services Commission requires payment of these costs from you now.

If there is anything in this letter which you do not understand, then do please discuss it with me when we next speak about your case.

Yours sincerely

[*Enc.*]

C015 Periodic letter to client not paying a contribution to CLS funding – no statutory charge

Dear [*client*]

This is a standard letter which I am required to write, as part of the terms of my firm's Community Legal Service Franchise, about the costs of your case.

I am required to inform you regularly of the amount of costs incurred in your case. Please note that you will not be required to pay these costs as the statutory charge will not apply in your case. I am only sending you this information to comply with the requirements under this firm's Community Legal Service Franchise.

Your costs incurred to date are as follows:

	VAT	£
Legal Help costs		
My firm's costs		
Expenses		
Barrister's fees		
Sub-totals	_____	_____
Total		_____

I now estimate that, if your case proceeds to a final hearing, your total costs are likely to be £[   ] including VAT and expenses. Needless to say, I hope it will be possible to resolve your case before the final hearing takes place.

Most cases do not go to a final court hearing.

[*I enclose a revised costs schedule for the future estimated costs in your case.*]

[*The estimate I have given is higher than I anticipated because [   ].*]

Please note that this is only a rough estimate based on approximate times, and not a detailed breakdown of all costs incurred and likely to be incurred in your case.

At the conclusion of your case, your costs will be assessed, normally by the court, and the court will only allow my firm those costs that it regards as reasonable. You will have an opportunity to express your views to the court if you wish, and, if necessary, have a formal court hearing about my firm's costs.

Neither my firm nor the Legal Services Commission requires payment of these costs from you now.

If there is anything in this letter which you do not understand, then do please discuss it with me when we next speak about your case.

Yours sincerely

[*Enc.*]

CO16   Periodic letter to client to whom statutory charge may apply, containing estimate of further fees

Dear [*client*]

This is a standard letter which I am required to write, as part of the terms of my firm's Community Legal Service Franchise, about your potential costs liability. I would draw your attention to my letter dated [   ] which explained my firm's terms of business and the operation of the statutory charge. Please re-read and consider that letter again.

I am required to inform you regularly of the amount of costs incurred because the statutory charge could apply in your case. If you recover or preserve any money or property in your case for which you get public funding, you will have to pay your costs out of that money or property at the end of your case, apart from any maintenance you receive. (Please refer to my letter dated [   ] about the circumstances in which enforcement of the statutory charge can be postponed.)

As you know, unless you have been assessed to pay a monthly contribution to the Legal Services Commission, you do not pay anything towards the cost of the case whilst it is continuing.

Your costs incurred to date are as follows:

	VAT	£
Legal Help costs		
My firm's costs		
Expenses		
Barrister's fees		
Sub-totals	———	———
Total		———

I now estimate that, if your case proceeds to a final hearing, your total costs are likely to be £[   ] including VAT and expenses. Needless to say, I hope it will be possible to resolve your case before the final hearing takes place.

Most cases do not go to a final court hearing.

[*I enclose a revised costs schedule for the future estimated costs in your case.*]

[*The estimate I have given is higher than I anticipated because [   ].*]

Please note that this is only a rough estimate based on approximate times, and not a detailed breakdown of all costs incurred and likely to be incurred in your case.

At the conclusion of your case, your costs will be assessed, normally by the court, and the court will only allow my firm those costs that it regards as reasonable. You will have an opportunity to express your views to the court if you wish, and, if necessary, have a formal court hearing about my firm's costs.

Neither my firm nor the Legal Services Commission requires payment of these costs from you now.

If there is anything in this letter which you do not understand, then do please discuss it with me when we next speak about your case.

Yours sincerely

[*Enc.*]

CO17   Periodic letter to client to whom statutory charge may apply, containing estimate of further fees and envisaging exceptional rates

Dear [*client*]

This is a standard letter which I am required to write, as part of the terms of my firm's Community Legal Service Franchise, about your potential costs liability. I would draw your attention to my letter dated [   ] which explained my firm's terms of business and the operation of the statutory charge. Please re-read and consider that letter again.

I am required to inform you regularly of the amount of costs incurred because the statutory charge could apply in your case. If you recover or preserve any money or property in your case for which you get public funding, you will have to pay your costs out of that money or property at the end of your case, apart from any maintenance you receive. (Please refer to my letter dated [   ] about the circumstances in which enforcement of the statutory charge can be postponed.)

As you know, unless you have been assessed to pay a monthly contribution to the Legal Services Commission, you do not pay anything towards the cost of the case whilst it is continuing.

Your costs incurred to date are as follows:

	VAT	£
Legal Help costs		
My firm's costs		
Expenses		
Barrister's fees		
Sub-totals	———	———
Total		———

I now estimate that, if your case proceeds to a final hearing, your total costs are likely to be £[   ] including VAT and expenses. Needless to say, I hope it will be possible to resolve your case before the final hearing takes place.

Most cases do not go to a final court hearing.

[*I enclose a revised costs schedule for the future estimated costs in your case.*]

[*The estimate I have given is higher than I anticipated because [   ].*]

Please note that this is only a rough estimate based on approximate times, and not a detailed breakdown of all costs incurred and likely to be incurred in your case.

I will be asking the court to allow a higher hourly rate mainly because of the complexity of the case.

At the moment, in publicly funded cases the Government allows my firm to charge approximately £[   ] per hour plus VAT and disbursements. If higher rates are allowed, the hourly rate could increase to £[   ] an hour or more and your total costs are therefore likely to be [50–80%] more than the figure referred to above.

At the conclusion of your case, your costs will be assessed, normally by the court, and the court will only allow my firm those costs that it regards as reasonable. You will have an opportunity to express your views to the court if you wish, and, if necessary, have a formal court hearing about my firm's costs.

Neither my firm nor the Legal Services Commission requires payment of these costs from you now.

If there is anything in this letter which you do not understand, then do please discuss it with me when we next speak about your case.

Yours sincerely

[*Enc.*]

CO18   Letter to privately paying client with six months' costs estimate

Dear [*client*]

Under the professional rules for solicitors, I am obliged to give you an estimate of the costs incurred and of the future costs in your case at least every six months.

[I enclose a note of my firm's charges to date together with a statement of account showing that a balance of £[   ] is now due from you. Please let me have another £[   ] on account of costs.

or

I estimate that since the last bill I sent you, I have done further work for about £[   ] and incurred the following expenses:

Including VAT this totals £[   ].]

Therefore your costs to date are a total of £[   ].

I also enclose an updated costs schedule showing my estimate of the further costs in your case.

[*You will see that I can only give you an estimate up to [   ] because [   ].*]

[*This estimate is higher than my initial estimate because [   ].*]

Yours sincerely

CO19 Letter to other party enclosing statement of costs for summary assessment

Dear Sirs

We enclose by way of service, statement of costs for summary assessment in respect of the hearing coming up on [   ].

Yours faithfully

Enc. statement of costs

CO20 Letter to court enclosing statement of costs for summary assessment

Dear Sir or Madam

We enclose statement of costs for summary assessment in respect of the hearing coming up on [   ].

Yours faithfully

Enc. statement of costs

CO21 Letter to client prior to Legal Services Commission's assessment of bill

Dear [*client*]

I have now had my firm's bill of costs prepared for assessment by the Legal Services Commission and I enclose a copy of the bill for your information.

You will see that if my firm's costs are allowed in full by the Legal Services Commission, they will amount to £[   ] plus VAT of £[   ] and expenses of £[   ], making a total of £[   ].

Because the statutory charge applies and/or you have paid a contribution to your case, you have a right to make written representations to the Legal Services Commission as to the amount of my firm's costs.

Please let me know if you want to make written representations to the Legal Services Commission, or whether you wish to rely on the Legal Services Commission to consider whether or not my firm's costs claimed are reasonable. The Commission does not just rubber-stamp our bills, but considers the files and papers before deciding whether our costs are reasonable.

If I do not hear from you within 21 days, I will presume that you do not want to make written representations.

Yours sincerely

Enc. copy bill

CO22   Letter to client prior to assessment of bill

Dear [*client*]

My firm is now about to have its legal charges, including barrister's fees and other expenses, assessed by the court.

As you have been made aware, the Legal Services Commission has a charge, known as the statutory charge, on all money or property recovered in the case, so that it will have a first claim on all money or property which has been recovered for you as a result of having public funding.

Since the statutory charge applies in your case and/or you have paid a contribution to your costs, you have a right to be heard at the assessment by the court or to write to the court with your views.

In assessing our costs, the court does not just rubber-stamp our bill. We have prepared an itemised bill for the court, in a form required by court rules, in which we detail every letter and all time which has been spent on the case. I enclose a copy for your information.

If you wish to be heard on assessment, or to make written representations, please write and tell me within the next 14 days. However, most clients do not attend the assessment hearing, since they rely on the court to consider whether our charges are reasonable.

To assist you, I have calculated all the totals and if the court allows our charges as claimed, they will amount to £[   ], plus VAT of £[   ] and expenses of £[   ], making a total of £[   ]. The statutory charge does not apply to the court fees of £[   ] for the assessment.

[*You will remember that the court ordered the other person in your case to pay your costs [of the hearing on [   ] from [   ] onwards]. Of course, unless the other person in your case pays the costs, you will have to start separate court proceedings to enforce the costs. You may not be granted public funding for this.*]

[*Since the other person in your case was publicly funded at the time, you will have to apply to the court separately for the judge to order that the other person in your case can actually pay the costs.*]

Yours sincerely

Enc. copy bill

CO23 Letter to client on public funding who has failed to give instructions

Dear [*client*]

I refer to my letter of [   ] to which I have received no reply.

Unless I hear from you within the next seven days, I shall assume that you require no further advice and shall close my file; I will request that the Legal Services Commission discharges your Certificate of Public Funding on the grounds that I have been unable to obtain your instructions; and I will claim payment from the Legal Services Commission for the work I have done for you.

[*As I am on the court record as your solicitor, I would be required to go to court hearings although I do not have your instructions. Please therefore sign and return to me the enclosed Notice of Acting in Person. I can then send it to the court and a copy to all other parties in your case. This means that the court and all other parties will contact you direct. If you do not return the document, I will need to make an application to the court to come off the court record. This will take considerable time and increase your overall costs, which you may have to pay indirectly as part of any contributions to your public funding or a statutory charge.*

Please remember that there is a court hearing coming up on [   ] and that if you do not attend, the court can order you to pay the costs of the hearing and/or make an order against you.]

Yours sincerely

[*Enc.   Notice of Acting in Person*]

CO24   Letter to new solicitors on transfer of Certificate of Public Funding

Dear Sirs

Thank you for your letter dated [   ], and [   ]'s authority enclosed with that letter.

The present position in these proceedings is [   ].

We are prepared to consent to transfer of the certificate to your firm and enclose a copy of our letter to the Legal Services Commission to this effect.

[*We do not however anticipate that detailed assessment will take place within six months and therefore intend to submit an interim bill to the Legal Services Commission for payment – we are therefore sending the papers at this stage to our costs draftsman to prepare the necessary itemised bill. Once the papers have been returned we can of course pass them to you.*].

To be able to pass our file of papers on to you, we require your written undertaking as follows:

(a)   to retain our papers in a manner which will enable our papers to be distinguished from those of your firm;

[(b) *to return them to us within 14 days of an order for detailed assessment or certificate of discharge to enable our bill to be prepared for detailed assessment*];

(c)   to process the claim for costs on our behalf with reasonable expedition. [*We will wish to arrange for our own costs draftsman to prepare our bill (the preferred course of action) or alternatively, we will agree to meet a proportionate part of your costs draftsman's bill within one month of receiving the draft bill of costs for approval prior to its being lodged at court*];

(d)   to preserve our lien (insofar as private costs fall to be paid) and that of the Legal Services Commission and, in particular, to take all steps necessary to ensure that the statutory charge is protected;

(e)   not to part with the papers save upon undertakings to the same effect as the above.

We look forward to hearing from you.

Yours faithfully

C025   Letter to new solicitors concerning payment of fees

Dear Sirs

We write to enquire when we may expect payment of our costs.

Please inform us if the bill has been lodged at court for detailed assessment, and if not, why not and when you anticipate the bill will be lodged.

Yours faithfully

C026   Letter to former solicitors concerning bill of costs

Dear Sirs

We enclose a copy of the relevant pages of the bill, as prepared by our costs draftsman, for your approval.

If we do not hear from you within seven days, we will presume that you approve the bill as drawn and will submit it to the court for detailed assessment.

Please inform us what payments on account of profit costs and/or disbursements you have received from the Legal Services Commission, so that we can deduct these amounts from the costs otherwise payable to you.

We enclose an invoice from our costs draftsman in respect of your part of the bill. Please send a cheque direct to him. When replying, please confirm that you have done so.

Yours faithfully

Enc. pages from bill invoice

CO27 Letter to agents concerning fees – publicly funded case

Dear Sirs

Since our client has the benefit of public funding, please confirm that you will calculate your charges to us in accordance with the prescribed rates.

Please note that, because our client is publicly funded, there may be some delay in payment of your fee pending receipt of money from the Legal Services Commission. We will not be able to pay you until we receive the money from the Legal Services Commission. Since agency fees are treated as profit costs and not in the same manner as other disbursements, we will not be able to claim payment on account. In the event that payment on account is not allowed, we will pay you as soon as we receive a payment on account of profit costs or following settlement of our final bill, whichever is sooner.

Your fees and our costs will have to be assessed by the court. Whilst we will pay your reasonable fee as soon as we receive payment from the Legal Services Commission, such payment can only be made on the condition that if your fees are reduced on detailed assessment, you will reimburse us with any overpayment we have made, such repayment to be made within 14 days of us notifying you of the reduction.

Please confirm that you are prepared to accept an instruction on these terms.

Yours faithfully

CO28 Reminder letter to client concerning non-payment of fees

Dear [*client*]

I refer to my firm's account dated [   ] of which £[   ] remains outstanding, and request payment without delay.

Please note that my firm charges interest at the rate of [8%] per year on any amount outstanding to us after one month from delivery of the bill.

If you dispute my firm's bill, you are entitled to apply to the court for the bill to be checked by an officer of the court, who will decide whether the amount claimed is reasonable. You must do so within 12 months from the date of receipt of this letter, although after the first month the court may impose terms on which you may exercise this right.

Yours sincerely

CO29 Second reminder letter to client concerning non-payment of fees

Dear [*client*]

I refer to my firm's account dated [   ] of which £[   ] remains outstanding.

Please pay this account without any further delay.

Yours sincerely

CO30 Letter to client before action

Dear [*client*]

I refer to my firm's account dated [   ] of which £[   ] remains outstanding.

If I do not hear from you within seven days with either payment in full or acceptable proposals for payment by instalments, I will [*pass the file to my firm's litigation department for them to*] commence proceedings against you for recovery of the outstanding amount due, together with interest.

In that case, you would also have to pay our costs of taking legal proceedings against you.

Yours sincerely

CO31   Letter to client with draft proceedings for recovery of debts

Dear [*client*]

[*Your file has been passed on to us by our colleagues in the family department.*]

You have not paid this firm's bill and interest, which now amount to £[   ].

We have now prepared the court papers necessary to start court proceedings against you and we enclose a draft. Unless we receive your cleared funds by cheque [*or BACS or debit card payment*] for the full amount within seven days, that means by [   ], we will send the papers to the court to start the proceedings. In that case, you will also have to pay the costs of those proceedings and the court fee of £[   ].

We look forward to hearing from you with payment forthwith.

Yours faithfully

Enc. claim form

CO32   Standing order by client to pay fees by instalments

From: [*client*]

The Manager

[*bank's or building society's name and address*]

Dear Sir

Please pay from my account numbered [   ], sort code [   ] to [   ], the sum of £[   ] (words – [   ] pounds) on the [   ] day of each month, starting on the [   ] day of [   ] 20xx.

The bank details of [*Messrs*] are:

[   ]

[*Client/Office*] A/c No [   ]

Sort Code [   ]

Please ensure that you quote reference number [   ].

Yours faithfully

SECTION 7

COHABITATION

Andrea Woelke

section 7 COHABITATION

Cohabitation

COH1 First letter to client setting out law on beneficial ownership – client is legal owner

Dear [*client*]

I write further to our meeting on [   ].

I enclose a statement which I have prepared from the information you gave me on the client questionnaire and during our meeting. I will not disclose this statement to your former partner but I will use it to remind myself and as a quick reference for any colleagues who may work on your file. I may also use it if it becomes necessary to instruct a barrister or an expert. Please go through the statement very carefully and check that everything is accurate and make any additions or amendments as are necessary. Please also fill in the gaps and answer the questions in the statement. Please then sign and date it and return it to me.

The law relating to beneficial ownership in a property

We discussed whether your former partner could claim a beneficial interest in your property. Essentially, the law relating to joint ownership is based on three broad principles, namely:

1. If you make an express declaration by deed about the beneficial ownership of a property, this is conclusive. If you do not, one of the following scenarios are possible:

2. If there is a common intention between the parties, *before* the property is bought, about the beneficial ownership, the court can imply a constructive trust. This means that the court will imply that the parties have come to an agreement and the court will effectively pretend there was a written trust. It is not necessary for the parties to have an explicit conversation about this agreement before the property is bought, but the court has to make a finding that they did come to such an agreement. It may be that the court will only make such a finding by looking at the conduct of the parties later on. Obviously if someone bought a property before they even met their new partner, this cannot apply. If the property was bought as a joint home, the court will certainly look more closely into the circumstances of why it was not put into joint names.

3. The court will also look at who contributed what and the beneficial ownership will be allocated accordingly. This is called resulting trust. Contributions can be either direct contributions to the purchase price or being a party to a mortgage. Direct contributions to the purchase price or deposit will nearly always result in a corresponding beneficial interest under this doctrine. Similarly, if someone takes on the burden of a mortgage, alone or jointly, this should also result in a corresponding share in the equity. Sometimes, however, someone only lends their name

to the mortgage while there is an agreement that they will not be liable to it as between the joint owners. In that case that person has no beneficial interest in the property as a result.

In your case, I understand that you did not sign an express deed of trust. It is therefore possible that either scenario 2 or 3 would come into effect. Under either scenario, you would be entitled to be reimbursed for the money that is not reflected in your beneficial interest by the doctrine of equitable accounting. This is not usually appropriate for mortgage payments and building insurance in cases where people have lived together and one party has taken on other responsibilities either by looking after the family or by paying for other outgoings from their income.

Therefore, if the court finds that there was an agreement between the two of you that you would hold the property jointly and equally, both of you would be entitled to half the equity in the property. However, before the equity is split you would be able to deduct from the net sale proceeds the money you spent on:

1. mortgage instalments;
2. improvements and repairs; and
3. building insurance.

The court does not usually make strict mathematical calculations but takes a more broad-brush approach and decides on what the fair shares in the equity would be, taking into account such contributions.

For me to be able to advise you in more detail I need to find out a number of things:

1. I will need to get the conveyancing file and consider it. I enclose a letter of authority to the conveyancing solicitors for you to sign and return to me.

2. Please send me the statements for your bank accounts at the time you bought the property to show where the deposit and the costs of buying the property came from.

3. [   ]

[*other and general advice*]

I look forward to hearing from you.

Yours sincerely

Enc. statement

COH2   First letter to client setting out law on beneficial ownership – client is not a legal owner

Dear [*client*]

I write further to our meeting on [   ].

I enclose a statement which I have prepared from the information you gave me on the client questionnaire and during our meeting. I will not disclose this statement to your former partner but I will use it to remind myself and as a quick reference for any colleagues who may work on your file. I may also use it if it becomes necessary to instruct a barrister or an expert. Please go through the statement very carefully and check that everything is accurate and make any additions or amendments as are necessary. Please also fill in the gaps and answer the questions in the statement. Please then sign and date it and return it to me.

The law relating to beneficial ownership in a property

We discussed whether you could bring a claim against your former partner for a beneficial share in the property. Essentially, the law relating to joint ownership is based on three broad principles, namely:

1.   If you make an express declaration by deed about the beneficial ownership of a property, this is conclusive. If you do not, one of the following scenarios are possible:

2.   If there is a common intention between the parties, *before* the property is bought, about the beneficial ownership, the court can imply a constructive trust. This means that the court will imply that the parties have come to an agreement and the court will effectively pretend there was a written trust. It is not necessary for the parties to have an explicit conversation about this agreement before the property is bought, but the court has to make a finding that they did come to such an agreement. It may be that the court will only make such a finding by looking at the conduct of the parties later on. Obviously if someone bought a property before they even met their new partner, this cannot apply. If the property was bought as a joint home, the court will certainly look more closely into the circumstances of why it was not put into joint names.

3.   The court will also look at who contributed what and the beneficial ownership will be allocated accordingly. This is called resulting trust. Contributions can be either direct contributions to the purchase price or being a party to a mortgage. Direct contributions to the purchase price or deposit will nearly always result in a corresponding beneficial interest under this doctrine. Similarly, if someone takes on the burden of a mortgage, alone or jointly, this should also result in a corresponding share in the equity. Sometimes, however, someone only lends their name

to the mortgage while there is an agreement that they will not be liable to it as between the joint owners. In that case that person has no beneficial interest in the property as a result.

In your case, I understand that you did not sign an express deed of trust. It is therefore possible that either scenario 2 or 3 would come into effect. Under either scenario, you would be entitled to be reimbursed for the money that is not reflected in your beneficial interest by the doctrine of equitable accounting. This is not usually appropriate for mortgage payments and building insurance in cases where people have lived together and one party has taken on other responsibilities either by looking after the family or by paying for other outgoings from their income.

Therefore, if the court finds that there was an agreement between the two of you that you would hold the property jointly and equally, both of you would be entitled to half the equity in the property. However, before the equity is split you would be able to deduct from the net sale proceeds the money you spent on:

1.   mortgage instalments;
2.   improvements and repairs; and
3.   building insurance.

The court does not usually make strict mathematical calculations but takes a more broad-brush approach and decides on what the fair shares in the equity would be taking into account such contributions.

For me to be able to advise you in more detail I need to find out a number of things:

1.   I will need to get a copy of the conveyancing file and consider it. You are not a client of the conveyancing solicitors and I therefore cannot request them to send it to me. I enclose a draft letter to your former partner asking them for a letter of authority and their agreement to release it.

2.   Please send me the statements for your bank accounts at the time you bought the property to show your contributions to the deposit and the costs of buying the property.

3.   [   ]

[*other and general advice*]

I look forward to hearing from you.

Yours sincerely

Enc. statement

COH3 First letter to client setting out law on beneficial ownership – property in joint names

Dear [*client*]

I write further to our meeting on [   ].

I enclose a statement which I have prepared from the information you gave me on the client questionnaire and during our meeting. I will not disclose this statement to your former partner but I will use it to remind myself and as a quick reference for any colleagues who may work on your file. I may also use it if it becomes necessary to instruct a barrister or an expert. Please go through the statement very carefully and check that everything is accurate and make any additions or amendments as are necessary. Please also fill in the gaps and answer the questions in the statement. Please then sign and date it and return it to me.

The law relating to beneficial ownership in a property

Essentially, the law relating to joint ownership is based on three broad principles, namely:

1. If you make an express declaration by deed about the beneficial ownership of a property, this is conclusive. If you do not, one of the following scenarios are possible:

2. If there is a common intention between the parties, *before* the property is bought, about the beneficial ownership, the court can imply a constructive trust. This means that the court will imply that the parties have come to an agreement and the court will effectively pretend there was a written trust. It is not necessary for the parties to have an explicit conversation about this agreement before the property is bought, but the court has to make a finding that they did come to such an agreement. It may be that the court will only make such a finding by looking at the conduct of the parties later on. The fact that two people buy a property in joint names gives the court a starting point of an equal share and there would need to be other circumstances to show the court that this was not the understanding between the parties.

3. The court will also look at who contributed what and the beneficial ownership will be allocated accordingly. This is called resulting trust. Contributions can be either direct contributions to the purchase price or being a party to a mortgage. Direct contributions to the purchase price or deposit will nearly always result in a corresponding beneficial interest under this doctrine. Similarly, if someone takes on the burden of a mortgage, alone or jointly, this should also result in a corresponding share in the equity. Sometimes, however, someone only lends their name to the mortgage while there is an agreement that they will not be liable to

it as between the joint owners. In that case that person has no beneficial interest in the property as a result.

In your case, I understand that you did not sign an express deed of trust. It is therefore possible that scenario 2 or 3 would come into effect. Under either scenario, you would be entitled to be reimbursed for the money that is not reflected in your beneficial interest by the doctrine of equitable accounting. This is not usually appropriate for mortgage payments and building insurance in cases where people have lived together and one party has taken on other responsibilities either by looking after the family or by paying for other outgoings from their income.

Therefore, if the court finds that there was an agreement between the two of you that you would hold the property jointly and equally, both of you would be entitled to half the equity in the property. However, before the equity is split you would be able to deduct from the net sale proceeds the money you spent on:

1. mortgage instalments;
2. improvements and repairs; and
3. building insurance.

The court does not usually make strict mathematical calculations but takes a more broad-brush approach and decides on what the fair shares in the equity would be taking into account such contributions.

For me to be able to advise you in more detail I need to find out a number of things:

1. I will need to get a copy of the conveyancing file and consider it. I enclose a letter of authority to the conveyancing solicitors for you to sign and return to me.

2. Please send me the statements for your bank accounts at the time you bought the property to show your contributions to the deposit and the costs of buying the property.

3. [   ]

[other and general advice]

I look forward to hearing from you.

Yours sincerely

Enc. statement

COH4   Letter explaining doctrine of proprietory estoppel

Dear [*client*]

Proprietory estoppel

Under the doctrine of proprietory estoppel, the court has a discretion to award a person a range of interests or rights, such as:

1.   grant a beneficial interest in the property;

2.   grant somebody a sum of money;

3.   grant somebody a right to live in a property for a specified time, for example for life.

The doctrine can arise if:

1.   the claimant mistakenly thinks they have a right in a property, and
2.   the claimant does something to their detriment relying on this mistake, and
3.   the owner knows that their ownership is inconsistent with the claimant's right, and
4.   the owner knows that the claimant mistakenly believes they have a right, and
5.   the owner either encourages the claimant to do something to their detriment (such as spending money on the property), or at least indirectly does so by not asserting their ownership.

Arguably, as far as this property is concerned, [you] [your former partner] may have relied on the promise by [her/him/you] that [he/she/you could live there for the rest of his/her/your life] and on that reliance [you] [your former partner] agreed to:

[   ]

If all the facts can be proven by evidence, preferably documentary evidence, and the court follows this line of argument, it may grant a number of rights to [you] [your former partner], for example [   ].

For me to advise you further on whether this applies in your case, I will need to investigate the circumstances in more detail. Please let me have the following documents:

[   ]

I look forward to hearing from you.

Yours sincerely

COH5   Letter explaining joint tenancy and inheritance

Dear [*client*]

Inheritance

I suspect that you and your former partner own the property as 'joint tenants'. This means that, if one of you dies, the survivor will be entitled to the whole property irrespective of any provision in a will or if there is no will irrespective of the intestacy rules.

You can prevent this by preparing a simple document called a notice of severance which you sign and which must be sent to your former partner for signature. Once you have both signed this, it will be lodged at the Land Registry. Even if your former partner does not sign it, the property will be owned by you both as 'tenants in common' if your former partner has received the notice. This means that, if you died before your former partner, your share in the property would pass according to the terms of your will or under the rules of intestacy if you had no valid will. To prove that your former partner has received the notice of severance, I need to send it by recorded delivery. Even if your former partner does not sign and return it, I can ask the Land Registry to put the appropriate restriction on the register.

If you have made a will in your former partner's favour, you will no doubt want to review this now. If you have not made a will, this is a good opportunity to do so. I can [*arrange for one of my colleagues to*] prepare a will for you. My firm's standard charges are about £[150] plus VAT for a straightforward will and more if it is more complicated.

As agreed I will also order Land Registry entries to ensure that there are no complications and so that you can prove ownership if you have to.

Please confirm that you want me to prepare a notice of severance and whether you would like to make a new will.

I look forward to hearing from you.

Yours sincerely

COH6   Letter to client enclosing Land Registry Entries

Dear [*client*]

Land Registry Entries

I have obtained Land Registry Entries and I enclose a copy. You will see that Section A sets out the property. I have not obtained a map at this stage. Do you know whether there could be some other bit of land that you bought but that is separately registered?

Section B sets out that [you are registered as the owner of the property] [you and your former partner are registered as the joint owners of the property] [your former partner is registered as the owner of the property].

[*There is [no] [a] restriction as to the receipt that a survivor could give. Therefore I advise you to serve a notice of severance so that if you die your former partner does not automatically own the property. I have prepared the notice and enclose it for you to sign.*] [*This means that if one of you dies, their share of the property forms part of their estate and passes under the provisions of their will or the intestacy rules. It will not automatically pass to the survivor of the two of you.*]

In section C you will find [*some restrictive covenants relating to the property and*] [*the mortgage with* [   ].] [*This also shows us the date of completion* [   ]].

Yours sincerely

[*Enc. notice of severance*]

COH7   First letter to other party – sole owner

Dear [   ]

[*address of property*]

Your former partner has come to me to seek advice on whether [he/she] has a
beneficial interest in [   ]. The law in this area is rather complex and
I will need some more information about the circumstances of your purchase
and ownership of the property to be able to advise your former partner on
whether [he/she] has a beneficial interest in the property and if so how much it
amounts to.

Your former partner does of course hope that all these matters can be agreed
between you without the need for court proceedings. Your former partner has
therefore agreed that after my preliminary investigation, I should write to you
to set out what your former partner's view is so that you can then seek your
own advice and consider the best way of coming to an agreement.

For me to be able to do this, I need further information, including a copy of the
conveyancing file. As you bought the property in your name, the conveyancing
solicitors will not send me a copy of the file without your authority or an
order from the court. Obviously, your former partner wants to avoid court
proceedings altogether if possible including the costs of an application for the
conveyancing file. I hope therefore that you will agree to sign an authority to
your conveyancing solicitors to send me a copy. I enclose a letter of authority
for you to sign and return to me. Please also let me have the name and address
of your conveyancing solicitors. I will check whether they are still at the same
address or whether the firm has merged with another firm and then insert the
current address on the letter. If you have a letter from your solicitor at the time,
it would help if you could let me have the name of the person who dealt with
the matter and the reference.

Your former partner tells me that you both contributed to the deposit [*and that
[he/she] transferred a sum into an account in your name that you then passed
on to your conveyancing solicitor*]. Could you please let me have copies of
your bank statements for the time of the purchase which show the cheques or
transfers to your conveyancing solicitor for the deposit and where that money
came from.

I strongly suggest that you seek independent legal advice from a solicitor
on this letter. I suggest that you consult an expert in the area of cohabitation
law. You will find details of family lawyers who take a non-confrontational
approach to family law and of experts in cohabitation by contacting Resolution
on www.resolution.org.uk or by calling 01689 820272. Resolution members
are normally specialists in family law and subscribe to a code of practice
which is geared towards encouraging a constructive and non-confrontational
approach in all family matters.

I look forward to hearing from you or a solicitor instructed by you in due course.

Yours sincerely

Enc. letter of authority

COH8   First letter to other party – joint owner

Dear [   ]

[*address of property*]

Your former partner has come to me to seek advice on [his/her] beneficial interest in [   ]. The law in this area is rather complex and I will need some more information about the circumstances of your purchase and ownership of the property to be able to advise your former partner on the extend of [his/her] beneficial interest.

Your former partner does of course hope that all these matters can be agreed between you without the need for court proceedings. Your former partner has therefore agreed that after my preliminary investigation, I should write to you to set out what your former partner's view is so that you can then seek your own advice and consider the best way of coming to an agreement.

For me to be able to do this, I need further information. Your former partner tells me that you both contributed to the deposit [*and that [he/she] transferred a sum into an account in your name that you then passed on to your conveyancing solicitor*]. Could you please let me have copies of your bank statements for the time of the purchase which show the cheques or transfers to your conveyancing solicitor for the deposit and where that money came from.

I strongly suggest that you seek independent legal advice from a solicitor on this letter. I suggest that you consult an expert in the area of cohabitation law. You will find details of family lawyers who take a non-confrontational approach to family law and of experts in cohabitation by contacting Resolution on www.resolution.org.uk or by calling 01689 820272. Resolution members are normally specialists in family law and subscribe to a code of practice which is geared towards encouraging a constructive and non-confrontational approach in all family matters.

I look forward to hearing from you or a solicitor instructed by you in due course.

Yours sincerely

Enc. letter of authority

COH9 Letter of authority for conveyancing file – client is owner or joint owner

[*address of client*]

[*name, address and reference of conveyancers*]

Dear Sirs

[*address of property*]

I hereby authorise and request you to send [a copy of the/the original] file of papers relating to the purchase of the above property to my solicitors [   ] including a copy of the ledger account and all dockets, file notes and telephone or other attendances. [*Alternatively, I authorise you to release the original file to them for copying and return.*]

Yours faithfully

_____

[*client's name*]

_____

Date

COH10 Letter of authority for conveyancing file by other party

[*address of other party*]

[*name, address and reference of conveyancers*]

Dear Sirs

[*address of property*]

I hereby authorise and request you to send a copy of the file of papers relating to the purchase of the above property to [   ] including a copy of the ledger account and all dockets, file notes and telephone or other attendances. Alternatively, I authorise you to release the original file to them for copying and return.

Yours faithfully

_____

[*owner's name*]

_____

Date

COH11　Letter to conveyancer – client is sole owner

Dear Sirs

[*address of property, reference*]

We act for [　　　　　], the owner of the above property and enclose a letter of authority in respect of the file of papers relating to the purchase.

The file is of course our client's property and there should therefore be no problem with releasing it to us forthwith.

If there are any papers relating to the purchase that you deem not to be our client's property, our client is of course entitled at any time to copies as this is data held about them. Please therefore ensure that we have a complete file and have a full picture of the transaction. We would prefer to receive the originals. As long as you indicate which parts of the file you consider to be your property, we are prepared to hold them to an appropriate undertaking.

There is at this stage no indication of any claim against your firm. The purpose of this request is to advise our client on an equitable claim for a beneficial share in the property. However, in order to do so, we must insist on receiving a complete set of papers including all attendance and file notes, dockets and ledgers either as originals or legible copies.

We look forward to hearing from you.

Yours faithfully

Enc. letter of authority

COH12 Letter to conveyancer – client is joint owner or other party is owner

Dear Sirs

[address of property, reference]

We enclose a letter of authority from [   ], the *[joint]* owner of the above property in respect of the file of papers relating to the purchase. We would prefer you to send us the original file to be held to your order for copying and return.

A solicitor's file is of course the client's property and the client can therefore authorise access to it at any time.

If there are any papers relating to the purchase that you deem not to be your client's property, your client is of course entitled at any time to copies as this is data held about them. Please therefore ensure that we have a complete file and have a full picture of the transaction.

There is at this stage no indication of any claim against your firm. The purpose of this request is to advise on beneficial shares in the property. However, in order to do so, we must insist on receiving a complete set of papers including all attendance and file notes, dockets and ledgers either as originals or legible copies.

We look forward to hearing from you.

Yours faithfully

Enc. letter of authority

COH13   Letter of claim to unrepresented party (property in other party's name – example)

Dear [   ]

I act for your former partner [   ] and I am writing this letter as a formal letter of claim to set out my client's case in relation to [   ]. This letter is written in accordance with the pre-action procedure in the Law Society Family Law Protocol (2nd ed.) section 5.5, a copy of which I enclose. Please confirm that you agree to follow it.

Background

[You met my client in [   ] and started a relationship in about [   ]. At the time you were living at [   ] and my client was living at [   ]. In [   ] you both decided to live together and buy a home together. You approached a mortgage broker, [   ], who for some reason which is unclear advised you that my client could not be a party to the mortgage because at the time [he/she] was a still a student and had no regular income. As a result you agreed to buy the house in your sole name. You also agreed that my client would start paying half the monthly mortgage payments and outgoings on bills on the house when he finished his Masters course in [   ], which [he/she] did.

I enclose a copy of the solicitor's file of the purchase of the house. From the completion statement (copy enclosed) it is clear that the deposit was £[   ] and the total costs of purchase was £[   ]. The mortgage with [   ] in your sole name was for £[   ]. I enclose copies of my client's bank statements at the time and you will see that a cheque for £[   ] was drawn on [   ], which corresponds to the entry on [   ] in the solicitors' ledger account.

After completion, you paid all the monthly mortgage instalments and bills for about six months and from then to date, you and my client both paid them in equal shares. In [   ] while my client was looking for work, [he/she] spent considerable time decorating the house including [   ].]

The Law

[Although the house was bought in your sole name, there was an agreement before you bought the property that you should buy it jointly as a joint home and contribute equally. You both contributed to the deposit to the best of your ability and put all your savings and efforts into the house. While you paid the monthly mortgage and bills initially, my client spent his own time decorating. Since then you have contributed equally, which confirms your initial agreement to own the house in equal shares. The only reason it is owned in your sole name is because of the advice of the mortgage broker (probably mistakenly) that my client could not be on the mortgage.

There is nothing specifically in the conveyancing file of the solicitors contradicting this. My client signed a deed of postponement for the benefit of the lender, but this is a standard feature and does not affect the rights between the two of you.

I have therefore advised my client that you hold the property on a constructive trust for both of you and my client is entitled to an equal share in the equity.]

My client's claim

[My client wants to realise his share of the equity because [he/she] will need to buy a new home. My client is entitled to do so and [he/she] can see nothing that indicates that the court would postpone a sale.

There is of course no reason why you should not buy the property and provided a value can be agreed and you can raise a mortgage to pay my client [his/her] half share of the equity, my client would agree to that. My client estimates that the house is worth £[   ] and the mortgage outstanding is about £[   ]. I enclose market appraisals from three estate agents and a mortgage redemption statement. I therefore calculate my client's share as follows:

Value of the house	£
Less Mortgage	(£)
Equity	£
Half Share	£
You would need to raise	£

Please confirm within four weeks whether you want to and can buy my client out. If so, please provide a copy of the mortgage offer.

If you cannot or do not want to buy my client out, the property has to be sold on the open market and my client proposes that it be marketed with [   ] estate agents as soon as possible.]

In accordance with the Law Society Protocol, please let me have an acknowledgement of this letter within two weeks, namely by [   ] and a full reply within four weeks, namely by [   ]. If for some reason you need more time, please write to me asking for more time giving the reasons why you need more time. If there are any other documents that you think my client has and that are relevant to the case, please let me know. If there are documents that you have that are relevant to this case, please let me have copies.

I recommend that you obtain independent legal advice about the contents of this letter. I recommend that you contact a member of Resolution in your area. You will find details of them on www.resolution.org.uk or by calling 01689 820272. Resolution members are normally specialists in family law and subscribe to a code of practice which is geared towards encouraging a constructive and non-confrontational approach in all family matters. A number of Resolution members have a specialist accreditation in cohabitation law and you can check whether there are accredited specialists in your area.

I look forward to hearing from you or a solicitor instructed by you.

Yours sincerely

Enc. [*documents*]

COH14   Letter of claim to solicitors (property in joint names – example)

Dear Sirs

As you know, we act for [   ] the former partner of your client. We are writing this letter as a formal letter of claim to set out our client's case in relation to [   ]. This letter is written in accordance with the pre-action procedure in the Law Society Family Law Protocol (2nd ed.) section 5.5, a copy of which we enclose. Please confirm that your client agrees to follow it.

Background

[Our clients met in [   ] and started a relationship in about [   ]. At the time your client was living in rented accommodation at [   ] and our client was living in a flat [he/she] owned at [   ]. In [   ] they both decided to live together and buy a home together. They decided that they would buy the house at [   ] together and our client sold [his/her] flat and the entire equity of £[   ] went towards the purchase of [   ] (equal to about [   ]% of the purchase price) the remainder of the purchase price of £[   ] was financed with a mortgage in joint names (about [   ]% of the purchase price). We enclose a copy of the conveyancing solicitor's file and refer to the completion statement and the docket dated [   ]. We also enclose the completion statement of the sale of our client's flat of the same date.

Since then our clients have contributed to the mortgage and the other outgoings on the house equally.

There is nothing on the solicitor's file indicating that our clients were given any advice on a deed of trust. There is not even a standard letter explaining the difference between a beneficial joint tenancy and a tenancy-in-common. It is our client's case that there was always an understanding that our client should have a stake in the house corresponding to his considerable deposit. There is nothing on the solicitor's file or in any other documents that seems to contradict this or to indicate that our client intended the considerable deposit so early in our clients' relationship as an outright gift.]

The Law

[Although the house was bought in joint names, we have advised our client that under the doctrine of resulting trust our client has a share corresponding to the original deposit, while the remainder is held equally, subject to the mortgage.]

Our client's claim

[Our client estimates that the house is worth £[   ] and the mortgage

outstanding is about £[   ]. We enclose market appraisals from three estate agents and a mortgage redemption statement. We have therefore advised our client that the shares are as follows:

Value of the house	£
Our client's share of [ ]% corresponding to the deposit (£)	£
Less Mortgage	(£_____)
Balance	£_____
Half Share and your client's share	£
Our client's share	**£**

Our client wants to remain in the house and therefore proposes that [he/she] buys your client out. Our client has obtained a mortgage offer of £[   ], which will allow [him/her] to redeem the existing mortgage and release your client from it and to pay your client [his/her] share of £ [   ].

Please confirm that your client agrees to a transfer of the property to our client as proposed.]

In accordance with the Law Society Protocol, please let us have an acknowledgement of this letter within two weeks, namely by [   ] and a full reply within four weeks, namely by [   ]. If for some reason you need more time, please write to us asking for more time giving the reasons why you need more time. If there are any other documents that your client thinks our client has and that are relevant to the case, please let us know. If there are documents that your client has that are relevant to this case, please let us have copies.

We look forward to hearing from you.

Yours faithfully

Enc. [*documents*]

COH15   Letter to client with draft letter of claim

Dear [   ]

I have now been able to consider all the documents including the solicitor's file of the purchase of your property and again the initial statement I prepared for you. I amended this following our meeting and I enclose a copy. Please check that this is all correct and let me know immediately if there are any mistakes in it or if it needs to be added to or amended. It is very important that I am clear in my mind what the facts are now that I am going to put your case to your former partner.

I also enclose a draft letter of claim. This is a fairly formal letter written in accordance with the Law Society Family Law Protocol. You will see that I will enclose copies of a large number of documents and that the letter itself goes into considerable detail about the background of the matter, the way you put your case in legal terms and what your claim is. Please check the letter carefully and let me have any amendments or questions you may have.

Please note that stating in the letter of claim that you have a good case does not mean that I necessarily think that you would have good chances of success if you bring the case to court. In this letter I am setting out your claim. At a later stage, I will consider with you whether or not it is worth bringing court proceedings. This will depend on a number of factors including what of your case is backed by documentary evidence and how I think any witnesses would perform in court.

Although under the protocol your former partner or solicitors instructed should reply within four weeks in full, it is likely that there will be a request for more time to consider the case. However, the protocol is a useful tool and guide to ensure that matters do not drift.

I look forward to hearing from you.

Yours sincerely

Enc. statement
    draft letter of claim

section 7 COHABITATION

COH16 Property interests – letter to client with draft statement for court proceedings (especially if issued under Part 8)

Dear [*client*]

Unfortunately the reply and further correspondence resulting from the letter of claim I sent to your former partner have not resulted in an agreement. You therefore instructed me to prepare the necessary papers to start court proceedings. By far the most important document is your statement. I now enclose the statement I have prepared for the court proceedings. This must be 100% correct because you could be cross-examined on it if the matter comes to a final hearing. If it later turns out that some of what you say is not entirely correct, this could alone mean that you lose your case and have to pay all your former partner's legal costs.

Please therefore go through the statement several times really carefully. Please feel free to write on it with any comments, corrections, amendments and additions that you may have. Please telephone me if you have any questions or if you think it is easier to discuss the issues you want to raise on the telephone or in a meeting. Please then return the statement to me so I can consider your comments and amend it.

I look forward to hearing from you.

Yours sincerely

Enc. draft statement

COH17 Letter to client with draft particulars of claim (if issued under Part 7)

Dear [*client*]

Unfortunately the reply and further correspondence resulting from the letter of claim I sent to your former partner have not resulted in an agreement. You therefore instructed me to prepare the necessary papers to start court proceedings. The most important document at this stage is the particulars of claim, which set out your case. At a later stage I will prepare a detailed statement for you. The particulars of claim set out your claim rather than the evidence you will give in court. Nevertheless it is vital that everything is 100% correct because you could be cross-examined on it if the matter comes to a final hearing. If it later turns out that some of what the particulars of claim say is not entirely correct, this could alone mean that you could lose your case and have to pay all your former partner's legal costs.

Please therefore go through the particulars of claim several times really carefully. Please feel free to write on it with any comments, corrections, amendments and additions that you may have. Please telephone me if you have any questions or if you think it is easier to discuss the issues you want to raise on the telephone or in a meeting. Please then return the particulars of claim to me so I can consider your comments and amend it.

I look forward to hearing from you.

Yours sincerely

Enc. draft particulars of claim

COH18   Letter to court – Trusts of Land Act (Part 8)

Dear Sir or Madam

We enclose for following documents for issuing and return to us for **solicitor service**:

1.   our client's Part 8 claim form dated [   ] for an order under the Trusts of Land and Appointment of Trustees Act 1996 with copies for the court and the respondent;

2.   our client's statement with exhibit and copies for the court file and the respondent;

3.   our cheque for £[   ] being the court fee.

We look forward to hearing from you.

Yours faithfully

Enc.

COH19   Letter to court – Trusts of Land Act (Part 7)

Dear Sir or Madam

We enclose for following documents for issuing and return to us for **solicitor service**:

1.   our client's Part 7 claim form dated [   ] for an order under the Trusts of Land and Appointment of Trustees Act 1996 with copies for the court and the respondent;

2.   particulars of claim and copies for the court file and the respondent;

3.   our cheque for £[   ] being the court fee.

We look forward to hearing from you.

Yours faithfully

Enc.

COH20   Letter to client re procedure – Trusts of Land Act (Part 7)

Dear [*client*]

I have now lodged your application at court for a declaration as to your beneficial interest in [   ] [*and an order for the sale of that property*].

Once the court returns your claim form and the particulars of claim, I can serve these on your former partner.

Your former partner must then file a formal court document, which is known as a defence, within 14 days, or, if [he/she] first files an acknowledgement form within 14 days, [he/she] can file the defence within 28 days from the day that [he/she] gets the court papers.

If appropriate, I will then prepare another formal court document, a reply, to deal with any new issues that your former partner has brought up in the defence.

The court will then send out a questionnaire about the case so that the judge can see how the case should be dealt with and what types of hearings should be listed. There is also likely to be a directions hearing where the judge will make an order for any steps that need to be taken to prepare the case for a final hearing, such as disclosure of documents, a joint valuation of the property and the exchange of witness statements. I will need to prepare a full witness statement for you and any other witnesses you want to give evidence at court on your behalf. This hearing is likely to be in about 3 months' time or so. Depending on the number of witnesses and the experts involved, I estimate that a final hearing will not be listed before [   ].

Yours sincerely

COH21 Letter to client re procedure – Trusts of Land Act (Part 8)

Dear [*client*]

I have now lodged your application at court for a declaration as to your beneficial interest in [   ] [*and an order for the sale of that property*].

Once the court returns your claim form and the particulars of claim, I can serve these on your former partner.

Your former partner must then file an acknowledgement form within 14 days together with any evidence [he/she] wants to rely on. In practice, there is likely to be a request for further time.

The court will also list a date for a hearing where the judge will make an order for any steps that need to be taken to prepare the case for a final hearing, such as disclosure of documents, a joint valuation of the property and the exchange of any other witness statements. This hearing is likely to be in about 2 to 3 months' time or so. Depending on the number of witnesses and the experts involved, I estimate that a final hearing will not be listed before [   ].

Yours sincerely

SECTION 8

CIVIL PARTNERSHIP

Mark Harper

Civil Partnership

section **8** CIVIL PARTNERSHIPS

CP1　Letter advising on effects of civil partnership

Dear [*client*]

I write to explain the legal effects of civil partnership.

Foreign same sex marriages, and almost all foreign registered partnerships or civil unions, are recognised as if they are a civil partnership. Civil partnership has all the rights and obligations that arise on marriage, and so as on divorce.

The differences between civil partnership and marriage are few. However a civil partnership cannot be entered into in religious premises and there cannot be a simultaneous religious ceremony at the time the partnership is registered. It is the signing of the civil partnership schedule which creates the legal relationship.

Further information can be obtained from www.womenandequalityunit.gov. uk/lgbt/partnership.htm.

A civil partnership can only be ended by way of formal dissolution, in the same way as divorce. The two most common facts which can be relied upon to obtain a dissolution are that one partner has behaved in such a way that the other cannot reasonably be expected to continue to live with him, or that the couple have been separated for two years and they consent to a dissolution. Obtaining a dissolution can be a lengthy process and a civil partnership cannot be ended by simply serving a notice.

Financial claims

In the same way that on divorce married couples have substantial rights and obligations, those exist on dissolution of civil partnership. They include a claim for a share of a property, payment of capital, sharing of pensions and payment of maintenance, in some cases for a substantial period of time.

It is likely that assets built up during the civil partnership, including earlier years of cohabitation, will be divided equally on dissolution.

Children issues

One of the significant differences between civil partnership and marriage is the legal consequences for same sex couples arising from having fertility treatment at a licensed clinic.

If a same sex couple have fertility treatment together, the non-biological parent will not automatically become a parent as a matter of law. In contrast if a married couple have fertility treatment, then the husband is automatically treated as the father as a matter of law.

After entering into a civil partnership a civil partner will have the same rights as if a step-parent in respect of children of the other partner. It will be possible to obtain parental responsibility by agreement for the non-biological parent.

section 8 CIVIL PARTNERSHIPS

Death and tax

Entering into a civil partnership automatically invalidates any existing Will. It is therefore important to make a new Will either in contemplation of registering the partnership, or immediately afterwards.

In all respects civil partnership is treated in the same way as marriage regarding tax. This is particularly important in the context of inheritance tax; all of a civil partner's estate can pass free of tax to the surviving partner. The only disadvantage of the equal tax treatment with married couples is that it is not possible to own more than one property as a principal private residence free of capital gains tax.

In summary civil partnership has many rights and obligations which some would regard as a potential burden. Therefore especially people who are more concerned with protecting their assets may prefer to simply cohabit, which will not create any rights and obligations on relationship breakdown under current law.

Yours sincerely

Index

References are to letters.